THE
EFFECTIVE
LEADER

HOW TO MAXIMIZE ENGAGEMENT AND
CULTIVATE A HIGH-PERFORMANCE TEAM

MW00990627

Published by Lorna Weston-Smyth

© **2023 Toronto, Canada**

All rights reserved. No part of this book may be reproduced or modified in any form, including photocopying, recording, or by any information storage and retrieval system, without permission in writing from the publisher.

UNLEASH YOUR LEADERSHIP POTENTIAL WITH OUR EXCLUSIVE DEVELOPMENT PLAN TEMPLATE - A PERFECT COMPANION TO "THE EFFECTIVE LEADER"!

Hey there, leader! Are you ready to take your leadership skills up a notch? Look no further, because we've got just the tool to help you level up! Introducing my Leadership Development Plan Template, designed to turbocharge the teachings from the book "The Effective Leader".

Imagine this: you, confidently guiding your team to unparalleled success and making a lasting impact in your organization. With this comprehensive template, you'll have the roadmap to become the influential leader you've always aspired to be.

So, why should you choose this Leadership Development Plan Template? Let me break it down for you:

1. Expertly Designed for Extraordinary Leaders: My template comes from my years of experience as an executive coach working with leaders just like yourself. I've distilled the most powerful strategies and techniques from "The Effective Leader" to create a masterful plan that's sure to take your leadership skills to new heights..

2. Customized for Your Success: This template is all about you and your unique leadership style. It's fully customizable, allowing you to tailor it to your specific needs and goals. Whether you're a bold visionary or a nurturing mentor, my template will help you tap into your strengths, address your weaknesses, and create a plan that's suited just for you.

3. Action-Oriented and Results-Driven: My template gets straight to the point, providing clear action steps and practical strategies to implement your plan with precision. Say goodbye to vague

intentions and hello to concrete results that will leave your colleagues and superiors in awe.

4. Build Stronger Bonds and Achieve Together: Effective leaders know the importance of building relationships and fostering a collaborative environment. This template goes beyond just task-oriented goals; it provides exercises and techniques to strengthen your interpersonal skills and forge genuine connections within your team. Prepare to witness a synergy that elevates the performance of everyone involved.

5. Ready to unlock your leadership potential and make a difference that truly matters? Don't miss out on this incredible opportunity - download this Leadership Development Plan Template today, the perfect companion to "The Effective Leader".

LornaWestonSmyth.com/Resources

Seize the chance to become the remarkable leader you were meant to be. Download this template now and ignite your leadership journey with confidence and purpose!

This book is dedicated to

Jim Edwards and Dexter Godfrey, without you this book would not exist.

Chris Robinson, thank you for being my friend and a shining example of how to live out each of these principles every day. I would not have come this far without you.

CONTENTS

INTRODUCTION

Congratulations. You have just made an incredible investment in yourself and your leadership journey by purchasing "The Effective Leader: How to Maximize Engagement and Cultivate a High-Performance Team." Get ready to take your leadership skills to the next level and achieve unprecedented success for yourself and your team.

As an Executive Coach, Trainer, and Speaker with years of experience in helping leaders like yourself, I wrote this book to equip you with the practical advice, tips, and examples that will transform your leadership style and inspire extraordinary results. Whether you are a seasoned leader looking to enhance your impact or an aspiring one aiming to navigate the overwhelming responsibilities of leadership, this book is your ultimate guide.

In the fast-paced and ever-evolving business world, creating effectiveness and engaging your employees is paramount to driving better results. And that's exactly what this book is designed to help you do. By drawing on my expertise as a member of the Forbes Coaches Council and Founder of LWS Coaching and Training, I will guide you on a transformative journey that will unlock the true potential of your team.

As you engage with this book, you will discover actionable strategies that will enable you to maximize engagement and foster a high-performance team. From cultivating a positive work environment to unlocking each individual's unique strengths, you will learn how to create a culture of trust, collaboration, and excellence.

But this book is not just about theories and abstract concepts. It's about real-world applications and tangible results. Through relatable stories, case studies*, and practical examples, you will gain a deeper understanding of how to put these principles into action. You'll be inspired by leaders who have achieved remarkable success by implementing the strategies outlined in this book.

What's more, I wrote this book in such a way as to effortlessly guide you through the content. It is conversational, akin to a friendly conversation with a trusted mentor. So, there's no need to feel overwhelmed by the weight of your leadership responsibilities. I'll be right there with you, offering guidance and support every step of the way.

Imagine the satisfaction of seeing your team members not only working together but collaborating seamlessly towards shared goals. Picture the moment when as a team you rely and support on each other to achieve those extraordinary results. With the insights shared in this book, you have the power to transform your leadership style and inspire your team to achieve greatness.

While there's no one-size-fits-all answer to the best order for a leader to work on these strategies, here's some of what we'll cover in this book:

Setting a clear vision: Start by establishing a compelling vision that serves as the guiding light for your team. Without a clear direction, it's challenging to engage and motivate your team effectively.

Fostering open communication: Creating a culture of open communication should be a priority from the start. When team members feel comfortable sharing their thoughts and concerns, it sets the stage for collaboration and trust.

Building trust: Trust is the foundation of an engaged and effective team. Work on building trust by being consistent, reliable, and fair in your actions. Encourage transparency and demonstrate integrity in your interactions.

Providing support and resources: Ensure your team has the tools, resources, and training necessary to succeed. Address any gaps or barriers that hinder their productivity and growth. This step sets the stage for engagement and effectiveness.

Recognizing achievements: Celebrate and recognize individual and team accomplishments regularly. This boosts morale and motivation, creating a positive work environment that fosters engagement and strengthens the team's bond.

Encouraging autonomy: Once trust is established, empower your team members to make decisions and take ownership of their work. This fosters accountability, creativity, and innovation while allowing individuals to develop leadership skills.

Fostering collaboration: Encourage teamwork and create opportunities for cross-functional collaboration. Collaboration enhances problem-solving, fosters diverse perspectives, and strengthens relationships among team members.

Encouraging professional growth: Support your team members' career development through mentoring, training, and growth opportunities. This shows your commitment to their success and helps them reach their full potential.

Leading by example: Set a positive example by embodying the values and behaviors you expect from your team. Be an active participant in the work and demonstrate your commitment and enthusiasm.

Providing regular feedback: Institute a feedback culture by providing constructive feedback regularly. Support your team members' growth by acknowledging their strengths and guiding them in areas for improvement.

Fostering work-life balance: Create an environment that values work-life balance by promoting flexibility and respecting personal boundaries. Encourage your team to prioritize their well-being to enhance engagement and effectiveness.

Embracing diversity and inclusion: Build a culture that embraces diversity and inclusion. Encourage diverse perspectives and create a safe and inclusive environment for all team members to thrive.

Adapting to change: Help your team navigate and adapt to change effectively. Provide support, communicate the benefits, and address concerns during periods of transition. This keeps the team engaged and focused during challenging times.

Encouraging innovation: Foster a culture of innovation by empowering your team to think creatively and embrace new ideas. Encourage experimentation, reward risk-taking, and create channels for idea sharing.

Showing appreciation: Continuously show genuine appreciation for your team members and their contributions. Small gestures go a long way in building morale and fostering a sense of belonging.

Remember that while the order of the chapters provides a logical progression, it's important to assess your team's unique needs and adapt accordingly. Prioritize the areas that require immediate attention, while also considering how different strategies may complement and reinforce each other.

So, my friend, I encourage you to begin reading the book that you are holding in your hands right now. Dive into the chapters, absorb the wisdom within, and let it ignite a fire within you to become the effective leader you always aspired to be.

Remember, by the end of this journey, you will possess the tools and knowledge to create a high-performance team that achieves remarkable results. The leadership success you have always dreamed of is within your grasp. It's time to unlock your full potential and embark on a transformative adventure.

Now, turn the page and let's unleash your extraordinary leadership potential.

THE CREED OF AN EFFECTIVE LEADER

We believe that our organization and community is only as strong as our team. We strive to create an environment that fosters collaboration, trust, and effective communication. We understand that through leadership development, we can further develop the skills of our team and create a culture of success.

We are committed to empowering ourselves and our leaders to take initiative and make decisions that will benefit the whole team. We understand that a strong team is rooted in trust and understanding, and that each individual has a responsibility to contribute to the success of the organization.

We recognize that our team is the foundation of our success, and we will prioritize leadership development that will help us reach our goals. We will continue to strive for excellence, and build a culture of collaboration and respect. We are confident that with our strong team and effective leadership, we will reach our goals and create a successful future that will benefit all.

AUTHOR BIO

LORNA WESTON-SMYTH:

Igniting High Performance Teams to Transform Leadership Styles and Propel Your Team Forward!

Lorna Weston-Smyth, Executive Coach, Trainer and Speaker, wrote this book, "The Effective Leader: How to Maximize Engagement and Cultivate a High-Performance Team" to help ordinary people become extraordinary leaders. She specializes in leadership development and communication to turn around culture and teams for mid-sized organizations. With her common-sense approach and framework, Lorna speaks in easy to understand, simple language and teaches practical, fundamental principles that are easy to understand and use and that get results right away when applied. Senior executives and other decision makers bring Lorna in when they are looking to create a high performance, cohesive team and extraordinary leaders, who can take their business to new levels.

If you're looking to improve your leadership skills and take them to the next level and achieve unprecedented success for yourself and your team in an inspirational way, Lorna is uniquely qualified to help you. With her years of experience leading people and teams, even in the toughest arena of all - volunteers - she can give you a truthful assessment of your people and leadership and will not accept payment to coach someone who is unwilling to grow and change.

Start reading "The Effective Leader" right now and discover the secrets to igniting high performance teams and transforming your leadership style to propel your team forward!

CHAPTER 1
UNLOCKING THE POWER OF LEADERSHIP
CREATING EFFECTIVE AND ENGAGED EMPLOYEES

"In the end, all business operations can be reduced to three words: people, product, and profits. Unless you've got a good team, you can't do much with the other two."

- Lee Iacocca

AT A GLANCE

Five Essential Points for Creating Effective and Engaged Employees

- Discover the fundamental connection between leaders and their teams to create effective and engaged employees.

- Unleash the power of clear communication to inspire your employees and align their individual contributions with the bigger picture.

- Empower your team with the necessary resources and support to excel in their roles and foster a culture of continuous learning and improvement.

- Acknowledge and appreciate the efforts of your team members to create a positive and engaged work atmosphere.
- Build trust, autonomy, and work-life balance to keep your employees committed, inspired, and achieving their full potential.

Five Questions Business Leaders Should Ask About Creating Effective and Engaged Employees

- What kind of work environment do you believe motivates and empowers your employees to perform at their best? What are you currently doing to create that?
- How do you think you can foster a greater sense of ownership and accountability among your employees? What strategies have you seen work effectively in the past?
- What do you believe are the most important qualities or skills that your employees should possess in order to be successful and engaged?
- How are you creating an inclusive and diverse workplace that fosters engagement and empowers all employees to contribute their best ideas and insights?
- How can you encourage and support your employees in finding meaning and purpose in their work? What steps do you take to align their individual goals with your organization's mission and values?

Creating effective and engaged employees is at the core of successful leadership. It goes beyond simply having a team that is productive and achieving outstanding results. It involves creating an environment where individuals are motivated, energized, and fully committed to their work, as well as to the team and the organization as a whole.

To define effective and engaged employees, it is important to consider both the quantitative and qualitative aspects. On one hand, effective employees are those who consistently meet or exceed their performance goals. They deliver high-quality work, demonstrate a strong work ethic, and are reliable and accountable for their actions. These individuals have a clear understanding of their roles and responsibilities and possess the necessary skills and knowledge to perform their jobs successfully.

On the other hand, engaged employees are emotionally invested in their work. They are enthusiastic, passionate, and inspired by their job and the purpose of the organization. They actively participate, contribute ideas, and take ownership of their work. Engaged employees believe in the goals and values of the organization and are aligned with its vision, mission, and culture. They feel valued and supported, knowing that their contributions are recognized and appreciated.

Creating effective and engaged employees requires a leader to focus on both results and relationships. Leaders must set clear expectations and provide their team members with the necessary resources and support to succeed. Regular feedback, coaching, and mentoring are also crucial for growth and development. By actively involving employees in decision-making processes and recognizing their achievements, leaders foster a sense of ownership and empowerment.

To further promote engagement, leaders should communicate a compelling vision and purpose that inspires and motivates employees. They should ensure that individuals understand how their work contributes to the bigger picture and how it aligns with the organization's goals. This sense of meaning and purpose drives employee engagement and fosters a strong sense of belonging and commitment to the organization.

Additionally, leaders should create a culture of trust, collaboration, and open communication. By fostering an environment where ideas and feedback are valued, employees feel safe to share their thoughts, take risks, and innovate. Building strong relationships based on trust and respect is paramount. Leaders should actively listen, show empathy, and provide support, creating a sense of psychological safety where everyone feels valued and included.

One company that exemplifies effective leadership in creating engaged employees is The Motley Fool, a renowned financial media and investment services company. Led by co-founders David and Tom Gardner, The Motley Fool has built a culture centered around individual empowerment, collaboration, and a passion for their mission.

At The Motley Fool, leaders understand that engaged employees are the backbone of their success. They prioritize open communication, ensuring that every employee's voice is heard and valued. Regular company-wide meetings serve as a platform for sharing updates, celebrating achievements, and fostering a sense of community. Employees feel a strong connection to the company's mission, which inspires them to go above and beyond in their roles.

Moreover, The Motley Fool places a significant emphasis on personal and professional growth. They offer generous training programs, mentorship opportunities, and support for employees to develop new skills and knowledge. By investing in their employees' growth, they not only equip them with the tools needed to succeed but also show a genuine interest in their long-term success and fulfillment.

The company also understands the importance of work-life balance and the impact it has on employee engagement. Leadership encourages a flexible work environment, promoting trust and autonomy. By empowering employees to manage their time and prioritize their personal lives, The Motley Fool fosters a healthy and harmonious work atmosphere.

Furthermore, The Motley Fool cultivates a culture of recognition and celebration. They regularly acknowledge employee contributions and achievements, both publicly and privately. Appreciation events, rewards, and incentives reinforce a sense of belonging and motivate individuals to continue their outstanding work.

The infectious enthusiasm and genuine care exhibited by The Motley Fool's leaders create a thriving and engaged workforce. Employees feel valued, empowered, and inspired to contribute their best efforts, which has resulted in remarkable business growth and a loyal community of investors and customers.

Overall, The Motley Fool stands out as a prime example of a company with leaders who have successfully created effective and engaged employees. Through open communication, investment in personal growth, support for work-life balance, and a culture of recognition, they have fostered an environment that both nurtures individual success and drives the company's overall accomplishments. Their leadership approach serves as an inspiring model for business leaders aiming to create a highly engaged and motivated workforce.

Creating effective and engaged employees in the context of leadership requires a combination of results-focused strategies and relationship-building efforts. By setting clear expectations, providing support and recognition, fostering a sense of purpose, and building strong relationships based on trust and collaboration, leaders can cultivate an environment where employees are fully engaged, delivering outstanding results, and contributing to the overall success of the team and organization.

Now that we have explored the key elements of creating effective and engaged employees within a leadership context, it's time to put these concepts into action. I have created a checklist that outlines specific strategies and practices that leaders can implement to foster employee engagement and drive exceptional performance. We'll dive in deeper to these in subsequent chapters.

> *"No one can whistle a symphony. It takes a whole orchestra to play it."*
>
> *- H.E. Luccock*

CHECKLIST

Checklist for Creating Effective and Engaged Employees:

- Clearly define performance goals and expectations: Clearly communicate the performance goals and expectations to employees, ensuring they understand what is expected from them.

- Provide necessary resources and support: Ensure that employees have access to the necessary resources, tools, and support they need to succeed in their roles. Invest in training for employees in both technical (hard skills) and essentials skills (soft skills).

- Regularly provide feedback, coaching, and mentoring: Schedule regular feedback sessions to provide constructive feedback, coaching, and mentoring to help employees grow and develop.

- Involve employees in decision-making processes: Actively involve employees in decision-making processes to empower them and give them a sense of ownership in their work.

- Recognize and appreciate achievements: Regularly recognize and appreciate the accomplishments and contributions of employees to make them feel valued and supported.

- Communicate a compelling vision and purpose: Clearly communicate the organization's vision and purpose, showing how employees' work contributes to the bigger picture and aligns with the organization's goals.

- Foster a culture of trust, collaboration, and open communication: Create an environment where ideas and feedback are valued, fostering trust, collaboration, and open communication.

- Listen actively and show empathy: Actively listen to employees, show empathy, and provide support to create a sense of psychological safety where everyone feels valued and included.

- Build strong relationships based on trust and respect: Build strong relationships with employees based on trust and respect, creating a supportive and positive work environment.

- Promote a sense of meaning and purpose: Help employees understand the meaning and purpose of their work, fostering a sense of engagement and commitment to the organization.

- Continuously monitor and adjust strategies: Regularly assess the effectiveness of the strategies implemented and make adjustments as needed to improve employee effectiveness and engagement.

By following these preparations, leaders can create an environment where employees are motivated, engaged, and fully committed to their work, team, and organization.

Now that we have gone through the checklist for creating effective and engaged employees, let's take a look at some examples that demonstrate how these preparations can be implemented in the workplace.

> *"Leadership is not about being in charge. It is about taking care of those in your charge."*
>
> *- Simon Sinek*

EXAMPLES

An effective employee: Sarah consistently meets her performance goals and delivers high-quality work. She is always reliable and accountable for her actions. Sarah has a clear understanding of her role and possesses the necessary skills and knowledge to perform her job successfully.

An engaged employee: Mark is emotionally invested in his work. He is enthusiastic, passionate, and inspired by his job and the purpose of the organization. Mark actively participates, contributes ideas, and takes ownership of his work. He believes in the goals and values of the organization and is aligned with its vision, mission, and culture.

A leader setting clear expectations: Jennifer, a team leader, holds regular meetings to communicate specific goals and expectations to her team members. She ensures that everyone understands their roles and responsibilities, as well as the desired outcomes. Jennifer provides clarity, so her team knows what is expected of them.

A leader providing support and recognition: Michael, a manager, regularly provides feedback, coaching, and mentorship to his team members. He supports their growth and development by identifying areas for improvement and guiding them towards success. Michael also recognizes and acknowledges their achievements and effort, boosting morale and motivation.

A leader fostering a sense of purpose: Emily, a department head, communicates a compelling vision and purpose to her team. She explains how their work contributes to the bigger picture and aligns with the organization's goals. Emily emphasizes the importance of their contributions, giving employees a sense of meaning and purpose in their work.

A leader building trust and collaboration: David, a team leader, creates a culture of trust, collaboration, and open communication. He encourages his team members to share their thoughts, ideas, and feedback. David actively listens, shows empathy, and supports his team, creating a safe and inclusive environment where everyone feels valued and respected.

Overall, effective and engaged employees are those who consistently meet performance goals, are emotionally invested in their work, and feel valued and supported by their leaders. It is the responsibility of leaders to set clear expectations, provide support and recognition, communicate a compelling vision and purpose, and foster trust and collaboration to cultivate a motivated and committed team.

With these examples in mind, let's explore some common mistakes to avoid when implementing similar strategies.

> *"Engaged, loyal employees are not only more productive, but they also contribute to a positive work culture and happy customers."*
>
> *- Richard Branson*

TYPICAL MISTAKES AND HOW TO AVOID THEM

Based on we've covered so far, one mistake that most people make in creating effective and engaged employees is focusing solely on the quantitative aspects of their performance. While meeting or exceeding performance goals is important, it is equally crucial to consider the qualitative aspects of engagement.

To avoid this mistake, leaders should take the time to understand the emotional investment employees have in their work. They should create an environment where employees feel passionate, inspired, and connected to the purpose of the organization. This can be achieved by communicating a compelling vision and purpose, explaining how their work contributes to the bigger picture, and aligning their goals with those of the organization.

Another mistake that can be made is neglecting the importance of building strong relationships with employees. Effective leadership goes beyond setting expectations and providing resources – it also involves actively listening, showing empathy, and providing support. Leaders should create a culture of trust, collaboration, and open communication, where employees feel valued and included.

To avoid this mistake, leaders should make an effort to foster an environment where ideas and feedback are welcomed. They should actively listen to their employees, show understanding and support, and provide opportunities for growth and development through coaching and mentoring.

The key mistakes to avoid when creating effective and engaged employees are solely focusing on quantitative performance and neglecting the importance of building strong relationships. By considering both the quantitative and qualitative aspects, and by fostering an environment of trust, collaboration, and purpose, leaders can create a workforce that is motivated, energized, and fully committed to their work and the organization as a whole.

MY #1 PIECE OF ADVICE

Now that we have discussed the mistakes to avoid in creating effective and engaged employees, it is important to give you the #1 piece of advice that encompasses both avoiding these mistakes and achieving the desired outcome.

My #1 piece of advice for improving leadership skills to effectively engage people is to prioritize active listening. By genuinely listening to others, understanding their perspectives, and valuing their input, you can begin to create a supportive and inclusive environment that fosters collaboration, trust, and effective communication.

"The key to successful leadership today is influence, not authority."

- Ken Blanchard

SUMMARY:

- Inspire others to go beyond productivity and strive for engagement, motivation, and commitment in their work.

- Encourage individuals to become effective employees by consistently exceeding performance goals, delivering high-quality work, and taking ownership of their responsibilities.

- Motivate employees to become engaged by finding purpose and passion in their job, actively participating, and aligning with the organization's vision and values.

- Empower leaders to foster engagement by setting clear expectations, providing support and recognition, and involving employees in decision-making processes.

- Create a culture of trust, collaboration, and open communication to inspire employees to share ideas, take risks, and feel valued and included in their work environment.

APPLICATION QUESTIONS

- How can you better leverage each employee's unique strengths and preferences to create a more engaging and productive work environment?

- What strategies will you employ to foster more open communication and collaboration among team members, ensuring everyone feels heard and valued?

- How can you create a bigger sense of purpose and meaning for your employees, connecting their individual roles to the bigger picture and organizational goals?

- What opportunities will you provide for professional growth and development, empowering employees to constantly learn and enhance their both their technical and their essential skills?
- How will you establish trust and credibility as leaders, allowing employees to feel comfortable expressing their concerns and ideas without fear of judgement?

QUIZ

1. What is one way that leaders can create effective and engaged employees?

   A. Set clear expectations
   B. Provide feedback and coaching
   C. Communicate a compelling vision
   D. All of the above

2. What is a qualitative aspect of effective employees?

   A. Consistently meeting performance goals
   B. Reliable and accountable
   C. Possessing necessary skills
   D. Demonstrating a strong work ethic

3. What is a characteristic of engaged employees?

   A. Enthusiastic
   B. Passionate
   C. Invested
   D. All of the above

4. What type of feedback is important for employee growth and development?

   A. Positive

   B. Constructive

   C. Regular

   D. All of the above

5. What type of relationships should leaders foster?

   A. Trusting

   B. Collaborative

   C. Open

   D. All of the above

Answer Key:

1. D - All of the above

2. D - Demonstrating a strong work ethic

4. D - All of the above

5. D - All of the above

As we conclude this chapter on defining effective and engaged employees, it's now time to delve into the practical application of these principles. In the next chapter, we will explore inspiring real-life examples of leaders who have successfully transformed their teams and organizations by implementing the very principles we have discussed here. Get ready to be inspired by the success stories that await you in the next chapter.

CHAPTER 2
TRANSFORMATIVE LEADERSHIP
INSPIRING STORIES OF LEADERS RESHAPING TEAMS AND ORGANIZATIONS

"Engaged employees are not just the satisfied ones. They have an emotional commitment to their organization and its goals. They genuinely care about their work and the mission of the company."

- Shari Harley

AT A GLANCE

Five Essential Points for Transformative Leadership

- Discover the transformative power of strategies that improve employee engagement with real-life examples from successful companies like Zappos and Adobe.

- Learn how Zappos goes above and beyond to create a positive work environment through their unique "Zappos Family Experience" system.

- Explore how Adobe's employee recognition program, "The Founders' Award," fosters a strong sense of camaraderie and motivation within their workforce.

- Find out how Patagonia encourages open and transparent communication to create a culture of trust and empowerment.

- Uncover the key to improving employee engagement by being curious, experimenting, and listening to your employees' feedback and needs.

Five Questions Business Leaders Should Ask About Transformative Leadership

- Have you come across any innovative approaches or strategies in other organizations that have successfully increased efficiency and employee engagement? How are you bringing them into your organization?

- What current challenges or pain points are there within the organization that are affecting efficiency or employee engagement? How do you envision addressing these issues to drive improvement?

- How well do you know your employees and their individual strengths and interests? In what ways are you leveraging this knowledge to enhance their engagement and boost overall productivity?

- What steps are you taking to foster a culture of continuous improvement and learning within the organization? How do you encourage employees to take ownership of their growth and development?

- How do you promote collaboration and cross-functional teamwork to maximize efficiency and engagement? Are there any initiatives or projects that would allow employees to work together more effectively?

Improving employee engagement is an essential goal for any organization that seeks to create a positive and productive work culture. As an executive coach and trainer, I have come across many programs and practices that have been proven to be successful in achieving this goal. Let me share with you some real-life examples that showcase the transformative power of these strategies. One remarkable company that stands out when it comes to employee engagement is Zappos.

Their commitment to fostering a positive work environment goes above and beyond. Their unique approach involves offering a "Zappos Family Experience," where they invite potential new hires to spend a week working alongside current employees, fully immersing themselves in the company's culture. This serves as a two-way assessment, as both the company and the potential employee can gain insight into whether they are a good fit for each other.

By creating this opportunity for mutual understanding and connection, Zappos ensures that their workforce is composed of individuals who genuinely believe in the company's values and are passionate about their work. Another successful practice in improving employee engagement is recognition and rewards. One fantastic example is the employee recognition program implemented by Adobe. They created an internal platform called "The Founders' Award," where employees can nominate each other for outstanding achievements.

This recognition extends beyond just small rewards or bonuses; it involves a formal presentation in front of the entire organization, highlighting the employee's accomplishments and their impact on the company. By providing a platform for peers to celebrate each other's successes, Adobe fosters a strong sense of camaraderie, motivation, and pride within their workforce. In addition to recognition, communication is another vital aspect of employee engagement. A shining example of this is the strategies employed by Patagonia, an outdoor clothing company known for their commitment to environmental sustainability.

They encourage a culture of open and transparent communication by hosting regular "town hall" meetings, where employees are updated on company goals, progress, and challenges. Beyond the typical Q&A sessions, Patagonia goes the extra mile by creating a safe space for employees to voice their concerns, share their ideas, and collectively problem-solve. By actively involving employees in the decision-making process and valuing their input, Patagonia instills a sense of ownership, trust, and empowerment. These examples illustrate the power of specific tactics and practices in improving employee engagement.

Whether it's offering immersive experiences to ensure cultural alignment like Zappos, implementing recognition programs that celebrate outstanding achievements like Adobe, or fostering open communication channels like Patagonia, each of these initiatives empowers employees, creates a positive and inclusive work culture, and ultimately leads to increased engagement and productivity.

Remember, every organization is unique, and what works for one may not work for another. The key is to be curious, willing to experiment, and to listen to your employees. By continuously evaluating and adapting your approach based on their feedback and needs, you can create a truly engaged culture that inspires and motivates your entire workforce.

Now that we have explored some real-life examples of successful strategies for improving employee engagement, let's dive into a checklist that can help you implement these ideas in your organization.

> *"Employees who believe that management is concerned about them as a whole person – not just an employee – are more productive, more satisfied, more fulfilled. Satisfied employees mean satisfied customers, which results in profitability."*
>
> *- Anne M. Mulcahy*

CHECKLIST

Checklist for Transformative Leadership

After reading about how some of the industry leaders do it, here is a checklist for improving employee engagement. We will dive deeper into each of these areas multiple times in this book.

- Assess your current work culture: Evaluate your organization's current work culture to identify areas that need improvement and opportunities for employee engagement.

- Empower employees: Encourage and empower employees to take ownership of their work and contribute to the organization's goals and objectives.

- Foster a growth mindset: Encourage a culture of continuous learning and growth, where employees are open to new ideas, willing to take risks, and embrace change.

- Encourage open communication: Promote transparency and open communication channels to foster trust, understanding, and effective problem-solving. Create a safe space for employees to voice their concerns, share ideas, and participate in collective problem-solving.

- Involve employees in decision-making: Actively involve employees in the decision-making process by seeking their input and valuing their ideas. This fosters a sense of ownership, trust, and empowerment.

- Tailor initiatives to your organization: Remember that every organization is unique, so adapt and customize these initiatives to fit the specific needs and culture of your company.

- Be open to experimentation: Be curious and willing to experiment with different strategies to improve employee engagement. Monitor the effectiveness of each initiative and make adjustments as needed based on employee feedback and needs.

- Continuously evaluate and adapt: Regularly evaluate the success of your employee engagement initiatives and gather feedback from employees. Make necessary changes and modifications to create a culture that inspires and motivates your entire workforce.

- Prioritize active listening: Actively listen to your employees, their concerns, and their ideas. Make communication a two-way street and ensure that their feedback is genuinely heard and considered.

Remember, improving employee engagement is an ongoing process that requires consistent effort and adaptation. Use this checklist as a framework to guide your actions, but be open to tailoring it to suit your organization's unique needs and requirements.

Now that we have gone over the action steps checklist for improving employee engagement, let's take a look at some examples that illustrate how these strategies can be implemented in real-world situations.

"Employees who are engaged, empowered, and inspired will take your organization to new heights."

- Tony Hsieh

EXAMPLES

Now that we've looked how big name companies have implemented transformative leadership principles here are some examples of how you might do it:

A tech start-up improved employee engagement by implementing a flexible work schedule policy. Employees were given the freedom to choose their own working hours as long as they met their deadlines and attended important meetings. This increased their sense of autonomy and work-life balance, resulting in higher job satisfaction and productivity.

A retail company focused on creating a strong sense of purpose and meaning for their employees. They organized regular volunteer events where employees could give back to their community. By aligning their work with a larger cause, employees felt a deeper sense of fulfillment and connection to the company, resulting in increased engagement and loyalty.

A manufacturing company implemented a mentorship program where senior leaders were paired with junior employees. This provided an opportunity for knowledge sharing, skill development, and career growth. The mentorship relationships built trust, improved communication, and allowed employees to feel supported and valued, resulting in higher engagement and retention rates.

A healthcare organization invested in professional development opportunities for their employees. They provided access to workshops, conferences, and training programs, allowing employees to enhance their skills and stay updated with industry trends. This investment in their growth and development made employees feel valued and motivated, resulting in increased engagement and a highly skilled workforce.

A financial services firm prioritized building a diverse and inclusive work culture. They implemented unconscious bias trainings, formed employee resource groups, and created a safe space for employees to share their experiences and perspectives. This inclusive environment fostered a sense of belonging and acceptance, leading to higher levels of engagement and overall employee satisfaction.

Based on these examples, let's now dive into the potential mistakes to avoid when undertaking similar efforts in improving employee engagement.

> *"Employee engagement is not about perks and benefits. It's about creating an environment where employees feel valued, trusted, and empowered."*
>
> *- Simon Sinek*

TYPICAL MISTAKES AND HOW TO AVOID THEM

One common mistake that most people make in transforming teams and organizations is neglecting the importance of cultural shift. Many individuals focus solely on making strategic changes without considering the impact of culture on the success of a transformation.

This mistake can hinder progress and limit the effectiveness of any changes implemented. To avoid this mistake, leaders should recognize the significance of cultural shift and understand that it goes hand in hand with strategic changes. They should prioritize creating an environment that encourages collaboration, innovation, and open communication. This can be done by empowering employees, fostering a growth mindset, and encouraging them to take risks and embrace change.

Another mistake that can be made is assuming that there is a one-size-fits-all solution for transforming teams and organizations. Every organization and leadership situation is unique, so blindly applying the principles discussed in a book or following the example of successful leaders may not yield the desired results. To avoid this mistake, leaders should take the time to understand the specific needs and dynamics of their teams. They should tailor the principles discussed in the material to their own context and make adjustments accordingly. By doing so, leaders can ensure that their transformation efforts align with the specific requirements of their organization and are more likely to inspire their teams to achieve greatness.

This is why I some franchised, pre-prepared one-size fits all canned content. I roll up my sleeves and get dirty, working with your team and your business right where you are with programs tailored specifically to your needs and your organization.

Another mistake people make is a lack of clear communication and transparency. When facing challenges, leaders should recognize the importance of open and honest communication. This can be achieved by implementing practices like weekly business review meetings, where leaders from different divisions openly discuss issues, successes, and challenges. Creating a collaborative environment fosters a sense of ownership and alignment among team members.

And yet another mistake is not embracing diversity and inclusivity. Leaders should understand the value of diverse perspectives and the impact it can have on driving meaningful change. By implementing initiatives that empower women and enhance diversity in senior leadership positions, organizations can foster innovation and drive growth.

MY #1 PIECE OF ADVICE

For those looking to enhance their leadership skills in employee engagement, my #1 advice is to lead by example. Show genuine care for your team by actively participating in their work, listening to their ideas, and valuing their contributions.

Foster a culture of open communication and trust where everyone feels heard and supported. Implement best practices, such as providing regular feedback, recognizing achievements, and promoting work-life balance. Remember, engaged employees are more motivated, productive, and committed, ultimately driving the success of your organization.

"The best way to engage your employees is to care about them and their success, both personally and professionally."

- Mary Kay Ash

SUMMARY:

- Improving employee engagement is critical for creating a positive and productive work culture.

- Zappos, a remarkable company, offers a "Zappos Family Experience" to ensure cultural alignment and passion among their workforce.

- Adobe's employee recognition program, "The Founders' Award," fosters camaraderie and motivation by celebrating outstanding achievements in front of the entire organization.

- Patagonia's open communication tactics, including "town hall" meetings, empower employees, instill trust, and create a sense of ownership.

- Remember, every organization is unique, so be curious, experiment, and listen to your employees to create an engaged culture that inspires and motivates.

Learn from your mistakes and actively seek out opportunities to grow and develop as a leader. With the right principles and strategies, you can lead your team to greatness.

APPLICATION QUESTIONS

- What strategies can you implement to ensure clear communication and alignment of goals across your organization?

- How are you providing your employees with the necessary resources, tools, and training to succeed and excel in their roles?

- How can you incorporate flexibility and autonomy into your work culture, enabling employees to work in ways that best suit their skills and preferences?

- How do you recognize and reward exceptional performance and contributions, motivating your team to go above and beyond? How can you improve it and make sure it fits how each employee wants to be appreciated?

- Are you regularly seeking feedback from your employees to identify areas for improvement and understand their needs and preferences? What are you doing with that feedback?

QUIZ

1. What should leaders not be looking for?

    A. A platform for transparency
    B. A one-size-fits-all solution
    C. A leader in cloud computing
    D. An example of successful transformation

2. What is the key to creating a truly engaged culture?

    A. Listening to employees
    B. Experimenting with different tactics
    C. Offering immersive experiences
    D. Implementing recognition programs

3. What is the most important thing for leaders to understand when transforming teams and organizations?

    A. The importance of implementing the principles discussed in the book
    B. The specific needs and dynamics of their teams
    C. The changing technology landscape

D. The need to take risks and embrace change

4. What is one example of a successful practice in improving employee engagement?

A. Offering immersive experiences

B. Implementing recognition programs

C. Hosting "town hall" meetings

D. All of the above

5. What is the key to improving employee engagement?

A. Offering recognition and rewards

B. Creating an internal platform

C. Listening to employees

D. Experimenting with different tactics

Answer Key:

1. B. - A one-size-fits-all solution

2. A. - Listening to employees

3. B. - The specific needs and dynamics of their teams

4. D. - All of the above

5. D. - Experimenting with different tactics

Now that we have explored real-life examples of leaders who have effectively transformed their teams and organizations, it is time to delve into the actionable strategies and techniques for developing and empowering high-performing teams who consistently deliver better results – are you ready to discover the key to achieving remarkable success by unlocking the true potential of your team?

CHAPTER 3

FROM GOOD TO GREAT

CULTIVATING A CULTURE OF CONTINUOUS IMPROVEMENT

"Innovation is seeing what everybody has seen and thinking what nobody has thought."

- Albert Szent-Györgyi

AT A GLANCE

Five Essential Points for Cultivating a Culture of Continuous Improvement

- Unlocking creativity and driving sustainable growth: Discover how organizational culture can serve as a powerful catalyst for fostering innovation and continuous improvement within teams and organizations.

- Embracing change and challenging the status quo: Learn how a culture that values innovation encourages employees to think outside the box and seek better ways of doing things.

- Collaboration and open communication: Explore how a culture that celebrates collaboration and diverse perspectives creates the ideal conditions for innovation to thrive, and enhances team dynamics.

- Leadership as a driving force: Understand the crucial role that leaders play in shaping and reinforcing an organizational culture that promotes continuous improvement and innovation.

- Actionable strategies that make a difference: Find out how organizations can implement practical approaches such as promoting a learning mindset, establishing feedback mechanisms, and recognizing and rewarding successful innovations, to foster a culture of innovation and continuous improvement.

Five Questions Business Leaders Should Ask About Cultivating a Culture of Continuous Improvement

- How do you think the overall organizational culture impacts your ability to embrace a mindset of continuous improvement and innovation?

- When reflecting on your organization's current culture, what aspects do you think are conducive to fostering innovation and continuous improvement? Are there any areas where you could improve or introduce new practices to enhance this culture?

- Can you recall any instances where an innovative idea or improvement was successfully implemented within our organization? What factors do you believe contributed to its success, both in terms of the idea itself and the organizational culture surrounding it?

- How do you think the way we communicate and collaborate as a team impacts our ability to generate new ideas, embrace change, and contribute to the overall vision of continuous improvement?

- How do you ensure that all employees feel empowered and encouraged to contribute their ideas for improvement, regardless of their level or role within the organization? Are there any practices or initiatives you could implement to better capture and leverage the knowledge and creativity of your entire workforce?

Organizational culture plays a pivotal role in fostering an environment of continuous improvement and innovation within teams or organizations. It sets the stage for employees to embrace new ideas, take risks, and challenge the status quo. When a culture of innovation is deeply embedded in the fabric of an organization, it becomes a powerful catalyst for unlocking creativity and driving sustainable growth.

First and foremost, a culture that values continuous improvement and innovation encourages employees to think outside the box and seek better ways of doing things. It promotes a mindset that embraces change and continuous learning, urging individuals to constantly question existing processes, products, and services. By nurturing an environment where experimentation is encouraged and failure is seen as a stepping stone towards progress, organizational culture sets the groundwork for fostering innovation and improvement.

Moreover, organizational culture shapes norms and values that guide employee behavior. A culture that celebrates collaboration, open communication, and diverse perspectives fosters the necessary conditions for innovation to thrive. It encourages individuals to share their ideas, collaborate with others, and build on each other's strengths. This collaborative approach not only leads to innovative solutions but also enhances team dynamics by building trust and fostering stronger relationships.

Leadership plays a crucial role in shaping and reinforcing the organizational culture that promotes continuous improvement and innovation. Leaders must embody and exemplify the values and behaviors they seek from their team members. They should provide a clear vision and purpose, communicate expectations, and set the tone for embracing change and taking calculated risks. When leaders actively encourage and support innovation, it sends a powerful message to the entire organization, signaling that creativity and improvement are not only welcomed but valued. To foster a culture of innovation and continuous improvement, organizations can implement a few actionable strategies. First, they should promote a learning mindset by providing opportunities for skill development, encouraging cross-functional collaboration, and creating platforms for sharing knowledge and best practices. This can be achieved through training programs, mentorship initiatives, or internal innovation challenges.

Secondly, organizations should establish feedback mechanisms that allow employees to contribute their ideas and suggestions for improvement. This can be done through regular feedback sessions, suggestion boxes, or digital platforms that facilitate idea sharing and evaluation. Encouraging employees to contribute their unique perspectives and tapping into their collective intelligence can lead to breakthrough innovations and continuous improvement.

Lastly, organizations should celebrate and reward successful innovations and improvements. Recognizing and acknowledging the efforts of individuals or teams who have made significant contributions to the organization's growth fuels motivation and reinforces the desired behaviors. By linking performance evaluations, promotions, or monetary incentives to innovative thinking and continuous improvement, organizations can drive a culture that actively supports and rewards these efforts.

One company that exemplifies a deep understanding of the role of organizational culture in fostering continuous improvement and innovation is Google. Renowned for its innovative products and services, Google has created a culture that not only encourages but also thrives on continuous learning, experimentation, and adaptability.

At Google, their organizational culture is centered around a few key pillars that contribute to an environment conducive to innovation. First and foremost, they prioritize openness and transparency, allowing employees to freely share ideas and collaborate across teams. This openness enables cross-pollination of knowledge and helps break down silos, fostering a culture of collective intelligence.

Furthermore, Google encourages a growth mindset among its employees, emphasizing the importance of learning from failures and embracing iterative approaches. They understand that innovation often involves taking risks, and they actively promote a safe space for employees to experiment and learn from mistakes without fear of repercussions.

To nurture a culture of continuous improvement, Google also invests heavily in employee development programs. They provide various learning opportunities such as internal training initiatives, hackathons, and innovation challenges, allowing employees to sharpen their skills and stay ahead in an ever-evolving industry.

Moreover, Google fosters a sense of autonomy and ownership among its employees. Engineers and other team members are given the freedom to pursue projects they are passionate about, which fosters intrinsic motivation and encourages creativity.

Google's organizational culture is further reinforced by their performance-based rewards system. They recognize and reward employees for their contributions to innovation, incentivizing them to continually strive for excellence.

While Google serves as an exceptional example, it is essential to note that every organization is unique, and what works for one may not work for another. However, understanding the significance of organizational culture in cultivating a culture of continuous improvement and innovation is crucial for any company seeking to thrive in today's dynamic business landscape. Organizational culture plays a crucial role in fostering continuous improvement and innovation within teams and organizations. It sets the stage for employees to embrace change, think creatively, and challenge the status quo. By promoting collaboration, providing opportunities for learning, and rewarding innovation, organizations can create a culture that inspires and empowers its members to strive for excellence and drive sustainable growth.

Now that we have explored the importance of organizational culture in fostering continuous improvement and innovation, let's dive into a checklist that can help organizations implement actionable strategies to cultivate this culture within their teams and organizations.

> *"The greatest enemy of progress is not failure, but complacency."*
>
> *- John C. Maxwell*

CHECKLIST

Checklist for Fostering a Culture of Continuous Improvement and Innovation:

- Assess the organizational culture: Evaluate the current culture within the organization to identify gaps or areas for improvement in fostering continuous improvement and innovation.

- Define the desired culture: Clearly define and articulate the values and behaviors that are desired for a culture that supports continuous improvement and innovation.

- Lead by example: Ensure that leaders exemplify the desired values and behaviors, acting as role models for employees.

- Encourage open dialogue: Foster an environment of open communication where employees feel comfortable sharing their ideas, insights, and concerns without fear of judgment or retribution.

- Empower employees: Provide the necessary resources, support, and recognition to empower employees to take risks and pursue innovative ideas.

- Reward contributions: Recognize and reward employees for their contributions towards continuous improvement and innovation to reinforce motivation and encourage active participation.

- Cultivate collaboration: Encourage collaboration among teams and departments to create a diverse pool of perspectives and knowledge that fuels creativity and generates unique solutions.

- Support experimentation: Embrace a culture that encourages experimentation and learning from failures as a means to drive continuous improvement and innovation.

- Provide continuous learning opportunities: Offer training and development programs that focus on building skills and knowledge in areas of improvement and innovation.

- Monitor and refine: Continuously assess and monitor the effectiveness of the culture in supporting continuous improvement and innovation, making adjustments as necessary.

By following this checklist, leaders can create a culture that supports continuous improvement and innovation, leading to increased creativity, collaboration, and success.

Now that we have gone through the checklist for fostering a culture of continuous improvement and innovation, let's examine some examples that demonstrate how these actions can be implemented in practice.

"A culture of innovation rewards intelligent failure; the reward is an exploratory mindset, a willingness to experiment and take risks."

- Linda Hill

EXAMPLES

Now not everyone is Google so here are a few other examples to show you what is possible to inspire you:

A culture that values continuous improvement and innovation: A technology company encourages its employees to think outside the box and experiment with new ideas. They provide regular training programs, mentorship opportunities, and platforms for knowledge sharing. Employees are encouraged to challenge existing processes and products, and their contributions are recognized and rewarded

A culture that celebrates collaboration and open communication: A marketing agency creates a culture where diverse perspectives are valued. Employees are encouraged to share their ideas and collaborate with colleagues from different departments.

This culture of collaboration not only leads to innovative solutions for clients but also strengthens team dynamics and trust. Leadership shaping and reinforcing organizational culture:

A manufacturing company's CEO actively promotes a culture of continuous improvement and innovation. They lead by example, encouraging employees to take calculated risks and embrace change. The CEO regularly communicates the organization's vision and purpose, inspiring employees to think creatively and contribute their ideas for improvement. Promoting a learning mindset:

A healthcare organization invests in training programs and cross-functional collaborations. They provide opportunities for employees to develop new skills and learn from experts within and outside the organization. Employees are encouraged to share their knowledge and best practices, fostering a culture of continuous learning and improvement. Establishing feedback mechanisms:

A retail company creates a digital platform where employees can share their ideas and suggestions for improvement. Regular feedback sessions are held, and a suggestion box system is implemented. This allows employees to contribute their unique perspectives and provides a structured way for evaluating and implementing innovative ideasCelebrating and rewarding successful innovations:

A financial institution rewards employees who come up with innovative ideas that improve customer satisfaction or operational efficiency. Successful innovations are recognized publicly, and individuals or teams behind the ideas are given promotions, monetary incentives or other forms of appreciation. This encourages a culture that values and rewards continuous improvement and innovation. Overall, these examples illustrate how organizational culture can create an environment that fosters continuous improvement and innovation.

Now that we have seen several examples of how organizational culture can foster continuous improvement and innovation, let's take a look at some common mistakes to avoid in order to ensure the sustainability of such a culture within an organization.

> *"Progress is impossible without change, and those who cannot change their minds cannot change anything."*
>
> *- George Bernard Shaw*

TYPICAL MISTAKES AND HOW TO AVOID THEM

One common mistake that most people make in fostering a culture of continuous improvement and innovation is sticking to traditional ways of thinking and doing things. Many individuals may be resistant to change and new ideas, preferring to stick to the status quo.

To avoid this mistake, it is important to promote a mindset that embraces change and continuous learning. Encourage individuals to constantly question existing processes, products, and services, and to seek better ways of doing things. Nurturing an environment where experimentation is encouraged and failure is seen as a stepping stone towards progress can help overcome this barrier.

Another mistake often made is not promoting collaboration and open communication within the organization. A culture that celebrates collaboration and diverse perspectives creates the necessary conditions for innovation to thrive. It is important to encourage individuals to share their ideas, collaborate with others, and build on each other's strengths. This not only leads to innovative solutions but also enhances team dynamics and fosters stronger relationships.

By promoting this collaborative approach, organizations can avoid the mistake of siloed thinking and foster creativity. Leadership also plays a crucial role in shaping and reinforcing the culture of continuous improvement and innovation. One mistake that leaders often make is not embodying and exemplifying the values and behaviors they seek from their team members.

To avoid this mistake, leaders should provide a clear vision and purpose, communicate expectations, and set the tone for embracing change and taking calculated risks. When leaders actively encourage and support innovation, it sends a powerful message to the entire organization. To foster a culture of innovation and continuous improvement, organizations can implement actionable strategies. One strategy is promoting a learning mindset by providing opportunities for skill development, encouraging cross-functional collaboration, and creating platforms for sharing knowledge and best practices.

Training programs, mentorship initiatives, or internal innovation challenges can be effective in achieving this. Establishing feedback mechanisms is another important strategy. By allowing employees to contribute their ideas and suggestions for improvement, organizations tap into their collective intelligence, which can lead to breakthrough innovations. Regular feedback sessions, suggestion boxes, or digital platforms that facilitate idea sharing and evaluation can be used to encourage employee contributions.

Lastly, organizations should celebrate and reward successful innovations and improvements. Recognizing and acknowledging the efforts of individuals or teams who have made significant contributions to the organization's growth fuels motivation and reinforces the desired behaviors.

By linking performance evaluations, promotions, monetary incentives or other forms of appreciation to innovative thinking and continuous improvement, organizations can drive a culture that actively supports and rewards these efforts. In conclusion, to avoid common mistakes, it is important to promote a mindset that embraces change, encourage collaboration and open communication, and have leadership that exemplifies and supports the values and behaviors required for continuous improvement and innovation.

Additionally, implementing strategies such as promoting a learning mindset, establishing feedback mechanisms, and celebrating successful innovations can help foster a culture of innovation and drive sustainable growth within organizations.

MY #1 PIECE OF ADVICE

After considering these mistakes to avoid my #1 piece of advice is to embrace diversity which in turn will foster collaboration and innovation in high-performance teams. That means not just cultural diversity but also gender, age, education, background and perspectives to get the best ideas for innovation and creativity.

> *"The art of progress is to preserve order amid change and to preserve change amid order."*
>
> *- Alfred North Whitehead*

SUMMARY:

- Embrace change and strive for excellence by fostering a culture that values continuous improvement and innovation.

- Think outside the box and challenge the status quo to discover better ways of doing things and unlock your creative potential.

- Celebrate collaboration, open communication, and diverse perspectives to fuel innovation and build stronger team dynamics.

- Lead by example, encourage calculated risks, and actively support innovation to inspire your team to reach new heights.

- Create a learning mindset, provide feedback opportunities, and reward innovative thinking to drive a culture that fuels growth and success.

APPLICATION QUESTIONS

- How can you create a culture of openness and transparency where employees feel comfortable sharing ideas and collaborating across teams? What specific steps can you take to break down silos and foster a sense of collective intelligence?

- What strategies or initiatives can you implement to encourage a growth mindset within your organization? How can you promote a culture where employees embrace failures as opportunities to learn and iterate, rather than fearing them?

- How can you actively involve employees at all levels in the decision-making process to foster a sense of ownership and engagement? Are there opportunities for cross-functional teams or task forces to work together on strategic initiatives that promote innovation?

- Are there any existing cultural norms or practices that might be hindering a culture of continuous improvement and innovation? How can you identify and address any potential barriers or resistance to change within your organization?

- As a leader, what steps can you personally take to model the behaviors and mindset required for a culture of continuous improvement and innovation? How can you communicate and reinforce these values to inspire and motivate the rest of the organization?

QUIZ

1. What is the most important factor for creating a culture of innovation and continuous improvement?

   A. Leadership
   B. Rewards
   C. Communication
   D. Collaboration

2. What is the primary goal of a culture that values continuous improvement and innovation?

   A. To increase profits
   B. To reduce costs

C. To challenge the status quo

D. To maintain the status quo

3. What should organizations do to foster a culture of innovation and continuous improvement?

A. Provide opportunities for skill development

B. Establish feedback mechanisms

C. Celebrate and reward successful innovations

D. All of the above

4. What message does active encouragement and support of innovation from leadership send to the organization?

A. Fear of failure

B. Creativity and improvement are not welcomed

C. Creativity and improvement are valued

D. Experimentation is discouraged

5. What values should leaders embody in order to build a culture that supports continuous improvement and innovation?

A. Risk-taking and learning from failures

B. Open dialogue and experimentation

C. Recognizing and rewarding contributions

D. All of the above

Answer Key:

1. A – Leadership

2. C - To challenge the status quo

3. D - All of the above

4. C - Creativity and improvement are valued

5. D - All of the above

In addition to organizational culture, another key factor in driving continuous improvement and innovation is employee engagement. This next chapter will explore the crucial role that engaged employees play in promoting efficiencies and effectiveness within teams, and how leaders can cultivate a culture of engagement to harness their full potential. So, let's continue reading to discover the power of employee engagement and its impact on organizational success.

CHAPTER 4

FUELING SUCCESS

THE IMPACT OF EMPLOYEE ENGAGEMENT ON ORGANIZATIONAL EFFECTIVENESS

"The difference between a successful company and a mediocre one often lies in the commitment and engagement of its employees."

- Andrew Carnegie

AT A GLANCE

Five Essential Points on the Impact of Employee Engagement has on Organizational Effectiveness:

- Discover the secret to unlocking higher levels of productivity and performance in your team through employee engagement.

- Learn how engaged employees are driven to go above and beyond their job descriptions, leading to improved efficiencies and quality of work.

- Find out why engaged team members actively seek opportunities for growth and development, contributing to a culture of continuous improvement.

- Unleash the power of collaboration and teamwork by fostering a supportive environment through employee engagement.

- Explore how employee engagement can impact retention and satisfaction, creating a loyal and committed workforce that maximizes efficiencies and effectiveness.

Five Questions Business Leaders Should Ask About the Impact of Employee Engagement has on Organizational Effectiveness

- How do you think employee engagement impacts your overall organizational effectiveness? What personal experiences or observations do you have that demonstrate the link between engaged employees and positive outcomes?

- In your opinion, what specific factors contribute to high levels of employee engagement within your organization? Are there any particular aspects of your workplace culture, leadership style, or employee development programs that you believe positively or negatively impact engagement?

- How are you ensuring that employees feel a sense of purpose and connection to the organization's mission? What initiatives or strategies do you have that foster a deeper sense of engagement and alignment with your core values?

- How do you promote a supportive and inclusive work environment that encourages employees to give their best? Are there any team-building activities, recognition programs, or feedback mechanisms that actively contribute to boosting engagement levels?

- How do the leaders at all levels of the organization actively contribute to fostering employee engagement? What specific actions do they take to empower and motivate their teams, while also building strong relationships and trust?

Employee engagement is a vital factor in driving efficiencies and effectiveness within an organization. When employees are engaged, they are more likely to be committed to their work, motivated to give their best, and aligned with the goals of the organization. This heightened level of engagement directly impacts productivity and overall performance.

Engaged employees are more focused and invested in their tasks, resulting in reduced errors, higher quality output, and increased efficiency. They go above and beyond their role requirements, seeking innovative solutions to problems and continuously looking for ways to streamline processes. Moreover, engaged employees are more resilient and adaptable, which is crucial in today's fast-paced and ever-changing business environment.

To foster a culture of engagement, leaders play a critical role. Firstly, they need to establish a clear vision and set well-defined goals for the organization. When employees understand the purpose and direction of their work, they feel a sense of meaning and are more likely to be engaged. Communicating this vision effectively and regularly is key to ensuring that everyone is aligned with the organization's goals.Leaders must also prioritize effective communication and transparent feedback channels.

They should encourage open dialogue, listen attentively to their employees' needs, ideas, and concerns, and provide constructive feedback that helps individuals grow and improve. By valuing and involving their employees in decision-making, leaders not only foster a sense of ownership and autonomy but also tap into their collective knowledge and creativity.

Recognizing and appreciating employees' efforts and achievements is another crucial aspect of building a culture of engagement. Leaders should make an effort to regularly celebrate successes, both big and small, and acknowledge the contributions of individuals and teams. This recognition not only boosts morale but also reinforces the connection between effort and results, driving further engagement and motivation.In addition to these practices, leaders can also consider incorporating opportunities for personal and professional growth within the workplace. Providing avenues for skill development, career advancement, and learning experiences not only demonstrates investment in employees' growth but also enhances their sense of purpose and engagement.

Ultimately, a culture of engagement is built on trust, respect, and a sense of belonging. Leaders must lead by example, demonstrating these values and instilling them in the team. By investing time and effort into building strong relationships based on trust, leaders create an environment where employees feel valued, supported, and empowered to contribute their best work.

Southwest Airlines has built its success on a strong foundation that recognizes the power of engaged employees. Their philosophy revolves around the belief that happy employees create happy customers, and this mantra permeates every aspect of the organization. By investing in their employees' well-being, Southwest has fostered a culture that not only boosts morale and retention but also enhances organizational effectiveness.

At the core of Southwest's employee engagement philosophy is the recognition that employees are not just workers but essential partners in the airline's success. This mindset is ingrained in the company's DNA, with leaders consistently emphasizing the importance of building relationships and providing support. Unlike other businesses that view employees as mere cogs in the wheel, Southwest sees them as valuable assets who can drive innovation, provide exceptional service, and deliver outstanding results.

This unique philosophy impacts Southwest's effectiveness in several ways. First and foremost, by prioritizing employee engagement, Southwest has created a positive and inclusive work environment. Employees feel valued, supported, and inspired, leading to higher levels of job satisfaction and engagement. When employees genuinely enjoy their work and feel a sense of purpose, they are more motivated to go above and beyond, consistently delivering exceptional service to customers.

Secondly, Southwest's employee engagement philosophy contributes to building strong relationships within the organization. Southwest fosters a sense of camaraderie and teamwork, encouraging employees to collaborate, share ideas, and support each other. This focus on building relationships at all levels of the organization creates a cohesive and united workforce. When employees trust and respect their colleagues, communication flows smoothly, conflicts are resolved more effectively, and teamwork flourishes, ultimately increasing productivity and efficiency.

Furthermore, Southwest Airlines recognizes the value of investing in its employees' growth and development. The company offers extensive training programs, career advancement opportunities, and a culture of continuous learning. By nurturing employees' professional growth, Southwest ensures that they are equipped with the skills and knowledge necessary to excel in their roles. This commitment to employee development not only enhances individual performance but also strengthens the collective capabilities of the organization.

The impact of Southwest's employee engagement philosophy is evident in their industry-leading customer satisfaction ratings. Happy and engaged employees genuinely care about their customers, going the extra mile to provide exceptional service. Southwest's employees are known for their friendly and personable demeanor, making the travel experience more enjoyable for passengers. This dedication to customer service has resulted in a strong customer base, increased loyalty, and positive word-of-mouth recommendations.

The point is, Southwest Airlines' philosophy around employee engagement programs has profoundly impacted the organization's effectiveness. By recognizing the importance of happy and engaged employees, Southwest has cultivated a work environment characterized by positivity, strong relationships, and continuous growth. Through their commitment to employee well-being, Southwest has unlocked the potential of their workforce, driving exceptional customer service and cementing their position as a leader in the airline industry. Other organizations can learn from Southwest's approach and prioritize employee engagement to enhance their own organizational effectiveness. With Southwest as a shining example, it's clear that investing in employees is a winning strategy for long-term success.

Employee engagement is a catalyst for driving efficiencies and effectiveness in an organization. By fostering a culture of engagement through clear vision, effective communication, transparent feedback, recognition, opportunities for growth, and building strong relationships, leaders can unleash the full potential of their teams and achieve outstanding results.

Now that we have explored the importance of employee engagement and the role leaders play in fostering it, let's take a look at a checklist I have created to help leaders cultivate a culture of engagement within their organizations

> *"Engagement is not something that can be demanded; it must be earned."*
>
> *- Unknown*

CHECKLIST

Driving Efficiencies and Effectiveness through Employee Engagement:

- Identify the problem: Clearly define the issue or challenge that needs to be addressed.

- Set goals: Establish clear objectives and measurable outcomes that align with the organization's vision and purpose.

- Communicate effectively: Ensure that employees understand the purpose and direction of their work by regularly communicating the organization's vision and goals.

- Encourage open dialogue: Create an environment where employees feel comfortable sharing their needs, ideas, and concerns.

- Provide constructive feedback: Offer feedback that helps individuals grow and improve, while also acknowledging their achievements and contributions.

- Foster a sense of ownership and autonomy: Involve employees in decision-making processes and value their input.

- Recognize and celebrate success: Regularly acknowledge and appreciate the efforts and achievements of individuals and teams.

- Provide opportunities for growth: Offer avenues for personal and professional development to enhance employees' sense of purpose and engagement.

- Build trust and respect: Lead by example and create an environment based on trust, respect, and a sense of belonging.

- Invest in strong relationships: Build strong relationships with employees based on trust, support, and empowerment.

By implementing these action steps, you can foster a culture of engagement and unleash the full potential of your teams to achieve outstanding results.

Now that we have gone through the checklist for driving efficiencies and effectiveness through employee engagement, let's take a look at some examples that illustrate these action steps in action.

> *"Coming together is a beginning. Keeping together is progress. Working together is success."*
>
> *- Henry Ford*

EXAMPLES

It may be hard to imagine how you could achieve the same results as Southwest Airlines but it is possible to do what they have done even if it is on a smaller scale. After all, they weren't always a big company. Here are several different examples to illustrate what happens when employees are engaged at work in any size of organization.

Reduced errors: An engaged employee working in a manufacturing company consistently double-checks their work, pays attention to detail, and follows quality control procedures. As a result, the number of defects in their products decreases, leading to cost savings and improved customer satisfaction.

Higher quality output: An engaged employee working in a software development team takes the initiative to thoroughly test their code, identify and fix bugs, and collaborate with their teammates to ensure the software meets the highest quality standards. This results in a more stable and reliable product, reducing the need for rework or customer complaints.

Increased efficiency: An engaged employee working in a customer service department consistently suggests process improvements, automates repetitive tasks, and finds ways to reduce customer response times. These proactive efforts lead to streamlined operations, quicker issue resolution, and improved customer satisfaction.

Resilience and adaptability: An engaged employee working in a marketing agency readily embraces changes in the industry, such as shifts in consumer preferences or emerging digital trends. They consistently seek opportunities to learn new skills, attend industry conferences, and adapt their strategies accordingly. This adaptability allows the company to stay ahead of the competition and seize new business opportunities.

Clear vision and goals: A leader in a nonprofit organization communicates a clear and compelling vision of the organization's mission to their employees. This vision inspires the employees to go the extra mile, and they feel a deep sense of purpose in their work. As a result, they are more engaged, motivated, and committed to achieving the organization's goals.

Effective communication and feedback: A leader in a sales team holds regular team meetings to gather input and ideas from their employees. They actively listen to their suggestions, provide constructive feedback, and implement changes based on their input. This open and transparent communication fosters trust and engagement among the team members, resulting in improved collaboration and sales performance.

Recognition and appreciation: A manager in a retail store acknowledges and rewards their employees' exceptional performance by publicly recognizing their achievements. This not only boosts the morale and motivation of the recognized employees but also inspires others to strive for excellence, leading to increased engagement and overall productivity.

Opportunities for growth: An employer in a technology company provides their employees with access to online learning platforms, encourages attendance at conferences and workshops, and supports them in pursuing certifications or advanced degrees. These growth opportunities signal to employees that their development is valued and nurtured, leading to increased engagement and loyalty.

Trust, respect, and belonging: A team lead in a corporate office creates a supportive and inclusive work environment. They actively listen to their team members' ideas, value their diverse perspectives, and promote a culture of respect and collaboration. As a result, team members feel trusted, appreciated, and encouraged to contribute their unique talents and abilities, leading to higher levels of engagement and performance.

These examples demonstrate how employee engagement is linked to various outcomes and how leaders can foster a culture of engagement in their organizations.

Now that we have explored several examples of engaged employees in different teams, let's delve into the mistakes to avoid in order to replicate their success. Here are some key lessons learned that can help guide organizations in their own employee engagement initiatives.

> *"To win in the marketplace, you must first win in the workplace."*
>
> *- Doug Conant*

TYPICAL MISTAKES AND HOW TO AVOID THEM

Based on the material covered, there are a few common mistakes that people make when it comes to employee engagement. Here are some ways to avoid them:

Lack of recognition: One mistake is not recognizing and valuing the efforts of team members. People want to feel appreciated for their hard work, so it's important to acknowledge their contributions and achievements. This can be done through simple gestures like saying thank you, giving praise, or providing opportunities for growth and development.

Failure to understand individual motivators: Another mistake is not taking the time to understand what motivates each team member. Everyone is motivated by different things, so it's essential for leaders to get to know their employees on a personal level. By understanding their strengths, aspirations, and interests, leaders can assign tasks and responsibilities that align with what motivates each individual, leading to higher levels of engagement and performance.

Lack of communication: Communication is key to fostering engagement within a team. When leaders fail to communicate effectively, team members can feel disconnected and disengaged. It's important for leaders to be transparent, provide clear expectations, and encourage open dialogue. Regular check-ins, team meetings, and feedback sessions are all great ways to enhance communication and improve engagement.

Ignoring professional development: People want to grow and develop in their careers, so ignoring opportunities for professional growth can lead to disengagement. Leaders should actively support and encourage their team members to enhance their skills and knowledge. This can be done through training programs, mentorship opportunities, or providing resources for continued learning. When team members feel like they are constantly improving, they are more likely to stay engaged and motivated.

Lack of trust and support: Building a collaborative and supportive environment is crucial for employee engagement. If team members don't feel supported or trusted, they are less likely to be engaged in their work. Leaders should foster trust by being available, approachable, and by creating an inclusive and positive work culture. When team members feel supported and valued, they are more likely to work well together, solve problems, and drive efficiencies.

Avoiding these common mistakes can help leaders drive employee engagement and foster a high-performing team. By recognizing and valuing team members, understanding individual motivators, improving communication, supporting professional development, and building trust and support, leaders can create an environment that promotes engagement, productivity, and overall team effectiveness.

MY #1 PIECE OF ADVICE

One of the most important aspects of improving leadership skills in understanding the connection between employee engagement and an effective team that consistently delivers outstanding results is to actively listen to your team members. By truly listening to their thoughts, concerns, and feedback, you can identify and address any barriers to engagement, foster a sense of trust and collaboration, and create an environment where everyone feels valued and motivated to deliver exceptional results.

> *"The strength of the team is each individual member. The strength of each member is the team."*
>
> *- Phil Jackson*

SUMMARY:

- When team members feel engaged, passionate, and connected to their work, they go above and beyond their job descriptions, leading to increased productivity and overall team performance. Be the kind of employee who brings passion and enthusiasm to every task, and watch your impact soar.

- Engaged employees are motivated and committed to their work, feeling a sense of purpose and fulfillment. Embrace your work with dedication and drive, and you'll unlock new levels of productivity you never thought possible.

- Engaged employees actively seek out opportunities to enhance their skills and knowledge, contributing to a culture of continuous improvement. Be hungry for knowledge and growth, and watch your skills soar to new heights.

- Employee engagement fosters a collaborative and supportive environment, where teamwork and communication thrive. When you build strong relationships and trust with your colleagues, you create a supportive network that fuels efficiency and effectiveness.

- By prioritizing building strong relationships with your team members, you can tailor tasks and responsibilities to their abilities and interests, maximizing engagement and performance. Be a leader who understands and values your team, and watch as their engagement and enthusiasm skyrocket.

APPLICATION QUESTIONS

- What steps will you take to create a more inclusive and diverse work environment where employees feel valued, respected, and motivated to excel and that celebrates different perspectives and promotes a sense of belonging?

- In what ways can you provide opportunities for growth and development that not only benefit the individual employees but also contribute to the organization's success?

- How can you recognize and reward employees' achievements in a way that is meaningful and motivating for them?

- What initiatives can you implement to promote work-life balance and support the overall well-being of your employees?

- How can you enhance the employee onboarding process to ensure new hires feel welcome, connected, and engaged from day one?

Remember, the key to improving employee engagement and organizational effectiveness lies in actively listening to employees, valuing their input, and taking meaningful action based on their feedback.

QUIZ

1. What is the most important thing for leaders to prioritize in order to drive engagement?

   A. Continuous learning

   B. Enhanced communication

   C. Building relationships

   D. Active listening

2. How can leaders demonstrate trust, respect, and a sense of belonging?

   A. Lead by example

   B. Prioritize communication

   C. Involve employees in decision-making

   D. All of the above

3. What does engagement lead to in terms of team performance?

   A. Improved communication

   B. Increased motivation

   C. Higher quality work

   D. Higher loyalty

4. What does engagement lead to in terms of employee retention?

   A. Lower costs

   B. Improved satisfaction

   C. Increased loyalty

   D. All of the above

5. What is a key element of building a culture of engagement?

   A. Communication

   B. Accountability

C. Trust

D. All of the above

Answer Key:

1. C - Building relationships

2. A - All of the above

3. C - Higher quality work

4. D - All of the above

5. D - All of the above

Now that we have explored the significance of employee engagement in driving efficiencies and effectiveness, it is time to delve into the crucial task of recognizing and rectifying any underlying organizational issues that may impede employee engagement, and uncovering areas where improvements can be made to enhance efficiency within our teams or organizations. Keep reading to discover valuable insights on tackling these challenges head-on and unlocking the true potential of your workforce.

CHAPTER 5
DIGGING DEEPER
IDENTIFYING AND RESOLVING ORGANIZATIONAL ISSUES THAT HINDER EFFICIENCY AND ENGAGEMENT

"A culture of engagement begins with leadership's understanding that engaged employees are the greatest asset to any organization."

- Robert K. Greenleaf

AT A GLANCE

Five Essential Points for Identifying and Resolving Organizational Issues that Hinder Efficiency and Engagement

- Discover the proven, world-class approach to addressing organizational issues that hinder employee engagement and creating a high-performance team.

- Understand the crucial role of observation and active listening in recognizing underlying challenges and obstacles faced by employees at all levels.

- Learn how open communication and trust-building can create a safe space for dialogue, foster a sense of belonging, and ignite employee engagement.

- Explore the power of short-term solutions and long-term strategies in tackling organizational issues, including redistributing tasks, implementing policy changes, and establishing employee recognition programs.

- Uncover the impact of personal anecdotes and stories in inspiring action and illustrating the positive outcomes that can be achieved when leaders actively address underlying issues.

Five Questions Business Leaders Should Ask About Identifying and Resolving Organizational Issues that Hinder Efficiency and Engagement

- Have you noticed any specific roadblocks or bottlenecks that hinder efficiency and engagement within your organization? How do these challenges impact your overall productivity and employee satisfaction?

- How do you think these issues are affecting our team's ability to achieve its goals and deliver results? Are there any missed opportunities or areas where you could improve if these obstacles were addressed?

- In your opinion, what are the underlying root causes of these organizational inefficiencies and disengagement? Are there any systemic factors that contribute to their persistence?

- How do you believe addressing these issues would benefit your employees on an individual level? Can you envision the positive impact it could have on their personal growth, job satisfaction, and overall sense of fulfillment within the organization?

- Imagine a scenario where these organizational obstacles were eliminated. What would the ideal work environment look like? How would it feel to work in a highly efficient and engaged team?

Identifying and addressing underlying organizational issues that hinder employee engagement is crucial for creating a high-performance team. As a world-class expert in this field, I have developed a proven approach that focuses on both results and building relationships. In this response, I will outline the steps and strategies that I recommend to effectively recognize and tackle these issues.

Firstly, recognizing underlying organizational issues requires a keen eye for observation and active listening skills. By regularly interacting with employees at all levels, conducting surveys, and holding one-on-one meetings, leaders can gain valuable insights into the challenges and obstacles faced by their team members. This includes identifying patterns such as high turnover rates, low morale, or lack of collaboration.

Once these issues are identified, it is essential to address them proactively. Rather than disregarding or trying to sweep them under the rug, leaders must take ownership and communicate openly with their team. Building trust and creating a safe space for open dialogue is crucial in this process. By actively listening to employees' concerns, leaders can demonstrate empathy and validate their experiences, fostering a sense of belonging and engagement.

To address the underlying issues effectively, leaders should implement a combination of short-term solutions and long-term strategies. Short-term solutions could include addressing any immediate concerns or implementing small changes that can have an immediate impact. For example, if employees are feeling overwhelmed with workload, redistributing tasks or providing additional resources can help alleviate stress and improve engagement.

Additionally, it is vital to implement long-term strategies that address the root causes of the issues. This might involve making changes to organizational policies, processes, or structures that hinder engagement. For example, leaders could evaluate and revamp performance management systems to ensure they are fair, transparent, and focused on growth rather than solely on outcomes.

Establishing regular feedback loops at various levels of your organization is essential. Encourage supervisors to provide constructive feedback and ensure employees have a platform to share their thoughts and concerns. Emphasize the importance of timely and actionable feedback that fosters growth, autonomy, and learning.

Often, the effectiveness of employee engagement initiatives heavily relies on middle management. Investing in their development and providing them with the necessary tools and resources can empower them to identify and address underlying organizational issues more effectively. Encourage them to actively support their teams, create a positive work environment, and drive continuous improvement.

Establish clear channels of communication throughout the organization. Transparency in decision-making processes and encouraging open dialogue build trust and engagement. Regularly update employees on company goals, progress, and any organizational changes, ensuring information is shared in a clear and accessible manner.

Celebrate and acknowledge exceptional performance and contributions. Recognition programs, rewards, and incentives not only motivate employees but also reinforce the positive behaviors and values you seek to instill within your organization. Tangible recognition also serves as a reminder of the importance placed on employee engagement.

One inspiring example of a company that successfully addressed their organizational issues to enhance efficiency and engagement is Zappos, the online shoe and clothing retailer. As they grew rapidly, they faced challenges that affected their employee morale and hindered their ability to provide exceptional customer service.

Recognizing the importance of creating a positive work environment, Zappos prioritized their company culture. They conducted thorough cultural assessments and solicited feedback from employees at all levels. Through this process, they identified several key areas that needed improvement, including communication, empowerment, and alignment with company values.

To address these issues, Zappos took bold and innovative steps. Instead of traditional hierarchical structures, they implemented a holacratic approach, empowering employees to make decisions and take ownership of their work. They introduced new channels for open communication, fostering transparency and trust among team members.

Furthermore, Zappos focused on aligning their company culture with individual passions and values. They provided opportunities for employees to pursue personal interests within their roles, promoting a sense of purpose and fulfillment. Recognizing the importance of professional growth, they invested heavily in training and development programs. This emphasis on growth and development not only improved employee engagement but also strengthened their ability to provide exceptional customer service.

The impact of these efforts was remarkable. Zappos witnessed improved employee morale and engagement, translating into exceptional customer service. They became widely recognized for their outstanding company culture and were consistently ranked as one of the best places to work.

This example highlights the transformative power of addressing organizational issues to drive efficiency and engagement. By valuing their employees, investing in their development, and fostering a culture of empowerment and communication, Zappos not only improved their working environment but also achieved exceptional business success.

In considering our own organizational challenges, we can draw inspiration from Zappos' approach. By prioritizing communication, empowering our employees, and aligning our culture with individual passions and values, we can create a thriving work environment that drives excellence and success.

Remember, addressing underlying organizational issues requires a continuous commitment. Stay vigilant, measure progress, and adapt your strategies as needed. By taking these steps and fostering an environment where employees feel heard, valued, and supported, you will establish a foundation for exceptional employee engagement and ultimately unlock the full potential of your organization.

Now that you have learned about the key strategies for addressing underlying organizational issues that hinder employee engagement, it's time to put them into action. I have created a comprehensive checklist that you can use to guide you in implementing these strategies in your own organization.

"In order to lead others, you must first learn to lead yourself."

- John Quincy Adams

CHECKLIST

Improving Employee Engagement by Addressing Organizational Issues:

- Observe and actively listen to employees at all levels to gain insights into their challenges and obstacles.

- Conduct surveys and hold one-on-one meetings to gather more specific information.

- Identify patterns such as high turnover rates, low morale, or lack of collaboration.

- Take ownership of the issues and communicate openly with the team.

- Build trust and create a safe space for open dialogue.

- Actively listen to employees' concerns and validate their experiences.

- Implement short-term solutions to address immediate concerns or make small changes.

- Consider redistributing tasks or providing additional resources to alleviate stress and improve engagement.

- Implement long-term strategies to address the root causes of the issues.

- Evaluate and revamp organizational policies, processes, or structures that hinder engagement.

- Establish employee recognition programs and foster a culture of appreciation.

- Publicly acknowledge and celebrate employees' contributions.

- Share personal anecdotes or stories to create a connection and inspire action.

- Use real-life scenarios that resonate with employees to illustrate positive outcomes when the issues are addressed.

- Focus on building relationships, demonstrating empathy, and taking action to create a highly engaged and high-performance team.

Remember to stay committed, measure progress, and adapt strategies as needed to continuously address underlying organizational issues and foster exceptional employee engagement.

Now that we have gone through the action steps checklist, let's take a look at some examples that illustrate how these steps can be implemented in practice. These examples will demonstrate the importance of listening attentively, assessing organizational culture, conducting regular feedback loops, analyzing data and metrics, empowering middle management, fostering transparency and communication, and recognizing and rewarding excellence in order to foster exceptional employee engagement.

"An organization that doesn't value open communication and actively listen to its employees is doomed to suffer from low engagement and a lack of innovation."

- Simon Sinek

EXAMPLES

Zappos is a great organization that has adopted many of these practices and made them their own but how can you do the same in your organization? Here are a few examples for you to consider how to do that:

A financial services company notices a decline in employee engagement and decides to implement a listening strategy. They conduct one-on-one discussions with employees, asking open-ended questions and actively listening to their concerns. Through these conversations, they uncover issues such as lack of communication and unclear goals that have been hindering employee engagement.

A pharmaceutical company that realizes their organizational culture is not aligned with promoting employee engagement. They assess their culture and find that there is a lack of collaboration and recognition. To address this, they introduce initiatives such as cross-functional projects and team-building activities to encourage collaboration. They also implement a recognition program that publicly acknowledges and rewards employees' contributions.

A call centre company establishes regular feedback loops to improve employee engagement. They encourage supervisors to provide constructive feedback to their team members and create a safe space for employees to share their thoughts and concerns. This feedback helps identify areas where employees need support or additional resources, leading to increased engagement and performance.

Using data analytics, a health care company discovers that employee engagement is low among a particular department. They analyze data from employee surveys and performance reviews and identify a lack of growth opportunities as a key issue. Based on this information, they develop targeted training programs and mentorship initiatives to provide employees in that department with the skills and knowledge they need to advance in their careers.

A logistics company recognizes the importance of empowering middle management to address organizational issues affecting employee engagement. They invest in leadership development programs for middle managers, providing them with the necessary tools and resources to support their teams. This investment pays off as middle managers actively drive continuous improvement, creating a positive work environment that fosters engagement.

A printing company acknowledges the need for transparency and communication to improve employee engagement. They implement regular town hall meetings where leadership shares updates on company goals, progress, and any changes within the organization. They also establish an online platform for employees to ask questions and provide feedback, ensuring information flows freely and employees feel informed and involved.

An insurance company realizes the importance of recognizing and rewarding excellence to improve employee engagement. They introduce a recognition program that highlights outstanding performance and contributions. This program includes tangible rewards such as bonuses, public recognition, and opportunities for career advancement. The recognition program boosts morale and motivates employees to continue excelling in their roles.

These examples demonstrate how different strategies can be implemented to address underlying organizational issues and improve employee engagement. By actively listening, assessing organizational culture, conducting feedback loops, analyzing data, empowering middle management, fostering transparency and communication, and recognizing excellence, companies can create a thriving work culture that promotes engagement and unlocks their organization's full potential.

Based on these examples, it is clear that there are various strategies organizations can implement to address underlying issues and enhance employee engagement. By actively listening to employees, assessing organizational culture, conducting feedback loops, analyzing data, empowering middle management, fostering transparency and communication, and recognizing excellence, companies can create a thriving work culture that promotes engagement. To further explore these strategies and their impact on employee engagement, it is important to discuss the mistakes to avoid.

"Recognizing and addressing organizational issues is not an option; it's an imperative for creating a work environment where employees can thrive and succeed."

– Unknown

TYPICAL MISTAKES AND HOW TO AVOID THEM

Based on the material covered, some mistakes that most people make in the area of employee engagement include:

Lack of active listening: Many organizations fail to actively listen to their employees and seek their feedback. This can result in a lack of trust and engagement. To avoid this mistake, make sure to engage in active listening by encouraging open and honest conversations, conducting surveys, and genuinely valuing employee feedback.

Dismissing frontline employees: Frontline employees often have valuable insights and firsthand experiences that can shed light on organizational issues. Make sure to actively seek their feedback and include them in problem-solving discussions.

Token involvement: When involving employees in problem-solving, ensure that their input is genuinely considered and incorporated into decision-making. Token involvement can lead to disengagement and cynicism.

Ignoring organizational culture: Organizations often overlook the impact of their culture on employee engagement. It is important to assess whether your culture promotes collaboration, communication, recognition, and growth opportunities. If there are misalignments, address them through targeted initiatives, training programs, or policy changes.

Neglecting feedback loops: Organizations should establish regular feedback loops at various levels. Encourage supervisors to provide constructive feedback and provide platforms for employees to share their thoughts and concerns. Emphasize the importance of timely and actionable feedback that promotes growth and learning.

Neglecting communication: Effective and transparent communication is crucial in addressing organizational issues. Organizations need to establish clear channels of communication and transparency in decision-making processes. Regularly update employees on company goals, progress, and any changes in a clear and accessible manner. This builds trust and engagement among employees.

Underestimating the role of middle management: Middle managers play a crucial role in driving employee engagement. Investing in their development and providing them with resources will enable them to effectively address organizational issues. Encourage them to actively support their teams, create a positive work environment, and drive continuous improvement.

Procrastination: Once you've identified the underlying issues, take action promptly. Delaying action can further erode engagement and perpetuate dissatisfaction.

Measure progress: Establish measurable outcomes and regularly review progress. Without tracking and measuring the impact of your actions, it's difficult to determine whether the changes are effective or if further adjustments are needed.

Neglecting recognition and rewards: Celebrating small achievements along the way is important to maintain employee morale and motivation. Recognize and appreciate the efforts of individuals and teams to foster a positive and engaging work environment. Implement recognition programs, rewards, and incentives to motivate employees and reinforce positive behaviors and values.

Expecting a quick fix: Addressing underlying organizational issues takes time and ongoing effort. Avoid expecting immediate results and be prepared for setbacks. Stay committed to the process and keep adapting your approach as needed.

Neglecting sustainability: Once you've successfully addressed the initial organizational issues, make sure to maintain the improvements. Continuously monitor engagement levels and address any new challenges that may arise to sustain employee engagement and organizational success.

To avoid these mistakes, commit to addressing organizational issues continuously. Stay vigilant, measure progress, and adapt your strategies as needed. By fostering an environment where employees feel heard, valued, and supported, you will achieve exceptional employee engagement and unlock your organization's full potential.

MY #1 PIECE OF ADVICE

My number one piece of advice for improving leadership skills and addressing blind spots in organizations that hinder employee engagement is to prioritize active listening. Actively listen to your team members, be open to their ideas and feedback without judgment or interruption. This will help uncover blind spots, foster a culture of trust and collaboration, and boost employee engagement.

> *"Beware of the silent epidemic of disengagement in the workplace. Ignoring it only leads to decay and dysfunction."*
> *– Unknown*

SUMMARY:

- Engage in active listening to uncover valuable insights and show employees that their voices are heard and valued.

- Evaluate and align your organizational culture to promote collaboration, open communication, recognition, and growth opportunities.

- Establish effective feedback loops at all levels of the organization to foster growth, autonomy, and learning.

- Use data analytics to measure employee engagement and tailor interventions to address specific issues.

- Empower middle management to identify and address underlying organizational issues effectively and create a positive work environment.

APPLICATION QUESTIONS

1. Are there any organizational processes or systems that are creating bottlenecks or hindering efficiency? How could you streamline or improve them?

2. What steps will you take to foster a culture of innovation and creative problem-solving within your organization?

3. Are your performance management and recognition systems effective in ensuring that your team members feel valued and engaged in their work? If not, what changes can you make?

4. How can you effectively align your organization's goals with the individual aspirations and professional growth of our team members?

5. Are there any conflicting priorities or unclear expectations that may be causing confusion or disengagement among your employees? How will you address them?

QUIZ

1. What is the first step in identifying underlying organizational issues that hinder employee engagement?

   A. Implement short-term solutions

   B. Establish employee recognition programs

   C. Active listening and observation

   D. Take ownership and communicate openly

2. Why is it important to invest in middle management development?

   A. To improve communication

   B. To foster collaboration

   C. To empower them to address organizational issues

   D. To create a positive work environment

3. What is the role of active listening in recognizing underlying organizational issues?

A. To help identify patterns

B. To create a safe space for open dialogue

C. To inspire team members to take action

D. To boost morale and motivation

4. How can leaders create a connection with employees?

A. By addressing immediate concerns

B. By implementing long-term strategies

C. By being transparent and sharing personal anecdotes and stories

D. By making changes to organizational policies

5. What is the ultimate goal of addressing underlying organizational issues?

A. To reduce turnover rates

B. To increase morale

C. To create a high-performance team

D. To foster a culture of appreciation

Answer key:

1. C - Active listening and observation

2. C - To empower them to address organizational issues

3. A - To help identify patterns

4. C - By being transparent and sharing personal anecdotes and stories

5. C - To create a high-performance team

As we have explored in the previous chapter, identifying and addressing underlying organizational issues is crucial in fostering employee engagement. In the next chapter, we will delve into real life examples of proven tactics and practices that have successfully enhanced employee engagement, inspiring you with practical strategies that can transform your organization. So keep reading to discover the transformative power of these examples and unlock the potential within your own workplace.

CHAPTER 6

BUILDING BRIDGES, BUILDING TRUST

STRATEGIES FOR STRONG EMPLOYEE RELATIONSHIPS

"Trust is the bedrock of any high-performing team. It allows individuals to take risks, be vulnerable, and support one another."

- Patrick Lencioni

AT A GLANCE

Five Essential Points for Strategies for Strong Employee Relationships

- Unlock the power of trust: Discover how trust can create efficiencies and engage employees in ways you never thought possible.

- The secret ingredient for success: Learn how trust acts as a lubricant, smoothing the wheels of collaboration and enhancing overall team performance.

- From chaos to harmony: See how trust breeds efficiency by streamlining workflows, delegating tasks effectively, and making decisions swiftly.

- A culture of trust: Find out how open communication and constructive feedback can thrive in an environment where trust is the foundation.

- Collaboration made easy: Explore how trust fosters teamwork and collaboration by encouraging the sharing of knowledge, resources, and expertise.

Five Questions Business Leaders Should Ask About Strategies for Strong Employee Relationships

- How do you ensure that your management style and communication approach are tailored to the unique needs and preferences of each employee? Are there any adjustments or improvements you could make in this area?

- What steps do you take to actively listen to your team members, understand their challenges, and provide support when needed? Can you recall an example of a time when practicing empathetic listening led to a better outcome?

- Can you identify any barriers or obstacles that may hinder the development of strong relationships with your team members? How might you overcome these challenges and create a more conducive environment for effective relationship-building?

- Reflecting on your leadership style, how do you balance accountability and fostering a sense of camaraderie among your team members? Is there room for improvement in promoting a positive and cohesive working atmosphere?

- What opportunities do you provide for your employees to connect with each other and build relationships within the team? How can you create more opportunities for collaboration and collaboration to strengthen these connections?

Trust plays a pivotal role in creating efficiencies and engaging employees within an organization. When there is a high level of trust among team members and their leaders, it leads to a more productive and harmonious work environment. Trust acts as a lubricant that smoothes the wheels of collaboration and enhances overall team performance.

First and foremost, trust breeds efficiency by eliminating unnecessary steps in the workflow. When team members trust each other's capabilities and intentions, they are more likely to streamline their work processes, delegate tasks effectively, and make decisions swiftly. Trust enables individuals to focus on their strengths and expertise, knowing that their colleagues will offer support and deliver quality work. This not only saves time but also reduces the need for constant supervision and micromanagement, ultimately leading to increased efficiency.

Moreover, trust encourages open communication and constructive feedback within teams. In an environment where trust thrives, employees feel comfortable expressing their opinions, ideas, and concerns without fear of judgment or retribution. This open dialogue facilitates the identification and resolution of issues, prevents misunderstandings, and promotes innovation. When employees trust that their contributions will be valued and respected, they become more engaged, actively participating in discussions and problem-solving. Engagement leads to higher job satisfaction and increased motivation, resulting in enhanced productivity and improved outcomes.

Trust also plays a crucial role in fostering collaboration and teamwork. When individuals trust each other, they are more likely to share knowledge, resources, and expertise willingly. Collaboration becomes seamless, as team members rely on one another's strengths and talents. Trust enables effective delegation, allowing tasks to be allocated to the most capable individuals, based on their skills and expertise. This division of labor not only improves efficiency but also deepens employee engagement, as individuals feel valued and recognized for their unique contributions.

One standout example of a company that excels in building trust and strong employee relationships is Microsoft. With its focus on fostering a culture of inclusion and collaboration, Microsoft has implemented effective strategies that nurture relationships and create a sense of camaraderie among its workforce.

One of the core components of Microsoft's approach is its commitment to diversity and inclusion. The company actively promotes a welcoming and inclusive environment where employees feel valued for their unique perspectives and contributions. Microsoft's employee resource groups provide a platform for networking, support, and professional development, fostering stronger relationships among employees from various backgrounds.

Another key strategy employed by Microsoft is its emphasis on transparency and communication. The company holds regular town hall meetings where senior leaders openly discuss updates, achievements, and challenges. These sessions create a sense of trust and enable employees to feel involved and informed, ultimately strengthening the employee-employer relationship.

Microsoft understands the significance of providing growth opportunities and investing in employee development. The company offers extensive training and learning resources, enabling employees to enhance their skills and advance their careers. By nurturing professional growth, Microsoft fosters a sense of loyalty and commitment, enhancing relationships between its employees and the organization.

Furthermore, Microsoft places great importance on creating a positive work environment and promoting work-life balance. The company offers flexible work arrangements and comprehensive benefits that support employee well-being. By prioritizing the holistic needs of its employees, Microsoft strengthens relationships and cultivates a culture of trust and mutual respect.

Microsoft's strategies for building trust and strong employee relationships revolve around fostering an inclusive culture, transparent communication, investing in employee development, and promoting work-life balance. By valuing diversity, encouraging open dialogue, prioritizing growth opportunities, and supporting employee well-being, Microsoft has created an environment where employees feel trusted, included, and empowered. Leaders can learn from their approach by prioritizing transparency, inclusion, growth, and work-life balance within their own organizations.

In short, trust acts as the foundation for creating efficiencies and engaging employees. It streamlines workflow by eliminating unnecessary steps, encourages open communication and feedback, fosters collaboration and teamwork, and ultimately leads to improved performance. As leaders, it is our responsibility to cultivate a culture of trust within our teams, as it will be a catalyst for success and a driver of sustainable results.

Now that we have explored the importance of trust in creating efficiencies and engaging employees, let's take a look at a checklist that can help you cultivate a culture of trust within your team. This checklist will provide you with practical steps and strategies to promote trust and enhance overall team performance.

> *"Trust is the currency of leadership. Without it, nothing gets done."*
>
> *- Joel Peterson*

CHECKLIST

- Assess the current level of trust within your team or organization. Conduct surveys, interviews, or other assessments to gauge the level of trust among team members and their leaders.

- Identify areas for improvement. Determine which aspects of trust are lacking or need to be strengthened, such as open communication, constructive feedback, collaboration, or delegation.

- Lead by example. Demonstrate trustworthiness by being transparent, honest, and reliable in your actions and communications.

- Create a safe and supportive environment. Encourage open dialogue, active listening, and respectful communication. Foster an environment where everyone's opinions, ideas, and concerns are valued and respected.

- Provide opportunities for team members to build trust. Facilitate team-building activities, such as icebreakers, trust exercises, or collaborative projects, to help team members develop trust in each other's capabilities and intentions.

- Promote accountability. Encourage team members to take ownership of their work and responsibilities. Provide opportunities for individuals to showcase their skills and expertise and recognize their contributions.

- Foster collaboration and teamwork. Create opportunities for team members to share knowledge, resources, and expertise. Support effective delegation and division of labor based on individual skills and expertise.

- Promote a feedback culture. Encourage regular feedback and constructive criticism. Provide training or resources on giving and receiving feedback effectively.

- Address conflicts and misunderstandings promptly. When issues arise, facilitate discussions and resolution in a timely manner. Encourage individuals to view conflicts as opportunities for growth and learning.

- Continuously evaluate and assess progress. Monitor the impact of trust-building efforts on efficiency, productivity, engagement, and overall team performance. Make adjustments as needed to further enhance trust within the team or organization.

Now that we have reviewed the checklist for building trust within a team or organization, let's take a look at some examples that illustrate these principles in action.

> *"Trust is the key to unlocking the full potential of a team. When trust is present, anything is possible."*
>
> *- Unknown*

EXAMPLES

Who wouldn't want to be Microsoft? After all they are a behemoth in the marketplace. But few companies have that kind of clout or budget for developing engagement and high performance. Let's look at a few examples of how other, not quite so large companies can implement these ideas to build trust in the workplace.

Trust eliminating unnecessary steps in the workflow:

In a software development team, the trust among team members allows them to effectively streamline their work processes. Each member trusts that their teammates have the necessary skills and expertise to complete their tasks efficiently. As a result, they delegate tasks effectively, eliminate redundant steps, and avoid unnecessary micromanagement. This increases the overall efficiency of the team and allows them to complete projects more quickly.

Trust promoting open communication and constructive feedback:

In a marketing team, trust among members encourages open communication and the sharing of ideas without fear of judgment. Team members trust that their opinions and ideas will be valued and respected, which leads to discussions and brainstorming sessions that generate innovative solutions. Constructive feedback is given and received in a supportive and non-judgmental manner, allowing team members to learn from each other's expertise and improve their work. This open communication and feedback loop result in more efficient execution of marketing campaigns and ultimately better outcomes.

Trust fostering collaboration and teamwork:

In a sales team, trust is crucial for effective collaboration and teamwork. When salespeople trust each other, they are more likely to share knowledge, resources, and best practices. They understand that their colleagues have their backs and are willing to help when needed. This collaborative environment allows salespeople to leverage each other's strengths, leading to more successful sales strategies and increased revenue. Trust also enables effective delegation of tasks, as team members trust that their colleagues will deliver quality work. This division of labor improves efficiency and ensures that the right people are working on the right tasks.

Trust leading to engagement and increased motivation:

In a customer service team, trust plays a significant role in employee engagement and motivation. When customer service representatives trust their team leaders and colleagues, they feel comfortable expressing their opinions and concerns. This open dialogue allows for the identification and resolution of customer service issues more quickly and effectively. Trust also leads to a sense of belonging and job satisfaction, as employees feel valued and respected for their contributions. This increased engagement and motivation result in higher productivity, improved customer satisfaction, and ultimately, business growth.

After examining these examples of trust in different work environments, let's take a look at some mistakes to avoid when trying to build trust and improve team performance. These mistakes are crucial to address in order to ensure the success and sustainability of trust-building efforts.

> *"Trust is the lubrication that makes it possible for organizations to work."*
>
> *- Warren Bennis*

TYPICAL MISTAKES AND HOW TO AVOID THEM

Based on the material covered in this chapter, one mistake that most people make is failing to actually cultivate trust within their teams. Trust is essential for creating efficiencies and engaging employees, but it is often overlooked or undervalued. To avoid this mistake, leaders should prioritize trust-building activities and foster a culture of trust within their organization.

Another mistake is micro-managing and not allowing team members to fully use their skills and expertise. When there is a high level of trust, leaders can delegate tasks effectively and empower their team members to take ownership of their work. By doing so, unnecessary steps in the workflow can be eliminated, saving time and increasing efficiency.

Additionally, not creating an open environment for communication and feedback is a common mistake. When employees feel comfortable expressing their ideas, concerns, and opinions without fear of judgment or retribution, it encourages collaboration, prevents misunderstandings, and promotes innovation. Leaders should encourage open dialogue and actively listen to their team members to ensure trust and effective communication.

Lastly, not recognizing and valuing individual contributions can hinder trust and engagement. When team members trust that their unique strengths and talents are respected and recognized, they are more likely to collaborate and contribute actively. Leaders should ensure that tasks are delegated based on individuals' skills and expertise, which not only improves efficiency but also deepens employee engagement.

To avoid mistakes in this area, it is crucial to prioritize trust-building activities, delegate tasks effectively, create an open communication environment, and recognize individual contributions. By doing so, leaders can cultivate a culture of trust within their teams, leading to increased efficiency, engagement, and overall improved performance.

With these mistakes in mind, it is crucial for leaders to prioritize trust-building activities, delegate tasks effectively, create an open communication environment, and recognize individual contributions. By doing so, they can cultivate a culture of trust within their teams, leading to increased efficiency, engagement, and overall improved performance.

MY #1 PIECE OF ADVICE

My #1 piece of advice to you is lead by example. Show your team that you trust them by being open, transparent, and accountable. Build relationships through effective communication and active listening. Encourage teamwork and collaboration while recognizing and valuing each member's contribution. Foster a safe and inclusive environment that promotes trust and mutual respect.

> "Trust is the ultimate litmus test of leadership. It determines whether people will follow you willingly or begrudgingly."
>
> - *Warren Bennis*

SUMMARY:

- Trust acts as a powerful catalyst for efficiency, eliminating unnecessary steps and streamlining workflow, saving time and reducing the need for constant supervision and micromanagement.

- In an environment built on trust, open communication and constructive feedback thrive, leading to better problem-solving, prevention of misunderstandings, and increased innovation.

- Trust fosters collaboration and teamwork, as individuals willingly share knowledge, resources, and expertise, allowing tasks to be allocated to the most capable individuals based on their skills and abilities.

- By cultivating a culture of trust, leaders can create a harmonious work environment where employees feel valued, recognized, and engaged, leading to higher job satisfaction, increased motivation, and improved outcomes.

- Trust is the foundation for success and sustainable results. As leaders, it is our responsibility to prioritize trust, as it is the key to creating efficiencies and engaging employees within our organizations.

APPLICATION QUESTIONS

- What steps are you willing to take to ensure open and transparent communication with your employees, fostering trust and keeping them informed about company goals, updates, and challenges?

- How can you actively listen more to your employees' needs and concerns, providing a platform for their voices to be heard and demonstrating your commitment to their satisfaction?

- How can you prioritize professional development opportunities that align with your employees' individual goals and aspirations, showing them that their growth and success matter to you?

- What specific behaviors or actions will you model as a leader to demonstrate your commitment to trust-building and effective communication?

- What specific actions can you take over the next month to deepen your relationships with each team member individually? How will you measure the impact of these efforts and adjust your approach accordingly?

QUIZ

1. What is the primary role of trust in an organization?

   A. To streamline workflow
   B. To eliminate unnecessary steps
   C. To foster collaboration and teamwork
   D. To enhance overall team performance

2. What is the responsibility of leaders in terms of trust?

   A. To provide constant supervision
   B. To cultivate a culture of trust
   C. To eliminate unnecessary steps
   D. To foster collaboration and teamwork

3. What does trust act as in terms of creating efficiencies and engaging employees?

   A. A foundation
   B. A lubricant
   C. A catalyst for success
   D. A driver of sustainable results

4. How does trust lead to improved performance?

   A. By eliminating unnecessary steps

   B. By encouraging open dialogue

   C. By increasing job satisfaction

   D. By all of the above

5. How does trust affect employee engagement?

   A. It increases motivation

   B. It facilitates the identification and resolution of issues

   C. It encourages active participation

   D. All of the above

Answer Key:

1. D - To enhance overall team performance

2. B - To cultivate a culture of trust

3. A - A foundation

4. D - By all of the above

5. D - All of the above

In order to foster open and transparent communication within teams, leaders must first understand the pivotal role that trust plays in creating efficiencies and engaging employees. In the next chapter, we will explore some effective practices and tools that can help leaders improve their communication skills and cultivate an environment of trust and transparency within their teams - keep reading to discover the keys to successful and inclusive communication.

CHAPTER 7

INSPIRING PERFORMANCE

EFFECTIVE COMMUNICATION STRATEGIES TO DRIVE TEAM GOALS AND EXPECTATIONS

"The art of communication is the language of leadership."

- James Humes

AT A GLANCE

Five Essential Points for Effective Communication Strategies to Drive Team Goals and Expectations

- Discover the key practices to cultivate an environment of openness and transparency in your team.

- Learn how active listening can make your team members feel valued and more likely to openly share their thoughts.

- Find out how to convey information in a clear and concise manner that is easily understood by everyone.

- Embrace a communication style that is open, honest, and transparent, and see how it encourages your team members to do the same.

- Create a safe space for communication, where individuals can express their thoughts and emotions without fear of judgment or retribution.

Five Questions Business Leaders Should Ask About Effective Communication Strategies to Drive Team Goals and Expectations

- How well do your communication strategies align with your team goals and expectations, while also fostering a positive and collaborative work environment?
- What are some common communication barriers you often encounter, and how do usually you overcome them to ensure clear and effective messaging?
- How do you ensure that your communication is inclusive and respectful of diverse perspectives and backgrounds?
- How do you use communication to motivate and inspire your team members towards achieving your collective goals?
- Are there any specific areas or topics where your team communication could benefit from improvement? How are you currently addressing these areas to drive better results?

I firmly believe that open and transparent communication is the cornerstone of effective leadership. It not only builds trust within teams but also promotes collaboration and, ultimately, leads to better results. Effective communication plays such an integral role in fostering trust, engagement, and success within a team. To improve communication skills as a leader, there are several key practices that can be implemented to cultivate an environment of openness and transparency.

Firstly, active listening is paramount. As a leader, it is important to genuinely listen to your team members, acknowledging their perspectives, ideas, and concerns. By demonstrating a genuine interest in what they have to say, you not only make them feel valued but also create an atmosphere where they are more likely to openly share their thoughts. Remember, effective listening isn't just about hearing the words being spoken but also understanding the underlying emotions and motivations.

Secondly, clear and concise communication is essential. As a leader, it is your responsibility to convey information, expectations, and feedback in a manner that is easily understood by all team members. Avoid using jargon or technical terms that could confuse or alienate individuals. Instead, break down complex concepts into digestible and relatable language. By doing so, you ensure that your message is effectively conveyed and understood by everyone.

Next, lead by example. As a leader, your actions speak louder than words. Embrace a communication style that is open, honest, and transparent, and consistently practice what you preach. When you model open communication, it encourages your team members to do the same. They will feel comfortable sharing their concerns, ideas, and feedback, knowing that you value their input and will genuinely consider it.

Alongside leading by example, creating a safe space for communication is crucial. Encourage an environment where individuals feel comfortable expressing their thoughts and emotions without fear of judgment or retribution. Foster a culture that celebrates diverse perspectives and encourages constructive dialogue. When team members feel safe to speak up, it enables healthy debate, increased innovation, and enhanced problem-solving abilities.

Additionally, regular and consistent communication is vital. Keep your team informed about important updates, goals, and strategies. Schedule regular check-ins and team meetings to provide updates, offer support, and address any questions or concerns. By keeping the lines of communication open, you ensure that everyone is on the same page, promoting unity and collaboration.

Lastly, be receptive to feedback and address concerns promptly. Encourage your team members to provide feedback openly and constructively. It is important to actively listen and take their feedback seriously. When issues or concerns arise, address them promptly and transparently. This demonstrates your commitment to open and transparent communication, building trust and fostering a culture of continuous improvement.

One great example of a company that excels in effective communication strategies is Buffer. This social media management platform prioritizes transparency, collaboration, and clear communication throughout its entire organization, even though I haven't personally used it before.

At Buffer, communication is ingrained in their culture, and they practice what they preach by openly sharing their internal processes and strategies with the public. They maintain an Open Blog, where team members regularly contribute articles on various topics, including communication best practices. By sharing their experiences and insights, Buffer not only exhibits thought leadership but also encourages open dialogue and knowledge sharing within their industry.

Additionally, Buffer places a strong emphasis on remote work, and as such, they have implemented communication tools specifically designed to facilitate effective remote collaboration. They use platforms like Slack and Zoom for real-time communication, fostering both synchronous and asynchronous communication across their distributed team, ensuring that everyone feels connected and informed regardless of their physical location.

Buffer also uses a framework called "Radical Candor" to encourage effective feedback and communication. This approach promotes honest and compassionate conversations, where individuals can express their opinions openly while also fostering a culture of respect and empathy.

Furthermore, Buffer organizes regular virtual "town hall" meetings where all team members can join and discuss important updates, company-wide goals, and address any concerns or questions. This interactive format allows for two-way communication, creating a sense of inclusivity and empowerment within the team.

Buffer's strategic approach to effective communication involves transparent knowledge-sharing, using remote collaboration tools, fostering a culture of feedback, and creating open communication platforms where everyone can actively participate and contribute. Through these initiatives, Buffer demonstrates their commitment to clear and effective communication, enabling their team to work cohesively towards achieving their goals while building meaningful relationships along the way.

John Maxwell's book "*Everyone Communicates Few Connect*", he delivers key insights on effective communication and connection. Here are the key points from his book:

1. Communication is more than just talking: Maxwell emphasizes that true communication goes beyond the exchange of words. It involves connecting with others on an emotional and relational level.

2. Building relationships is essential: Effective communication means building relationships with others. Maxwell explains that understanding and connecting with people's values, beliefs, and needs is crucial to establish meaningful connections.

3. Connectors find common ground: Connectors seek common ground with their audience by finding shared experiences, interests, or goals. By emphasizing similarities, they bridge the gap between themselves and others, fostering a sense of trust and understanding.

4. Listening is key: Successful communication begins with active listening. Maxwell encourages readers to set aside distractions,

show genuine interest, and listen to others with the intention to understand, not just respond.

5. Authenticity is vital: Being authentic is foundational to connecting with others. Maxwell emphasizes the importance of staying true to oneself, being transparent, and expressing vulnerability. Authenticity builds trust and makes connections more meaningful.

6. Connectors adapt their communication style: Effective communicators adjust their approach to fit the needs of their audience. Maxwell advises readers to be flexible in their communication style, whether it means simplifying complex concepts or adapting their tone to different personality types.

7. Creating memorable experiences: Memorable communication experiences make a lasting impact. Maxwell suggests incorporating stories, metaphors, and visuals to engage audiences and make messages more memorable and relatable.

8. Connecting requires empathy: Empathy plays a central role in connecting with others. Maxwell encourages readers to practice empathy by understanding and valuing the perspectives and emotions of others, creating a strong bond between individuals.

9. Practice and repetition are key: Improvement in communication skills comes with practice and repetition. Maxwell advises readers to continually refine their communication techniques, seek feedback, and learn from both successes and failures.

10. Connecting leads to influence: By focusing on connecting rather than simply communicating, individuals can influence and positively impact those around them. Maxwell believes that true influence comes from building relationships and connecting on a deeper level.

Effective communication skills are crucial for leaders looking to foster open and transparent communication within their teams. By actively listening, communicating clearly, leading by example, creating a safe space, maintaining regular communication, and being receptive to feedback, leaders can build strong relationships and achieve optimal engagement and results within their teams.

Now that we have explored the key practices for fostering open and transparent communication, I have created a checklist that outlines these practices. The checklist will serve as a helpful tool to guide you in improving your communication skills as a leader and creating an environment of openness and transparency within your team.

"Great communication begins with connection."

- Oprah Winfrey

CHECKLIST

Checklist for Fostering Open and Transparent Communication within Your Team:

- Practice Active Listening: Focus on understanding the perspectives and concerns of your team members by giving your full attention, maintaining eye contact, and avoiding interruptions or judgments. Active listening shows that you value their input and encourages them to express their thoughts freely.

- Set Clear Expectations and Provide Regular Feedback: Clearly communicate your goals, expectations, and requirements to your team. This clarity helps prevent misunderstandings and ensures everyone is on the same page. Additionally, provide constructive feedback regularly to help individuals grow and align their actions with team objectives.

- Lead by Example: Embrace open, honest, and transparent communication and consistently practice what you preach.

- Create a Safe and Inclusive Environment: Foster a culture where everyone feels comfortable speaking up by encouraging diverse opinions and perspectives. Avoid penalizing mistakes or differences of opinion. By valuing and respecting each team member, you create an environment of open communication and trust.

- Maintain Regular Communication: Keep the team informed about updates, goals, and strategies through regular check-ins and team meetings.

- Be Receptive to Feedback: Encourage team members to provide feedback openly and constructively, actively listen, and address concerns promptly and transparently.

In the workplace, applying the key points from John Maxwell's book *"Everyone Communicates Few Connect"* can significantly enhance trust and engagement among team members. Here's how you can put these points into action:

- Foster relationships: Prioritize building relationships with your colleagues. Take the time to understand their values, beliefs, and needs, and find common ground. Engage in meaningful conversations and show genuine interest in their thoughts and ideas.

- Active listening: Practice active listening by giving your full attention and showing genuine curiosity. Avoid distractions, maintain eye contact, and provide verbal and non-verbal cues to demonstrate that you are fully engaged in the conversation. This will make others feel heard and valued.

- Be authentic: Authenticity is key to gaining trust in the workplace. Be true to yourself, share your genuine thoughts and feelings, and admit when you don't have all the answers. This vulnerability creates an open and honest environment where trust can thrive.

- Adapt your communication style: Recognize that different colleagues have unique communication preferences. Adapt your style to meet their needs, whether it means simplifying complex concepts for some or providing more data for others. By flexing your communication approach, you'll create a more inclusive and engaging environment.

- Create memorable experiences: Enhance engagement by creating memorable moments in your communication. Incorporate stories, metaphors, or visuals to make your messages more relatable and impactful. Engaging your colleagues on an emotional level will make the content more memorable and encourage active participation.

- Practice empathy: Empathy is a powerful tool for building trust. Put yourself in your colleagues' shoes, understand their perspectives, and validate their feelings and experiences. By showing empathy, you establish a strong connection and foster an environment where everyone feels understood and valued.

- Seek feedback and improvement: Continually seek feedback on your communication skills and be open to constructive criticism. Actively work on refining your techniques and practices. Embrace both successes and failures as opportunities for growth and learning.

- Lead by example: Embody the principles of effective communication and connection as a leader. Demonstrate active listening, authenticity, and empathy in your interactions. Encourage others to do the same, and recognize and reward effective communication efforts within your team.

When you follow these practices and using the recommended tools, you can promote open and transparent communication within your team. This will not only enhance your leadership skills but also build stronger relationships with your team members, resulting in improved communication and better outcomes.

Now that we have gone through the checklist for fostering open and transparent communication within your team, let's take a look at some examples that illustrate how these practices can be implemented effectively.

> *"The most important thing in communication is hearing what isn't said."*
>
> *- Peter Drucker*

EXAMPLES

Imagine a marketing team leader who actively listens to their team members during a brainstorming session. They ask open-ended questions and encourage each person to share their ideas without any judgment or interruption. This leader truly values their team's input and makes an effort to understand the underlying emotions and motivations behind each idea. As a result, team members feel valued and empowered to share their thoughts openly, leading to a more collaborative and innovative environment.

An IT team leader communicates a new project to everyone in their company in a clear and concise manner. Instead of using technical terminology that only a few team members understand, they break down complex concepts into relatable language. By doing so, everyone on the team is able to understand the project's objectives, expectations, and timeline. This enhances team alignment and ensures that everyone is on the same page, leading to better results and productivity.

A production team leader leads by example by consistently practicing open and transparent communication. They share updates, challenges, and successes with their team, demonstrating vulnerability and honesty. When mistakes are made, they take responsibility and openly address them. This kind of transparency builds trust among team members and encourages them to also be open and transparent in their communication with each other and the leader.

A customer service team leader creates a safe space for communication by fostering a culture that celebrates diverse perspectives and encourages constructive dialogue. They encourage team members to express their thoughts and emotions without fear of judgment or retribution. This kind of environment enables healthy debate, increases innovation, and enhances problem-solving abilities within the team.

A sales team leader maintains regular and consistent communication with their team. They schedule regular check-ins and team meetings to provide updates, offer support, and address any questions or concerns. By keeping the lines of communication open, team members feel informed and connected, which promotes unity and collaboration.

A management team leader is receptive to feedback and addresses concerns promptly. They actively listen to their team members' feedback, taking it seriously and incorporating it into decision-making and problem-solving processes. When issues or concerns arise, they address them transparently, seeking resolution and improvement. This kind of response demonstrates the leader's commitment to open communication and fosters a culture of continuous improvement within the team.

Now that we have explored various examples of effective communication and leadership, let's explore some of the key mistakes to avoid in order to ensure effective communication within a company.

"The single biggest problem in communication is the illusion that it has taken place."

- George Bernard Shaw

TYPICAL MISTAKES AND HOW TO AVOID THEM

The most common mistake people make in this area is not actively listening to their team members. Many leaders may hear their team members speak, but they don't truly listen to what they are saying. To avoid this mistake, leaders should make an effort to genuinely listen to their team members, acknowledging their perspectives, ideas, and concerns. By demonstrating a genuine interest in what they have to say, leaders can create an atmosphere where team members feel valued and are more likely to openly share their thoughts.

Another mistake is not communicating clearly and concisely. Leaders have a responsibility to convey information, expectations, and feedback in a way that is easily understood by all team members. To avoid confusing or alienating individuals, leaders should avoid using jargon or technical terms. Instead, they should break down complex concepts into simple and relatable language. This ensures that the message is effectively conveyed and understood by everyone.

A common mistake is not leading by example. As a leader, your actions speak louder than words. It is important to embrace a communication style that is open, honest, and transparent, and consistently practice what you preach. When you model open communication, it encourages team members to do the same. They will feel comfortable sharing their concerns, ideas, and feedback, knowing that you value their input and will genuinely consider it.

Many people also make the mistake of not creating a safe space for communication. It is crucial to encourage an environment where individuals feel comfortable expressing their thoughts and emotions without fear of judgment or retribution. Leaders should foster a culture that celebrates diverse perspectives and encourages constructive dialogue.

When team members feel safe to speak up, it enables healthy debate, increased innovation, and enhanced problem-solving abilities.

Another mistake is not maintaining regular and consistent communication. Keeping the team informed about important updates, goals, and strategies is vital. Leaders should schedule regular check-ins and team meetings to provide updates, offer support, and address any questions or concerns. By keeping the lines of communication open, everyone is on the same page, promoting unity and collaboration.

Lastly, many people make the mistake of not being receptive to feedback and not addressing concerns promptly. Leaders should actively encourage their team members to provide feedback openly and constructively. It is important to actively listen and take their feedback seriously. When issues or concerns arise, leaders should address them promptly and transparently. This demonstrates a commitment to open and transparent communication, building trust and fostering a culture of continuous improvement.

To avoid these common mistakes, leaders should actively listen, communicate clearly, lead by example, create a safe space, maintain regular communication, and be receptive to feedback. By implementing these practices, leaders can build strong relationships and achieve optimal engagement and results within their teams.

MY #1 PIECE OF ADVICE

My #1 piece of advice would be to listen actively and empathetically to truly understand others, fostering open and inclusive communication that builds trust and strengthens relationships.

> *"When you make a commitment, you create hope. When you keep a commitment, you create trust."*
>
> — *John C. Maxwell*

SUMMARY:

- Embrace the power of active listening - truly value your team's ideas, concerns, and perspectives, and watch the trust and openness soar.

- Communicate with clarity - break down complex concepts into relatable language, ensuring everyone understands your message and feels included.

- Lead by example - be the beacon of open and honest communication, inspiring your team to do the same and creating a culture of trust and collaboration.

- Create a safe space for communication - celebrate diverse perspectives, encourage constructive dialogue, and watch innovation and problem-solving thrive.

- Keep the lines of communication open - regularly update your team, hold check-ins and meetings, and show your commitment to transparent communication, fostering unity and continuous improvement.

APPLICATION QUESTIONS

- How can you better foster a culture of transparency and knowledge-sharing within your organization to drive effective communication and collaboration among team members?

- Are there any existing barriers or communication gaps within your team that are hindering your progress towards achieving your goals? How can you overcome these challenges and bridge those gaps?

- How can you ensure that your communication strategies are aligned with your team's diverse needs and preferences, taking into account cultural differences and communication styles?

- How can you promote a culture of active listening within your team, where all voices are heard and valued, fostering a collaborative and inclusive environment?

- What steps can you take to regularly evaluate and gather feedback on your communication strategies, ensuring that you continuously improve and adapt to the changing needs of your team and organization?

QUIZ

1. What is an important practice for leaders to implement to foster an environment of openness and transparency?

   A. Active listening
   B. Clear and concise communication
   C. Leading by example
   D. All of the above

2. What is an important step in actively listening?

   A. Acknowledging perspectives, ideas and concerns
   B. Asking questions
   C. Providing feedback
   D. Paraphrasing

3. Why is it important for leaders to lead by example when it comes to communication?

   A. To promote unity and collaboration
   B. To encourage team members to speak up
   C. To foster a culture of continuous improvement
   D. All of the above

4. What is the purpose of creating a safe space for communication?

A. To promote healthy debate

B. To encourage constructive dialogue

C. To enable individuals to express their thoughts without fear of judgment or retribution

D. All of the above

5. What is the importance of maintaining regular communication?

A. To ensure everyone is on the same page

B. To provide updates and offer support

C. To address any questions or concerns

D. All of the above

Answer Key:

1. D - All of the above

2. A - Acknowledging perspectives, ideas and concerns

3. D - All of the above

4. D - All of the above

5. D - All of the above

Now that we have explored effective practices for improving communication skills as a leader, let us turn our attention to another crucial aspect of leadership - empowering employees to actively contribute to the efficiency improvement process. By understanding how leaders can create an environment that encourages their team members to participate and innovate, you will gain valuable insights and strategies to enhance your organization's overall performance. So, let's dive in and discover the power of empowering your employees.

CHAPTER 8
EMPOWERMENT REVOLUTION
HOW LEADERS DRIVE EFFECTIVENESS AND EFFICIENCY THROUGH
EMPLOYEE INVOLVEMENT

"None of us is as smart as all of us."

- Ken Blanchard

AT A GLANCE

Five Essential Points for How Leaders Drive Effectiveness and Efficiency
Through Employee Involvement

- Cultivating a culture of trust and open communication is essential
  for empowering employees and unlocking new possibilities for
  efficiency improvement.

- Involving employees in decision-making processes not only
  enhances their commitment, but also brings diverse perspectives to
  the table, leading to more robust and innovative ideas.

- Providing necessary resources and support, such as training and
  development opportunities, helps employees feel equipped to
  proactively seek out opportunities for improvement and take
  ownership of their work.

- Recognizing and celebrating the efforts and achievements of employees boosts morale and reinforces the idea that everyone has a role to play in the efficiency improvement process.

- Leaders who actively participate and lead by example inspire their team to embrace the improvement process, drive innovation, and achieve exceptional results while building strong and collaborative relationships.

Five Questions Business Leaders Should Ask About How Leaders Drive Effectiveness and Efficiency Through Employee Involvement

- How do you currently involve and engage your employees in decision-making processes and problem-solving discussions and ensure that all employees have equal opportunities to participate and contribute?

- How do you currently facilitate a culture of collaboration and open communication within your team or organization?

- Have you noticed any barriers or challenges that prevent employees from actively participating in driving effectiveness and efficiency? If so, what steps have you taken to overcome these obstacles?

- How do you as the leader ensure that employee involvement in driving effectiveness and efficiency is integrated into the organization's long-term strategy and goals? How can it be sustained and scaled for maximum impact?

- How do you as the leader inspire and motivate employees to take ownership and accountability for their roles in driving effectiveness and efficiency?

Empowering employees to actively contribute to the efficiency improvement process is essential for building a high-performing team that leads itself. It not only drives innovation and continuous improvement but also fosters a sense of ownership and engagement among employees. Here are several key strategies leaders can employ to empower their employees in this process.

First and foremost, leaders must cultivate a culture of trust and open communication. Employees need to feel comfortable sharing their ideas, concerns, and suggestions without fear of retribution. By creating a safe environment where diverse opinions are encouraged and respected, leaders can tap into the collective intelligence of their team, unlocking new possibilities for efficiency improvement.

Another effective way to empower employees is by involving them in decision-making processes. When employees have a say in identifying problems, generating solutions, and selecting improvement initiatives, they feel a sense of ownership and responsibility. This involvement not only enhances their commitment but also brings diverse perspectives to the table, leading to more robust and innovative ideas.

Furthermore, leaders can provide the necessary resources and support for employees to actively contribute to the efficiency improvement process. This includes providing training and development opportunities so employees can enhance their skills and knowledge. When employees feel equipped to take on new challenges, they are more likely to proactively seek out opportunities for improvement and take ownership of their work.

In addition to these strategies, leaders should recognize and celebrate the efforts and achievements of their employees. Publicly acknowledging and rewarding their contributions not only boosts morale but also reinforces the idea that every individual has a role to play in the efficiency improvement process. By highlighting success stories and sharing them with the team, leaders inspire others to follow suit and actively engage in the improvement initiatives.

Lastly, leaders should lead by example and demonstrate their commitment to improvement. When leaders actively participate in the efficiency improvement process, it sends a strong message to employees that this is a priority and expected behavior. By sharing their own personal experiences, challenges, and successes, leaders establish a connection with their team, inspiring them to actively contribute and take ownership of their work.

One company that stands out for its leaders driving effectiveness and efficiency through employee involvement is Home Depot. With a focus on empowering their workforce and fostering a culture of collaboration, Home Depot has achieved remarkable success.

The leaders at Home Depot understand the value of including employees in decision-making processes. They actively involve their frontline employees in identifying areas for improvement and coming up with innovative solutions. Through regular team meetings, suggestion programs, and employee feedback forums, they create opportunities for employees to contribute their ideas and insights.

One powerful example of their commitment to employee involvement is their "Manager's Walk," where leaders engage in walk-throughs with employees to gain valuable insights and feedback. This practice not only allows leaders to identify areas where efficiency can be enhanced but also demonstrates their dedication to hearing and implementing employee suggestions.

Furthermore, Home Depot prioritizes employee training and development, equipping them with the necessary skills and knowledge to excel in their roles. By investing in their employees' growth and success, leaders at Home Depot inspire a sense of ownership and accountability, aligning everyone towards the shared goal of driving efficiency and effectiveness.

To further foster a collaborative environment, Home Depot recognizes and rewards employee contributions. They have programs in place to celebrate and showcase exceptional performances, motivating employees to go above and beyond to drive results. This recognition serves as a testament to their commitment to employee involvement and appreciation.

By embracing employee involvement as a core value, Home Depot has experienced improvements in productivity, customer satisfaction, and overall business success. Their leaders understand that engaged and empowered employees are key drivers of effectiveness and efficiency.

Taking a page from The Home Depot's playbook, leaders in any organization can drive effectiveness and efficiency by involving employees in decision-making, providing opportunities for feedback and suggestions, investing in training and development, and recognizing employees' contributions. Together, these initiatives can create a culture of collaboration and ownership, ultimately leading to enhanced performance and success.

To sum up, leaders can empower their employees to actively contribute to the efficiency improvement process by fostering a culture of trust and open communication, involving them in decision-making, providing necessary resources and support, recognizing their contributions, and leading by example. By implementing these strategies, leaders can inspire their team to embrace the improvement process, drive innovation, and achieve exceptional results while building strong and collaborative relationships.

Now that we've explored several strategies leaders can employ to empower their employees in the efficiency improvement process, let's recap by taking a look at a helpful checklist I've created to guide you in implementing these strategies effectively.

"The function of leadership is to produce more leaders, not more followers."

- Ralph Nader

CHECKLIST

Empowering Employees to Drive Efficiency Improvement

- Cultivate a culture of trust and open communication: Create a safe environment where employees feel comfortable sharing their ideas, concerns, and suggestions without fear of retribution.

- Involve employees in decision-making processes: Allow employees to have a say in identifying problems, generating solutions, and selecting improvement initiatives.

- Provide necessary resources and support: Offer training and development opportunities to equip employees with the skills and knowledge they need to actively contribute to the efficiency improvement process.

- Recognize and celebrate employee efforts and achievements: Publicly acknowledge and reward employee contributions to boost morale and reinforce the idea that every individual has a role to play in the process.

- Lead by example: Actively participate in the efficiency improvement process and share personal experiences, challenges, and successes to inspire employees to do the same.

- Foster a sense of ownership and engagement among employees: Empower employees to take ownership of their work and actively seek out opportunities for improvement.

- Encourage diverse opinions and perspectives: Create an environment where diverse ideas are encouraged and respected, tapping into the collective intelligence of the team for more robust and innovative solutions.

By following these steps, leaders can empower their employees to take ownership of their work and drive positive change in the efficiency improvement process.

Now that we have gone over the checklist for empowering employees to drive efficiency improvement, let's look at some examples that demonstrate how these steps can be put into practice. These examples will highlight the importance of clear communication, fostering a culture of trust, delegating decision-making authority, encouraging open communication and collaboration, providing resources and support, and recognizing and celebrating contributions. By implementing these strategies, leaders can empower their employees to take ownership of their work and make meaningful contributions to the efficiency improvement process.

> *"The best teamwork comes from men who are working independently toward one goal in unison."*
>
> *- James Cash Penney*

EXAMPLES

A manager at a software development company holds a team meeting to clearly communicate the purpose and goals of a new project to the developers. He explains how their work will contribute to the overall success of the company and encourages them to actively participate in finding ways to improve efficiency throughout the development process.

A team leader at a healthcare organization creates a safe and supportive environment for her team. During weekly team meetings, she actively listens to her team members' ideas and concerns without judgment. She encourages open dialogue and ensures that everyone's opinions are valued and respected, fostering a culture of trust and psychological safety.

The CEO of a manufacturing company delegates decision-making authority to his engineers. He trusts them to identify and implement improvements on the production line without constant micromanagement. This empowerment not only boosts employee morale but also allows the engineers to take ownership of their work and find innovative solutions to increase efficiency.

A project manager at a marketing agency encourages open communication and collaboration among team members. She organizes regular brainstorming sessions where everyone can freely share their ideas and perspectives. She also promotes cross-functional collaborations, allowing employees from different departments to work together and leverage their diverse expertise for more efficient project outcomes.

The director of a sales team ensures that his sales representatives have access to resources and support to improve their efficiency. He invests in sales training programs to enhance their selling skills and provides them with the necessary tools and technology to streamline their workflow. Additionally, he holds regular one-on-one coaching sessions to offer guidance and support whenever needed.

The manager of a customer service team recognizes and celebrates her employees' contributions. She publicly acknowledges the achievements of her team members during team gatherings and sends personalized emails to express her appreciation privately. This recognition not only motivates her employees but also creates a positive work environment where everyone feels valued and encouraged to actively participate in improving efficiency.

Based on these examples, it is important to also consider the potential mistakes that should be avoided in this process. These mistakes can hinder the progress towards efficiency improvement and may diminish the impact of employee empowerment strategies. Let's explore some of these mistakes to ensure a successful implementation of similar initiatives.

"Teamwork makes the dream work."

- John C. Maxwell

TYPICAL MISTAKES AND HOW TO AVOID THEM

A common mistake people make in empowering employees is not clearly communicating the purpose and goals of the organization. To avoid this, leaders should provide a clear understanding of the organization's purpose and goals to employees. When employees have a sense of purpose and know how their work contributes to the bigger picture, they are more likely to actively participate in the efficiency improvement process.

Another mistake is not fostering a culture of trust and psychological safety. To avoid this, leaders should create a safe and supportive environment where employees feel comfortable sharing their ideas, opinions, and concerns without fear of negative consequences. When employees feel trusted and valued, they are more motivated to actively participate in the efficiency improvement process.

Additionally, leaders often make the mistake of not delegating decision-making authority. To avoid this, leaders should delegate decision-making authority to their employees whenever possible. By granting employees autonomy and responsibility, they feel trusted and valued, which leads to increased confidence and motivation to actively contribute to efficiency improvements.

Another mistake is not encouraging open communication and collaboration. To avoid this, leaders should promote open communication and collaboration among employees. This can be done through regular team meetings, brainstorming sessions, and cross-functional collaborations. By encouraging employees to work together and share their ideas and knowledge, leaders can tap into diverse perspectives and experiences that contribute to the efficiency improvement process.

Leaders also make the mistake of not providing necessary resources and support for employees. To avoid this, leaders should ensure that employees have access to the necessary resources, training, and support to actively contribute to efficiency improvements. This may include providing relevant tools, training programs, or external resources to enhance employees' skills and knowledge. Additionally, leaders should be available to provide guidance and support whenever needed, serving as a resource and mentor to their team.

Lastly, leaders often fail to recognize and celebrate employees' contributions. To avoid this mistake, leaders should acknowledge and appreciate the efforts and achievements of their team members, publicly and privately. This not only motivates employees to continue taking initiative but also creates a positive and engaging work environment.

In conclusion, by avoiding these common mistakes and implementing the strategies discussed here, leaders can empower their employees to actively contribute to the efficiency improvement process and drive meaningful improvements.

MY #1 PIECE OF ADVICE

If you want to excel as a leader then my #1 piece of advice to you is to delegate tasks and responsibilities effectively. Trust your employees and empower them to make decisions and take ownership of their work.

> *"Great things in business are never done by one person; they're done by a team of people."*
>
> *- Steve Jobs*

SUMMARY:

- Cultivate a culture of trust and open communication, allowing employees to freely share their ideas and suggestions without fear of retribution.

- Involve employees in decision-making processes, giving them a sense of ownership and responsibility, and bringing diverse perspectives to the table for more innovative ideas.

- Provide necessary resources and support for employees to actively contribute, including training and development opportunities to enhance their skills and knowledge.

- Recognize and celebrate the efforts and achievements of employees, boosting morale and reinforcing the idea that everyone has a role to play in efficiency improvement.

- Lead by example and demonstrate commitment to improvement, inspiring employees to actively contribute and take ownership of their work.

Remember, by creating a supportive and empowering environment, recognizing and celebrating contributions, and encouraging active participation, you can unleash the potential of your team to drive meaningful improvements and achieve success.

APPLICATION QUESTIONS

- Have you considered implementing regular feedback sessions or suggestion programs to encourage open communication and involvement from your employees? If not, how can you incorporate these practices into your leadership style?

- How can you invest in the training and development of your employees to equip them with the necessary skills and knowledge to excel in their roles and contribute to increased effectiveness and efficiency?

- Can you identify specific areas within your team or organization where frontline employees can play a more active role in decision-making? How can you involve them in these processes?

- How can you incorporate regular "walk-throughs" or informal conversations with employees to gain valuable insights, identify areas for improvement, and demonstrate your commitment to employee involvement?

- What steps can you take to foster a collaborative environment where every team member feels heard, valued, and empowered to actively participate and contribute to driving effectiveness and efficiency?

QUIZ

1. What is one benefit of involving employees in decision-making processes?

   A. It improves employee morale

   B. It encourages diverse opinions

   C. It reinforces the idea that everyone has a role to play in the efficiency improvement process

   D. It enhances their commitment to the team

2. What can happen when employees feel equipped to take on new challenges?

   A. They become more proactive in seeking out opportunities for improvement

   B. They become more engaged and committed to the team

   C. They become more innovative and creative

   D. They become more involved in decision-making processes

3. What is a key strategy to empower employees in the efficiency improvement process?

   A. Creating a safe environment where diverse opinions are encouraged and respected

B. Highlighting success stories and sharing them with the team

C. Involving employees in decision-making processes

D. Rewarding their contributions

4. What is the first step in empowering employees?

A. Delegating decision-making authority

B. Providing a clear understanding of the organization's purpose and goals

C. Encouraging open communication and collaboration

D. Recognizing and celebrating contributions

5. What is the goal of empowering employees?

A. To create a positive and engaging work environment.

B. To foster a culture of shared ideas and collective problem-solving.

C. To recognize and celebrate their contributions.

D. To unleash the full potential of their teams to drive positive change

Answer Key:

1. D - It enhances their commitment to the team

2. A - They become more proactive in seeking out opportunities for improvement

3. A - Creating a safe environment where diverse opinions are encouraged and respected

4. B - Providing a clear understanding of the organization's purpose and goals

5. D - To unleash the full potential of their teams to drive positive change

Now that we've explored how leaders can empower their employees to actively contribute to efficiency improvement, let's dive into the crucial topic of how leaders can effectively delegate tasks and responsibilities that inspire ownership without overwhelming their team members - ensuring they continue to thrive and remain motivated. Keep reading to discover the key strategies that can transform the way you delegate and propel your team towards optimal productivity.

CHAPTER 9
DELEGATION MASTERY
INSPIRING EMPLOYEES TO TAKE OWNERSHIP AND DELIVER EXCEPTIONAL RESULTS

"The best executive is the one who has sense enough to pick good men to do what he wants done and the self-restraint to keep from meddling with them while they do it."

- Theodore Roosevelt

AT A GLANCE

Five Essential Points for Inspiring Employees to Take Ownership and Deliver Exceptional Results

- Empower your employees by clearly defining expectations and outcomes for delegated tasks.

- Match tasks to your employees' skills and interests to boost engagement and pride in their work.

- Build trust by allowing employees the freedom to make decisions and take initiative.

- Provide necessary resources and support through mentorship and feedback to help employees succeed.

- Encourage autonomy and creativity by allowing employees to find their own approaches to completing tasks.

Five Questions Business Leaders Should Ask About Inspiring Employees to Take Ownership and Deliver Exceptional Results

- What strategies or tools do you currently find most effective in inspiring your team to take ownership of their work? How do you ensure that they feel genuinely motivated and engaged?
- In your opinion, what role does trust play in inspiring employees to take ownership? How do you continue to build trust and create an environment where individuals feel comfortable taking ownership and initiative?
- As a leader, how do you encourage and support employees to set their own goals and take ownership of their professional development?
- How do you foster a culture of accountability within your team or organization? How do you encourage individuals to take ownership of their actions and outcomes, even in the face of setbacks or obstacles?
- When it comes to inspiring employees to take ownership, what have you found to be the most common barriers or challenges?

To effectively delegate tasks and responsibilities in a way that inspires employees to take ownership of their work, leaders must follow a few key principles. By balancing clarity, trust, and support, leaders can cultivate a sense of ownership and motivation among their employees. Here are some actionable recommendations:

Begin by providing clear expectations and objectives. Clearly communicate what needs to be achieved, along with any relevant deadlines or milestones. When employees understand the expectations, they can step up and take responsibility for their work. Take the time to discuss the task in detail, answer any questions they may have, and provide any necessary resources or support.

Next, it's essential to match the right task with the right person. Each team member has unique talents, strengths, and interests, so taking the time to understand their skills and aspirations is crucial. Once identified, it is essential for leaders to actively leverage these strengths by allocating tasks and projects accordingly. Employees should be given opportunities to work in their strength zones as much as possible.

To identify the strengths of employees, leaders should adopt a multifaceted approach. First, they should have open and ongoing conversations with team members to understand their career aspirations, skills, and interests. This will provide insights into what energizes and motivates each employee. Additionally, conducting formal assessments are a great way to understand hidden talents and preferences of communication and work styles. I've used the Maxwell Method of DISC and the Working Genius assessment to provide remarkable insights with teams. By aligning tasks with an individual's strengths, leaders foster engagement, enthusiasm, and exceptional performance.

Leaders should also encourage employees to further develop and refine their strengths as well. When we invest in developing our strengths, they become our superpowers. This can be achieved through ongoing training, workshops, and coaching sessions. By investing in the growth and advancement of their team members, leaders not only enhance individual performance but also create a culture of continuous learning and improvement within the team.

It is essential to ensure that employees have the resources, tools, and training required to complete the delegated tasks successfully. Offering support through mentorship, regular check-ins, and feedback can help employees feel supported and confident in their work. This support also demonstrates your investment in their growth and development.

Trust is crucial to successful delegation. Once you delegate a task, trust your team to get it done. Micromanaging not only hinders productivity but also diminishes the sense of ownership. Instead, empower your employees to make decisions and take initiative. Let them know that you trust their judgment and encourage them to come up with creative solutions.

Allow employees the freedom to find their own approaches to completing delegated tasks. Encourage them to bring their ideas and insights to the table, fostering a sense of ownership and creativity. When employees have autonomy and the opportunity to contribute their unique perspectives, they are more likely to take ownership of their work.

Finally, provide support and feedback throughout the process. Check-in regularly to see if your team members have any questions or need any assistance. Offer guidance and be available for discussions. Recognize and appreciate their efforts, providing constructive feedback and encouragement. By supporting your team along the way, you build a sense of partnership and foster their ownership of the tasks.

One exemplary company whose leaders are renowned for inspiring employees to take ownership and achieve exceptional results is Netflix. Led by CEO Reed Hastings, Netflix has built a culture that encourages individuals to be self-motivated, innovative, and customer-focused.

At Netflix, leaders prioritize a high degree of freedom and responsibility. They believe in setting clear expectations and allowing employees to work autonomously, taking ownership of their projects and decisions. By promoting a culture where employees are trusted and empowered, Netflix has created an environment where exceptional results can thrive.

One notable example of inspiring leadership at Netflix is demonstrated through their "Culture Deck." This widely circulated document, crafted by former Netflix Chief Talent Officer Patty McCord, transparently outlines the company's values and expectations. By clearly communicating the company's vision, principles, and the key behaviors required to succeed, leaders at Netflix inspire employees to take ownership of their roles and drive exceptional outcomes.

Furthermore, Netflix is known for its commitment to amplifying the voices of its employees. They actively seek feedback, value diverse perspectives, and encourage communication at all levels. This inclusive approach to leadership not only empowers individuals to take ownership of their work but also fosters a sense of belonging and shared purpose throughout the organization.

Importantly, Netflix's leaders also recognize the importance of continuous learning and growth. They invest in employee development programs, encourage individuals to explore new ideas, and learn from failures. This emphasis on personal and professional growth inspires employees to take ownership of their success and push the limits of what they can achieve.

Netflix is an excellent example of a company whose leaders excel at inspiring employees to take ownership and achieve exceptional results. By cultivating a culture of autonomy, transparency, inclusivity, and continuous learning, they foster an environment where individuals are empowered to deliver their best work and drive the company's success.

Incorporating these practices into your delegation approach will not only empower and inspire your employees but also foster stronger relationships and a more productive work environment. Remember, effective delegation is not just about offloading tasks but also about establishing a culture of trust, collaboration, and shared ownership.

Now that you've learned about the key principles of effective delegation, let's take a look at a checklist I've created to help you implement these practices in your own leadership style.

> *"If you want to do a few small things right, do them yourself. If you want to do great things and make a big impact, learn to delegate."*
>
> *- John C. Maxwell*

CHECKLIST

Checklist for Effective Delegation:

- Understand your team members: Take the time to know each team member's unique talents, strengths, and interests.

- Use assessments to not only identify their strengths but to find strength gaps within the team.

- Match tasks with individuals: Assign tasks that align with each employee's abilities and interests to increase motivation and ownership.

- Communicate expectations: Clearly communicate what needs to be achieved, along with deadlines and milestones.

- Provide necessary resources and support: Discuss the task in detail, answer questions, and offer any needed resources or assistance.

- Embrace autonomy: Trust your team to get the task done and empower them to make decisions and take initiative.

- Avoid micromanagement: Allow your team members to work independently and demonstrate trust in their judgment.

- Provide support and feedback: Regularly check in with your team members to see if they have any questions or need assistance. Offer guidance and constructive feedback.

- Recognize and appreciate efforts: Acknowledge and appreciate your team members' efforts. Provide positive feedback and encouragement.

- Lead by example: Show passion and commitment towards your work and demonstrate ownership and accountability. Be a role model for your team members to follow.

By following this checklist, leaders can learn to effectively delegate tasks and responsibilities, inspire employees to take ownership, and build a trusted and empowered team.

Now that we have gone through the preparations checklist for effective delegation, let's take a look at some examples that showcase how these principles can be applied in real-life situations.

> *"I not only use all the brains that I have, but all that I can borrow."*
>
> *- **Woodrow Wilson***

EXAMPLES

You might be thinking, 'well, I'm not Netflix' so here are other examples to further illustrate the points:

As a team leader in a marketing agency, you have a team member named Sarah who is exceptionally skilled at graphic design. You delegate the task of creating a new promotional banner for a client's website to her. Because you took the time to understand her skills and interests, you know that she enjoys design work and has a keen eye for aesthetics. Sarah feels motivated and takes ownership of the task, using her talents to create an impressive banner that exceeds the client's expectations.

In a software development team, there is a team member named John who has strong coding skills and a passion for problem-solving. You delegate the task of fixing a complex bug in the system to him. By discussing the task in detail and providing any necessary resources, John understands the expectations and takes responsibility for solving the issue. He uses his technical expertise and creativity to come up with an innovative solution, demonstrating ownership of the problem.

As a manager in a retail store, you delegate the responsibility of organizing a product launch event to one of your team members, Emily. Knowing that Emily has excellent organizational skills and enjoys event planning, you trust her to handle the task. By giving her autonomy and encouraging her to make decisions, you empower Emily to come up with creative ideas for the event and take ownership of the planning process.

In a busy call center, there is a team member named Alex who has been handling a high volume of customer calls. You delegate the task of training a new employee to Alex, considering their workload capacity. By spreading the responsibilities evenly and avoiding overburdening Alex, you give him the chance to balance his existing responsibilities while taking ownership of training the new team member.

As a project manager, you delegate the responsibility of presenting the team's progress to a client to one of your team members named Lisa. Throughout the process, you provide support and feedback, offering guidance on how to effectively communicate the project's achievements and challenges. By recognizing Lisa's efforts and providing constructive feedback, you encourage her ownership of the presentation and empower her to represent the team with confidence.

As a leader in a nonprofit organization, you personally take on the task of fundraising and actively demonstrate ownership and accountability. By sharing updates on your progress, discussing your strategies with the team, and showing your passion for the cause, you inspire your team members to also take ownership of their responsibilities within the organization. They feel a sense of partnership and are motivated to contribute towards the organization's goals.

These examples demonstrate how applying the principles of effective delegation can create a sense of ownership, trust, and motivation among employees.

Now that we have explored several examples highlighting the principles of effective delegation, let's take a look at the list of mistakes to avoid when delegating tasks to ensure success and maintain a positive work environment.

> *"Delegating work means letting others become the experts and hence the best."*
>
> *- Stephen R. Covey*

TYPICAL MISTAKES AND HOW TO AVOID THEM

Based on the ground we've covered so far, one mistake that most people make in delegation is not taking the time to understand their team members' unique talents, strengths, and interests. By doing so, leaders can assign tasks that align with employees' abilities and interests, which in turn motivates them to take ownership of their work. To avoid this mistake, leaders should invest time in getting to know their team members and their skills.

Another common mistake is not providing clear expectations and objectives when delegating tasks. Without clear communication, employees may not fully understand what needs to be achieved or what the deadlines are. To avoid this, leaders should clearly communicate the expectations, discuss the task in detail, and provide any necessary resources or support.

Micromanagement is another mistake that should be avoided. Micromanaging not only hinders productivity but also diminishes the sense of ownership among team members. Instead, leaders should trust their team to get the task done and empower them to make decisions and take initiative.

Providing support and feedback throughout the delegation process is crucial. Leaders should regularly check in with their team members, offer guidance, and be available for discussions. Recognizing and appreciating their efforts, as well as providing constructive feedback and encouragement, helps build a sense of partnership and fosters ownership.

Lastly, leaders should lead by example. Showing passion and commitment towards their own work and actively demonstrating ownership and accountability inspire team members to adopt the same mindset.

In summary, to avoid common mistakes in delegation, leaders should match tasks with individuals' strengths and interests, set clear expectations, embrace autonomy, avoid micromanagement, consider workload capacity, provide support and feedback, and lead by example. By following these principles, leaders can inspire their employees to take ownership of their work and build a trusted and empowered team.

MY #1 PIECE OF ADVICE

My #1 piece of advice that can help you overcome these pitfalls and ensure successful delegation is trust your team and empower them to take ownership of their tasks. When delegating, clearly communicate expectations, provide support, and give room for autonomy. By doing so, you'll foster growth, build a cohesive team, and achieve better results.

> *"Great leaders are willing to sacrifice their own personal interests for the good of the organization. They are willing to delegate authority and empower others to make decisions and take action."*
>
> *- Brian Tracy*

SUMMARY:

- Clearly define expectations: Provide a clear explanation of the task or responsibility, including desired outcomes, deadlines, and specific requirements. Empower employees to take ownership of their work by clearly communicating what is expected of them.

- Match skills and interests: Understand your employees' strengths, skills, and interests to assign tasks that align with their abilities and goals. When employees work on tasks they are passionate about, they become more engaged and take pride in their work.

- Establish trust: Trust your employees' abilities to accomplish delegated tasks. Avoid micromanaging and allow them the freedom to make decisions and take initiative. When employees feel trusted, they are more likely to take ownership of their work and go the extra mile.

- Provide necessary resources and support: Ensure employees have the resources, tools, and training they need to successfully complete their tasks. Offer support through mentorship, regular check-ins, and feedback. This demonstrates your investment in their growth and development.

- Encourage autonomy and creativity: Foster a culture where employees can find their own approaches to tasks and contribute their unique perspectives. Encourage them to bring their ideas and insights to the table, fostering a sense of ownership and creativity.

APPLICATION QUESTIONS

- Imagine your team members feeling a strong sense of autonomy and empowerment, just like the employees at Netflix. How do you believe this would impact their motivation and drive to deliver exceptional results?

- In your leadership journey, think of someone who inspired you to take ownership and achieve exceptional results. What qualities or actions made them an effective leader? How can you incorporate those leadership traits into your own approach to inspire and empower your employees?

- Imagine a future where your team operates with a high level of autonomy, trust, and shared purpose, just like the companies we've discussed. How would that impact their sense of ownership and the results they deliver? What measures can you take to integrate a that level of autonomy into your team's day-to-day operations?

- Reflect on your own leadership style and behaviors. How can you lead by example, demonstrating the values and actions that inspire ownership and exceptional results? Share any concrete actions or changes you plan to implement.

- Consider the importance of communication and transparency in inspiring employees to take ownership. How can you effectively communicate expectations and provide clarity while still empowering individuals to make decisions and take ownership?

QUIZ

1. What is the main goal of delegation?

   A. Assigning tasks
   B. Building a sense of trust
   C. Improving productivity
   D. All of the above

2. What is the first step to successful delegation?

   A. Providing support and feedback
   B. Matching the right task with the right person
   C. Setting clear expectations

D. Prioritizing tasks

3. What should leaders avoid when delegating tasks?

   A. Leading by example
   B. Embracing autonomy
   C. Micromanaging
   D. Offering guidance

4. What is the last step to successful delegation?

   A. Leading by example
   B. Prioritizing tasks
   C. Matching the right task with the right person
   D. Checking in regularly

5. How can leaders build a sense of partnership and foster ownership of tasks?

   A. Recognize and appreciate efforts
   B. Offer guidance
   C. Set clear expectations
   D. All of the above

Answer Key:

1. B - Building a sense of trust

2. B - Matching the right task with the right person

3. C - Micromanaging

4. A - Leading by example

5. D - All of the above

Having established the foundations of effective delegation, it is now crucial for leaders to understand and develop the strengths of your employees. In the next chapter, we will explore how training and development play a vital role in enhancing employee skills, equipping them with the necessary knowledge to drive better results. Keep reading to discover the significance of ongoing growth and how it can empower your team.

CHAPTER 10

INVESTING IN SKILLS, REAPING RESULTS

THE POWER OF TRAINING AND DEVELOPMENT

"The single biggest way to impact an organization is to focus on leadership development. There is almost no limit to the potential of an organization that recruits good people, raises them up as leaders and continually develops them."

- John Maxwell

AT A GLANCE

Five Essential Points for the Power of Training and Development

- Unleash your full potential: Discover how ongoing training and development can help you unlock your hidden talents and contribute to your team's success.

- Stay ahead of the game: Find out how acquiring new skills and knowledge through training programs can help you adapt to changing demands and tackle complex challenges in today's fast-paced business world.

- Be part of a culture of continuous learning: Learn how organizations that prioritize employee growth and development create a motivating environment that boosts productivity and attracts top talent.

- Bridge the gaps and soar high: See how training and development programs can identify and address skill gaps, ensuring you have the competencies needed to excel in your role and achieve better results.

- Join a community of innovation: Explore how nurturing a supportive learning culture can not only enhance your skills but also inspire creativity and innovation within your team.

Five Questions Business Leaders Should Ask About Training and Development

- What are your thoughts on the current training and development initiatives in your organization? How do you believe they align with your overall goals and vision?

- What do you see as the top skills or knowledge gaps that need to be addressed through training and development?

- How do you envision your training and development programs evolving to meet the changing needs of your employees and industry?

- Are there any emerging trends or technologies in your industry that you believe your employees should be trained in to stay ahead of the curve?

- What role do you believe leadership should play in supporting and promoting a strong training and development culture within your organization?

Training and development play a crucial role in enhancing employee skills and ensuring that they have the necessary knowledge to drive better results. In today's fast-paced and competitive business environment, it is essential for organizations to invest in their employees' growth and progress.

Firstly, training and development programs provide employees with the opportunity to acquire new skills and enhance their existing ones. By participating in these programs, employees can learn the latest industry trends, technologies, and best practices. This continuous learning approach enables employees to stay ahead of the game and adapt to changes in their respective fields. They become equipped with cutting-edge tools and techniques, which ultimately leads to improved productivity, efficiency, and innovation within the organization.

Moreover, training and development initiatives help employees stay motivated and engaged in their roles. When employees are given the opportunity to expand their skill set and develop professionally, they feel valued and recognized. This recognition fosters a positive work environment and a sense of loyalty towards the organization. When employees are engaged, they are more likely to invest their energy and effort into their work, leading to better overall performance and results.

Additionally, training and development contribute to employee retention and attraction. Employees are more likely to stay with an organization that invests in their growth and development. By offering comprehensive training programs, organizations demonstrate their commitment to their employees' success and provide them with a clear pathway for career advancement. This not only helps in retaining top talent but also attracts high-potential individuals who are seeking opportunities for personal and professional growth.

To ensure training and development initiatives drive better results, it is crucial to tailor these programs to meet the specific needs of both the individual employees and the organization as a whole. Conducting a thorough needs analysis and identifying competency gaps and developmental areas will enable organizations to design training programs that address these areas effectively. Furthermore, incorporating practical and hands-on exercises into the training sessions will enhance employees' ability to apply their knowledge in real-life situations, further boosting their capabilities.

One company that stands out for its dedication to investing in training and development is HubSpot. Their leaders have shown a strong commitment to nurturing their employees' growth and ensuring continuous learning opportunities.

Through their HubSpot Academy, they offer a wide range of free online courses and certifications, covering topics such as inbound marketing, sales, customer service, and more. This extensive educational platform allows employees to enhance their skills and stay ahead of industry trends.

Not only does HubSpot provide employees with access to valuable learning resources, but they also encourage a culture of learning within their organization. They have designated "learning pods" that bring together employees with similar learning interests, enabling them to collaborate, share knowledge, and support each other's growth.

Moreover, HubSpot's leaders actively participate in training and development efforts. They lead by example, often sharing their expertise and insights through workshops, webinars, and internal mentorship programs. By being actively involved in the growth of their employees, the leaders at HubSpot foster a strong sense of engagement and commitment within the organization.

Overall, HubSpot's investment in training and development showcases their dedication to cultivating a skilled workforce and empowering their employees to reach their full potential. Their leaders' commitment, coupled with a comprehensive and accessible learning platform, make HubSpot a company that exemplifies the importance of investing in training and development for sustainable success.

Training and development programs are indispensable for enhancing employee skills, knowledge, and motivation, ultimately driving better results for organizations. By investing in their employees' growth, organizations not only equip them with the necessary tools to excel in their roles but also foster a culture of continuous learning and improvement. It is through this investment in their workforce that organizations can ensure long-term success and build a team that is both equipped and engaged to exceed expectations.

Now that we have discussed the importance of training and development programs in enhancing employee skills and driving better results, it is important to have a checklist in place to ensure the success of these initiatives. This checklist will help organizations tailor their training programs to meet the specific needs of their employees and the organization as a whole, leading to improved productivity, efficiency, and innovation.

"Leadership and learning are indispensable to each other."

- John F. Kennedy

CHECKLIST

Checklist for Driving Better Results through Training and Development:

- Identify goals and objectives: Define the specific goals and objectives of the training and development programs. Identify the skills and knowledge gaps that need to be addressed.

- Conduct a needs analysis: Conduct a thorough needs analysis to determine the specific training needs of individual employees and the organization as a whole. Identify competency gaps and developmental areas that require attention.

- Budget allocation: Allocate a budget for training and development programs. Consider the costs associated with trainers, materials, technology, and any other resources required.

- Design customized programs: Tailor the training and development programs to meet the specific needs of individual employees and the organization. Ensure that the content and delivery methods are relevant and engaging.

- Set clear objectives: Clearly define the learning objectives for each training program. Ensure that the objectives are measurable and achievable.

- Identify trainers: Select trainers who have the necessary expertise and experience to deliver effective training sessions. Consider hiring external trainers if you do not have anyone internally with the necessary expertise.

- Schedule training sessions: Determine the timing, duration, and frequency of the training sessions. Consider the availability of employees and the impact on daily operations.

- Communicate with participants: Inform the participants about the training programs well in advance. Clearly communicate the purpose, schedule, and expectations of the training sessions.

- Provide necessary resources: Ensure that the training sessions have the necessary resources, such as training rooms, equipment, and technology, to facilitate effective learning.

- Incorporate practical exercises: Your trainer should include practical and hands-on exercises in the training sessions to enhance employees' ability to apply their knowledge in real-life situations.

- Monitor progress: Regularly monitor the progress of employees throughout the training programs. Provide feedback and support as needed to ensure effective learning.

- Evaluate the effectiveness: Conduct post-training evaluations to assess the effectiveness of the training and development programs. Gather feedback from participants and make necessary improvements for future programs.

- Follow-up and reinforcement: Implement follow-up measures to reinforce the learning and ensure that employees are able to apply their new skills and knowledge in their roles.

- Continuously improve: Continuously evaluate and improve the training and development programs based on feedback and the changing needs of the organization.

By following this checklist, organizations can ensure that their training and development programs are well-prepared, effective, and contribute to the growth and success of employees and the organization as a whole.

Now that we have gone through the comprehensive checklist for preparing training and development programs, let's take a look at some examples that demonstrate how these steps can be implemented effectively. These examples will provide a clear understanding of how organizations can tailor their programs to meet the specific needs of their employees and ensure successful outcomes.

> *"The key to success is to keep growing in all areas of life - mental, emotional, spiritual, as well as physical."*
>
> *- Julius Erving*

EXAMPLES

Even if you do not have the capacity to implement training and development programs on the scale of HubSpot, you can still find ways that to get started right now. Here are some examples of how you could do that.

Acquiring new skills: A software development company offers a training program on machine learning and artificial intelligence. Employees who participate in the program learn the latest algorithms and techniques in these fields, allowing them to stay ahead of the competition and develop innovative solutions for clients.

Enhancing existing skills: A retail company provides a customer service training workshop for its employees. Through the workshop, employees learn effective communication techniques, conflict resolution strategies, and problem-solving skills. As a result, they are better equipped to handle customer inquiries and provide top-notch service, leading to increased customer satisfaction and repeat business.

Motivation and engagement: An accounting firm offers a mentorship program where junior employees are paired with senior professionals in the company. Through regular meetings and guidance from their mentors, employees gain valuable insights into their industry and specific career paths. This support and recognition fuel their motivation, making them more engaged in their work and eager to excel in their roles.

Employee retention and attraction: A healthcare organization provides professional development opportunities for its medical staff, including subsidized continuing education courses and certifications. This investment in their growth and development not only helps to retain experienced physicians and nurses but also attracts new talent who are seeking opportunities for career advancement and staying updated with the latest medical practices.

Tailored training programs: A manufacturing company conducts a training needs analysis and identifies a gap in its employees' knowledge of lean manufacturing principles. As a result, the company develops a customized training program focused on lean manufacturing techniques and tools. By incorporating hands-on simulations and practical exercises, employees gain a deep understanding of lean practices and can implement them effectively on the shop floor, leading to improved efficiency and reduced waste.

These examples demonstrate how training and development initiatives contribute to employee growth, motivation, retention, and overall organizational success.

Now that we have explored the successful training and development initiatives examples, it is important to also consider the mistakes that should be avoided in order to ensure the effectiveness and success of such initiatives. Here are some key mistakes to avoid when implementing training and development programs.

> *"The only thing worse than training employees and losing them is to not train them and keep them."*
>
> *- Zig Ziglar*

TYPICAL MISTAKES AND HOW TO AVOID THEM

One common mistake that people make in the area of training and development is not investing enough in their employees' growth. Some organizations may see these programs as unnecessary expenses or may not prioritize them. However, this is a short-sighted approach that can hinder the long-term success of the organization. Investing in employee development helps in attracting and retaining top talent, as individuals seek organizations that support their personal and professional growth.

To avoid this mistake, organizations should recognize the importance of training and development in enhancing employee skills and knowledge.

They should allocate sufficient resources and budget for these programs, understanding that the investment will lead to improved productivity, efficiency, and innovation.

Another mistake is not tailoring the training programs to meet the specific needs of employees and the organization. One-size-fits-all approaches may not effectively address the competency gaps and developmental areas of individuals. Conducting a thorough needs analysis and identifying these gaps will enable organizations to design training programs that are more impactful and relevant. By addressing these skill gaps, organizations ensure that employees have the necessary competencies and knowledge to perform their roles effectively, leading to improved performance and better results.

To avoid this, organizations should take the time to understand the specific skills and knowledge that employees need to succeed in their roles. This can be done through surveys, interviews, or performance evaluations. By customizing the training programs to address these specific needs, organizations can ensure that employees acquire the necessary skills and knowledge to excel.

Additionally, a mistake that most people make in the area of training and development is solely focusing on the provision of programs without creating a supportive learning environment. Simply providing training programs is not enough to enhance employee skills and drive better results. In today's fast-paced and competitive business landscape, leaders must prioritize their employees' growth and provide them with the necessary tools and knowledge to excel.

To avoid this mistake, organizations should prioritize creating a culture of collaboration, providing opportunities for employees to apply their newly acquired skills, and offering continuous feedback and recognition. By nurturing a learning culture, organizations not only enhance employee skills but also foster innovation and creativity within their teams.

The key mistakes that most people make in the area of training and development include neglecting to create a supportive learning environment, not addressing skill gaps, and failing to invest in employees' growth. To avoid these mistakes, organizations should foster a culture of collaboration, assess and address skill gaps, and prioritize employee development. By doing so, they can enhance employee skills, drive better results, and create a talented and engaged workforce that is capable of adapting to change, addressing challenges, and achieving success.

MY #1 PIECE OF ADVICE

While taking all of this into consideration, here is my #1 piece of advice for you: invest time to understand individual strengths, provide clear expectations, and offer support and feedback consistently to empower employees for optimal performance and a sense of worth.

> *"The most important investment you can make is in yourself."*
> *- Warren Buffett*

SUMMARY:

- Unlock your full potential and contribute to the success of your team and organization by investing in training and development programs.

- Acquire new skills and knowledge vital for your role through ongoing training and development, and become part of a talented and adaptable workforce.

- Foster a culture of continuous learning and engagement by prioritizing employee growth and development, leading to increased productivity and better results.

- Bridge skill gaps within your team through targeted training and support, ensuring everyone has the necessary competencies to excel in their roles.

- Create a supportive and innovative learning environment that encourages collaboration, feedback, and recognition, enhancing employee skills and driving better results.

APPLICATION QUESTIONS

- How can you create a learning culture within your organization, like HubSpot has done with its 'learning pods' initiative, to foster continuous development and collaboration among your employees?
- As leaders, how can you actively participate in training and development efforts, whether through sharing your expertise, leading workshops, or mentoring employees, to inspire and support their growth?
- In what ways can you encourage and incentivize your employees to take advantage of training and development opportunities, making it not only accessible but also enticing and engaging for them?
- What strategies can you implement to create a strong support system, such as mentorship programs or peer-to-peer learning, that encourages knowledge-sharing, collaboration, and growth among your employees?
- How can you effectively communicate the value and importance of training and development to your employees, ensuring that they view it as an investment in their own career growth and success?

QUIZ

1. What is the importance of fostering a supportive learning environment?

   A. Enhancing employee skills

   B. Encouraging continuous improvement

C. Facilitating collaboration

D. All of the above

2. What is the primary goal of training and development programs?

A. To bridge skill gaps

B. To create a culture of continuous learning

C. To provide employees with the opportunity to acquire new skills

D. To maximize the impact of training and development

3. How can training and development initiatives benefit organizations?

A. They help to attract high-potential individuals

B. They help to retain top talent

C. They help to improve productivity and efficiency

D. All of the above

4. What does investing in employee growth create?

A. A sense of motivation

B. A culture of innovation

C. A supportive learning environment

D. All of the above

5. What is the ultimate goal of providing employees with training and development opportunities?

A. To create a culture of innovation

B. To reduce costs

C. To enable employees to acquire new skills

D. To drive better results

Answer Key

1. D - All of the above

2. C - To provide employees with the opportunity to acquire new skills

3. D - All of the above

4. D - All of the above

5. D - To drive better results

As we have seen in this chapter, training and development play a crucial role in equipping employees with the skills and knowledge needed for success. However, the journey towards exceptional performance goes beyond mere skills and knowledge, which is what we will explore in the next chapter. Let's dig into the realm of leadership styles and approaches that have shown exceptional effectiveness in cultivating engaged and effective employees, unveiling the secrets to inspiring teams to achieve greatness. So, keep reading and be prepared to uncover valuable insights that will revolutionize your leadership approach.

CHAPTER 11

THE LEADERSHIP X-FACTOR

ESSENTIAL TRAITS FOR CREATING EFFECTIVE AND ENGAGED EMPLOYEES

"A great leader leads by example, setting high standards and demonstrating integrity in their actions and decisions."

- Nelson Mandela

AT A GLANCE

Five Essential Points for Essential Traits for Creating Effective and Engaged Employees

- Discover the secret qualities that make leaders truly effective and able to engage their teams for outstanding results.

- Learn how exceptional communication skills can create an atmosphere of trust and drive employee engagement.

- Explore the power of empathy and emotional intelligence in fostering a sense of belonging, motivation, and loyalty among team members.

- Uncover the transformational and servant leadership styles that inspire and empower employees to go above and beyond.

- Find out how coaching and mentoring can unleash the full potential of your team, driving high performance, loyalty, and commitment.

Five Questions Business Leaders Should Ask About Essential Traits for Creating Effective and Engaged Employees

- How would you describe your leadership style and how it contributes to creating an engaged and high-performing team?
- In your experience, what are the key leadership traits that have consistently led to the highest levels of employee engagement and productivity?
- How do you promote an environment of trust and open communication within your team? What strategies or techniques have you found to be effective in building and maintaining this type of culture?
- How do you engage with your employees on an individual level to understand their strengths, goals, and development needs? How does this personalized approach contribute to their overall engagement and growth within the organization?
- When it comes to employee development and growth, what actions do you take to cultivate a learning culture within your organization? How do you encourage continuous learning and skill development among your team members?

When it comes to creating effective and engaged employees, there are several abilities, qualities, leadership styles, and approaches that have proven to be particularly effective. By cultivating these attributes, aspiring leaders can motivate their teams to achieve outstanding results and foster a culture of engagement and productivity.

First and foremost, effective leaders possess excellent communication skills. They understand the importance of articulating clear expectations, actively listening to their employees, and providing constructive feedback. By being transparent in their communication, leaders create an atmosphere of trust, which promotes employee engagement and drives positive outcomes.

Furthermore, successful leaders demonstrate empathy and emotional intelligence. They are able to understand and relate to their employees' emotions, needs, and individual circumstances. By showing genuine care and support, leaders can foster a sense of belonging, motivation, and loyalty among their team members. This encourages employees to go above and beyond their job requirements and become passionate contributors to the organization's success.

Moreover, leaders who exhibit a transformational leadership style have been shown to effectively create engaged employees. Transformational leaders inspire and motivate their teams through their own enthusiasm and passion. They set a compelling vision and empower their employees to innovate, take risks, and grow both personally and professionally. By being charismatic and optimistic, these leaders create a positive and energizing work environment that fosters employee engagement and a drive for excellence.

In today's rapidly changing business environment, leaders need to be flexible and adaptable. They embrace new challenges, encourage innovation, and are open to different perspectives. By fostering a culture of adaptability, leaders create engaged employees who are willing to embrace change, take risks, and explore new opportunities.

Trust is the foundation of any successful team. Leaders who are transparent, honest, and trustworthy create a safe environment where employees feel comfortable taking risks, sharing ideas, and collaborating. By trusting their team members and giving them autonomy, leaders empower their employees and foster a sense of ownership and engagement.

In addition, leaders who adopt a servant leadership approach are highly effective at building engaged employees. By putting the needs of their team members first and focusing on their development, servant leaders create a culture of support, collaboration, and personal growth. These leaders actively listen to their employees, provide guidance and resources, and promote a sense of ownership and autonomy. By fostering a climate of empowerment, servant leaders motivate their employees to reach their full potential and achieve exceptional results.

Leaders also set the tone for their team. They need to embody the behaviors and values they expect from their employees. By leading by example, leaders inspire and motivate their team members to follow suit. When employees witness their leader's dedication, professionalism, and positive attitude, it generates a ripple effect throughout the team, creating a culture of excellence and engagement.

Lastly, leaders who emphasize a coaching and mentoring approach are instrumental in creating effective and engaged employees. They invest time and effort in developing their team members' skills and competencies. By providing ongoing guidance, feedback, and opportunities for growth, these leaders empower their employees to take ownership of their professional development. This approach not only drives high performance but also cultivates a sense of loyalty, commitment, and engagement within the team.

One company that exemplifies exceptional leadership traits for creating effective and engaged employees is Adobe Systems Incorporated. Led by its CEO, Shantanu Narayen, Adobe has established itself as a global leader in software solutions.

Narayen's leadership style incorporates several essential traits that contribute to a motivated and high-performing workforce. First and foremost, he emphasizes the importance of fostering a culture of innovation. By encouraging employees to explore new ideas and take calculated risks, Narayen inspires a sense of creativity and engagement throughout the organization.

Another crucial trait demonstrated by Adobe's leaders is their commitment to continuous learning and development. They provide extensive opportunities for skill-building and professional growth, ensuring that employees stay ahead of industry trends. This investment in their employees' development not only enhances their expertise but also boosts motivation and engagement.

Adobe's leaders also prioritize diversity and inclusion. They actively seek out diverse perspectives and create an inclusive environment where all employees feel valued and heard. By fostering a sense of belonging, Adobe's leaders enhance engagement and collaboration among their teams.

In terms of communication, Narayen and his team emphasize transparency and open dialogue. They provide clear and frequent updates on company strategies and objectives, ensuring that employees understand the broader vision. This transparent communication enables employees to align their individual goals with the company's mission, fostering a sense of purpose and engagement.

Furthermore, Adobe's leaders actively recognize and reward exceptional performance. They have implemented comprehensive recognition programs that celebrate achievements, whether big or small. This acknowledgment reinforces motivation, encourages a culture of excellence, and cultivates a sense of pride among employees.

Ultimately, Adobe serves as an excellent example of a company with leaders who embody essential leadership traits for creating effective and engaged employees. Through a focus on innovation, learning and development, diversity and inclusion, transparent communication, and meaningful recognition, Adobe's leaders inspire their workforce to consistently deliver exceptional results and drive the company's continued success.

Remember, leadership is not simply about achieving results; it is about building relationships and inspiring others to perform at their best. By incorporating these abilities, qualities, leadership styles, and approaches into your leadership toolkit, you can lead your team exceptionally well and create a highly engaged and productive workforce.

Now that we have explored the key abilities, qualities, and leadership styles that contribute to creating effective and engaged employees, I have created a checklist that will help aspiring leaders incorporate these principles into their own leadership approach. By following this checklist, you will be able to cultivate a culture of engagement and productivity within your teams and drive exceptional results.

> *"Effective leaders understand the importance of open communication and actively listen to their employees, fostering trust and collaboration."*
>
> *- Warren Buffett*

CHECKLIST

Checklist for Creating Effective and Engaged Employees:

- Enhance your communication skills by practicing both verbal and written communication. Seek feedback and actively listen to others to improve your communication abilities.

- Develop empathy and emotional intelligence by understanding and acknowledging the emotions, perspectives, and needs of your team members. Show genuine interest and support to foster a sense of belonging and motivation.

- Define a clear vision and purpose that inspires and motivates your employees. Communicate the bigger picture and link their work to the organization's mission to increase engagement.

- Build trust and transparency by being honest, open, and trustworthy. Create a safe environment that encourages risk-taking, idea-sharing, and collaboration.

- Embrace the role of a coach and mentor by providing regular feedback, recognizing achievements, and offering constructive criticism. Invest in your employees' professional development to foster a culture of continuous learning.

- Cultivate flexibility and adaptability to navigate the rapidly changing business environment. Encourage innovation, embrace new challenges, and be open to different perspectives.

- Be a Servant Leader by putting the needs of team members first. Focus on their development fostering support, collaboration, and personal growth. Actively listen, provide guidance, and promote ownership and autonomy whenever possible.

- Lead by example by embodying the behaviors and values you expect from your employees. Set the tone for your team by demonstrating dedication, professionalism, and a positive attitude.

By developing these abilities, qualities, leadership styles, and approaches into your leadership toolkit, you can become an effective leader who builds engaged and productive employees and fosters a powerful, positive work culture.

Now that we have reviewed the checklist for the leadership qualities that create effective and engaged employees, let's take a look at some examples that demonstrate how these abilities, qualities, and leadership styles can be put into practice.

"Leadership is not about being the best. It is about making everyone else better."

- Bill Gates

EXAMPLES

Although you may aspire to have a company the size of Adobe, you may not be there quite yet. Here are some other examples of how you can apply these principles to move you toward that level of success though.

John is a manager at a marketing firm. He always ensures that he clearly communicates the goals and expectations to his team members at the beginning of each project. He actively listens to their ideas and concerns, and provides constructive feedback to help them improve. John's transparent communication creates trust within the team, leading to increased employee engagement and productivity.

Sara is a department head at a tech company. She takes the time to understand her employees' emotions, needs, and personal circumstances. When one of her team members is going through a difficult time, Sara offers support and flexibility, showing genuine care. This fosters a sense of belonging and loyalty among her employees, resulting in a highly engaged and motivated team.

Mike is a CEO at a start-up company. He exhibits a transformational leadership style by setting a compelling vision and inspiring his team through his enthusiasm and passion. Mike encourages his employees to think outside the box, take risks, and be innovative. His charismatic and optimistic approach creates a positive work environment that drives employee engagement and a strong commitment to excellence.

Emily is a supervisor at a retail store. She follows a servant leadership approach by always putting her team members' needs first. Emily actively listens to her employees, provides guidance and resources, and encourages collaboration and personal growth. Her supportive and empowering leadership style creates engaged employees who strive to reach their full potential and achieve exceptional results.

Mark is a project manager at a consulting firm. He adopts a coaching and mentoring approach with his team members. Mark invests time in developing their skills and competencies, and provides ongoing guidance and feedback. By empowering his employees to take ownership of their professional development, Mark cultivates a sense of loyalty, commitment, and engagement within his team, resulting in high performance and success.

After exploring these examples of effective leadership, it is important to consider some mistakes to avoid when implementing this approach. These mistakes can hinder the effectiveness of transformational leadership and hinder its ability to drive employee engagement and organizational success. Here are a few key mistakes to be mindful of and avoid.

> *"Leadership is not about being in control. It is about creating a culture of service and selflessness."*
>
> *- Richard Branson*

TYPICAL MISTAKES AND HOW TO AVOID THEM

Based on we have talked about here, one mistake that most people make in creating effective and engaged employees is lacking communication skills. Effective leaders understand the importance of clear expectations, active listening, and providing constructive feedback. To avoid this mistake, aspiring leaders should focus on improving their communication skills and being transparent in their communication.

Another mistake is lacking empathy and emotional intelligence. Successful leaders are able to understand and relate to their employees' emotions and needs. To avoid this mistake, leaders should show genuine care and support for their team members, fostering a sense of belonging, motivation, and loyalty.

Additionally, not adopting a transformational leadership style can hinder the creation of engaged employees. Transformational leaders inspire and motivate their teams through their own enthusiasm and passion. They set a compelling vision and empower their employees to grow both personally and professionally. To avoid this mistake, leaders should strive to be charismatic and optimistic, creating a positive and energizing work environment.

Leaders who do not embrace a servant leadership approach may also struggle to build engaged employees. Servant leaders prioritize the needs of their team members and focus on their development. By actively listening, providing guidance and resources, and promoting a sense of ownership, servant leaders can motivate their employees to reach their full potential. To avoid this mistake, leaders should put the needs of their team members first and foster a culture of support and collaboration.

Lastly, not emphasizing a coaching and mentoring approach can hinder the creation of effective and engaged employees. Leaders who invest time and effort in developing their team members' skills and competencies empower their employees to take ownership of their professional development. To avoid this mistake, leaders should provide ongoing guidance, feedback, and opportunities for growth.

To avoid these mistakes and create effective and engaged employees, it is important for leaders to have exceptional communication skills, empathy, and emotional intelligence. Adopting transformational, servant, and coaching leadership styles can help inspire and motivate teams, foster a supportive work environment, and drive outstanding results. By avoiding these common mistakes and adopting these effective approaches, aspiring leaders can unlock the true potential of their employees and drive positive change within their organizations.

MY #1 PIECE OF ADVICE

My #1 piece of advice to you is to learn from your mistakes, take ownership of them, and use them as opportunities for growth.

> *"A leader is not defined by their title, but by their ability to empower others and achieve collective goals."*
>
> *- Oprah Winfrey*

SUMMARY:

- Cultivate exceptional communication skills to create an atmosphere of trust and promote employee engagement and positive outcomes.

- Show empathy and emotional intelligence to foster a sense of belonging, motivation, and loyalty among team members.

- Embrace a transformational leadership style to inspire and motivate teams, setting a compelling vision and empowering employees to innovate and grow.

- Adopt a servant leadership approach to prioritize the needs of team members, creating a culture of support, collaboration, and personal growth.

- Emphasize coaching and mentoring to develop employees' skills and competencies, empowering them to take ownership of their professional development and driving high performance.

APPLICATION QUESTIONS

- How can you better manage and resolve conflicts within your teams, promoting a healthy and productive work environment?

- How can you lead by example better and model the desired behaviors and values, inspiring your employees to follow suit and become more engaged and committed to their work?

- How can you more effectively communicate your vision and goals to employees in a way that inspires and engages them?

- How can you improve your communication with your team members to ensure transparency and open dialogue? What specific measures can you take to keep them informed about company strategies, objectives, and changes, while also encouraging their input and feedback?

- How can you ensure that your leadership style reflects the essential traits for creating effective and engaged employees we discussed? What steps will you take to continuously develop and improve your own leadership skills and behaviors for the benefit of your team?

Remember, implementing these essential leadership traits requires action and commitment. It is crucial to find concrete ways to apply these principles within your specific context and organization to create a positive and engaging work environment that drives success and employee satisfaction.

QUIZ

1. What is the primary ability required for leaders to create effective and engaged employees?

   A. Empathy
   B. Emotional intelligence
   C. Communication skills
   D. Charismatic behavior

2. What leadership style is known for inspiring and motivating employees?

   A. Transformational
   B. Servant
   C. Coaching

D. Autocratic

3. What is a primary focus of servant leaders?

    A. Autonomy

    B. Taking risks

    C. Innovating

    D. Putting employees' needs first

4. What are the primary communication skills that effective leaders possess?

    A. Verbal and written communication

    B. Listening and providing feedback

    C. Articulating expectations

    D. All of the above

5. How can leaders create a culture of excellence and engagement?

    A. Setting clear expectations

    B. Investing in employees' professional development

    C. Linking work to the organization's mission

    D. All of the above

Answer Key:

1. C - Communication skills

2. A - Transformational

3. D - Putting employees' needs first

4. D - All of the above

5. D - All of the above

As we have explored the important qualities and leadership styles that create effective and engaged employees, it is essential for you to continually evaluate your own skills and knowledge. In the next chapter, we will delve into specific training and development programs that will not only help identify any gaps, but also equip you with the tools needed to address them. Keep reading to discover the transformative power of personal growth and development in leadership.

CHAPTER 12

CLOSING THE GAP

IDENTIFYING AND ADDRESSING LEADERSHIP SKILLS GAPS THAT DRIVE
EFFICIENCY AND EMPLOYEE ENGAGEMENT

"The single biggest way to impact an organization is to focus on leadership development. There is almost no limit to the potential of an organization when its leaders are constantly learning, growing, and evolving."

- John C. Maxwell

AT A GLANCE

Five Essential Points for Identifying and Addressing Leadership Skills Gaps

- Discover how executive coaching can provide personalized feedback and support to help leaders gain insights into their strengths and areas for improvement.

- Uncover the power of interactive leadership workshops and seminars where leaders can learn from each other, gain new perspectives, and build relationships with like-minded professionals.

-165-

- Explore investing in general leadership development programs that provide comprehensive instruction and experiential learning opportunities, offering a chance to connect with like-minded professionals and share best practices.

- Learn how self-directed learning through books, podcasts, and networking groups can help leaders identify and address their own skills or knowledge gaps.

- Embrace the importance of continuous learning and feedback loops in improving leadership skills, bridging gaps, and making a positive impact on teams and organizations.

Five Questions Business Leaders Should Ask About Identifying and Addressing Leadership Skills Gaps

- As a business leader, how do you currently assess and identify gaps in leadership skills within your organization? What strategies or initiatives do you currently have in place to address these gaps and improve leadership skills?

- Have you noticed any patterns or common challenges that leaders face within your organization when it comes to driving efficiency and employee engagement?

- What resources, support, or training do you currently provide to develop and enhance the leadership skills of your team?

- How do you involve and empower employees in the process of identifying and addressing leadership skill gaps?

- How do you communicate the importance of developing strong leadership skills to your team and foster a culture that values and prioritizes this development?

It's crucial for leaders to be proactive in identifying and addressing any gaps in their skills or knowledge. Fortunately, there are several training and development options that can help them do just that.

Leaders can start where they are by engaging in self-directed learning to identify and address their skills or knowledge gaps. They can read books, listen to podcasts, or watch videos on leadership topics that interest and challenge them. Additionally, joining professional associations or networking groups can provide access to resources, workshops, and mentors who can offer valuable insights and support.

Their next step may be to consider investing in general leadership development programs offered by respected names in the industry. These programs are often a combined group of individuals with a shared interest in leadership development.

They may include classroom instruction with sharing of best practices and insights into real-world situations, and experiential learning activities. They provide leaders with a comprehensive understanding of leadership theories, frameworks, and best practices, while also offering opportunities for connection with other like-minded professionals.

Another option is leadership workshops or seminars for everyone on the team. These interactive sessions bring leaders and future leaders together to learn and share experiences in a group setting. A well-designed workshop focuses on specific leadership competencies and provides participants with practical tools, frameworks, and strategies specific to their own organization. It creates a dynamic learning environment where people can explore their strengths and weaknesses, gain new perspectives, and build relationships with others within the company. Furthermore, workshops with expert facilitators can offer valuable insights based on their own leadership experiences.

Furthermore, the most effective program is executive coaching. This involves working one-on-one with a qualified coach who can provide objective feedback, guidance, and support. A skilled coach can help leaders gain insights into their strengths and areas for improvement, identify specific leadership gaps, and create a tailored action plan to address those gaps. By collaborating with a coach, leaders can fine-tune their skills, enhance their self-awareness, and accelerate their personal and professional growth.

Finally, I encourage leaders to embrace continuous learning and seek regular feedback from their team members, colleagues, and mentors. Feedback is a powerful tool for identifying blind spots and areas for improvement. Leaders should actively solicit feedback and create a safe and supportive environment for their team members to share their observations and suggestions. By valuing feedback and taking action on it, leaders can continuously improve their skills and bridge any gaps.

One prime example of a company renowned for its exceptional leaders who address gaps in leadership skills, driving efficiency and employee engagement, is Toyota. Widely recognized for their commitment to quality and continuous improvement, Toyota's leaders have played a pivotal role in establishing their sterling reputation.

Toyota's leaders understand that effective leadership is essential for optimizing efficiency and engaging employees. They prioritize developing leaders who can foster a culture of continuous improvement, proactivity, and teamwork throughout the organization.

One standout strategy used by Toyota is their Lean Leadership approach. This approach focuses on empowering leaders to identify and solve problems, encourage employee engagement, and streamline processes to boost efficiency. Toyota leaders embody the principles of Lean Leadership by actively seeking input from employees, facilitating open communication, and supporting their teams in implementing improvements.

Toyota leaders also invest heavily in developing their own skills through programs like the Toyota Way 2001 Global Leadership Competence Model. This program equips leaders with the necessary skills to address leadership gaps effectively, such as problem-solving, decision-making, and communication.

Furthermore, Toyota leaders emphasize the importance of employee engagement by creating a supportive work environment. They encourage collaboration, respect, and continuous learning. By fostering a culture where employees feel valued, motivated, and empowered, Toyota's leaders achieve high levels of efficiency and employee engagement.

Toyota leaders continuously evaluate their own performance and seek feedback from their teams. Regular performance reviews, coaching sessions, and professional development opportunities enable leaders to identify areas for growth and enhance their leadership skills. This iterative approach ensures that any skill gaps are addressed promptly and effectively.

In conclusion, Toyota exemplifies a company with leaders who excel at driving efficiency and employee engagement through their commitment to Lean Leadership principles and continuous improvement. Their focus on developing their own skills, creating a supportive work environment, and valuing employee input leads to a culture of excellence and optimal performance within the organization. By investing in leadership development and fostering employee engagement, Toyota's leaders have established a strong foundation for their continued success.

Ultimately, leaders have an array of training and development programs at their disposal to identify and address gaps in their skills or knowledge. Executive coaching, leadership workshops for their company, public programs, self-directed learning, and feedback loops are all effective approaches. The key is to proactively invest in one's own development, collaborate with experts, and constantly seek opportunities to grow. Remember, great leaders are not born, they are developed. With the right mindset and commitment, anyone can improve their leadership skills and make a positive impact on their teams and organizations.

Now that we have discussed various approaches to leadership development, it's time to take a closer look at a checklist that can help leaders proactively identify and address any gaps in their skills or knowledge.

"Successful leaders create a culture of accountability, where individuals take ownership of their actions and outcomes."

- Stephen Covey

CHECKLIST

Checklist for Leadership Development:

- Research and explore executive coaching programs: Look for qualified coaches who specialize in leadership development and can provide objective feedback, guidance, and support.
- Identify specific leadership gaps: Reflect on your strengths and areas for improvement and combine with personal assessments and then work with a coach to gain insights into specific leadership gaps that need to be addressed.
- Create a tailored action plan: Collaborate with your coach to develop a customized action plan that outlines steps to address the identified leadership gaps.
- Attend leadership workshops or seminars: Look for opportunities to participate in interactive sessions that focus on specific leadership competencies and provide practical tools, frameworks, and strategies.

- Engage in self-directed learning: Read books, listen to podcasts, and watch videos on leadership topics that interest and challenge you, and apply the knowledge gained in your leadership role.

- Consider internal programs: Look for recognized leadership development facilitators who can create tailored programs for your organization that focuses on specific leadership competencies and provides you with practical tools, frameworks, and strategies specific to your needs.

- Embrace continuous learning: Maintain a mindset of perpetual growth and seek regular feedback from your team members, colleagues, and mentors to identify blind spots and areas for improvement.

- Create a safe and supportive environment for feedback: Actively solicit feedback from your team members and create a culture that encourages open and honest communication, where feedback is valued and acted upon.

- Invest time and effort in your development: Commit to consistently investing in your own development and seize opportunities to grow as a leader.

Remember, leadership skills can be developed with the right mindset, commitment, and investment in self-improvement.

Now that we have gone through the checklist for leadership development, let's take a look at some examples that demonstrate how these steps can be applied in real-life situations.

> *"The ability to adapt and embrace change is a fundamental leadership trait in today's fast-paced world."*
>
> *- Jack Welch*

EXAMPLES

Since you may feel intimidated by how Toyota has done it, here are other examples of how to implement their ideas.

Executive coaching: A CEO realizes that they struggle with effective communication and decision-making. They enlist the help of an executive coach who provides them with objective feedback and guidance on improving these specific areas. Through this coaching, the CEO gains insights into their communication style, learns strategies to enhance their decision-making process, and develops an action plan to address these gaps.

A general leadership workshop: An organization sends one of its high-potential leaders to a public leadership program specifically designed for executives. Throughout the workshop, they engage in various interactive activities and discussions that help them understand the importance of emotional intelligence in leadership. They learn practical tools and strategies for self-awareness, empathy, and relationship-building. By the end of the workshop, these managers have gained new perspectives, enhanced their emotional intelligence skills, and built relationships with fellow participants.

An internal leadership development program: A group of mid-level managers attend an internal leadership development program focused on developing their communication skills. This program combines sharing of experiences, best practices and experiential learning activities. They increase their communication skills and awareness of how to embrace different perspectives. They also have the opportunity to assess their own communication style and receive valuable feedback from each other. Upon completion of the program, they have not only developed new skills and knowledge but also received a certificate that adds credibility to their professional profile.

Self-directed learning: A team leader wants to improve their conflict resolution skills. They start by reading books on conflict management, exploring different theories and strategies. They then listen to podcasts featuring experts in the field, gaining further insights and practical advice. Finally, they watch video tutorials on active listening and mediating techniques. Through this self-directed learning process, the team leader acquires new techniques and approaches for effectively managing and resolving conflicts within their team.

Feedback loops: A manager regularly seeks feedback from their direct reports, peers, and mentors about their leadership style and performance. They create a safe and supportive environment where team members feel comfortable providing constructive feedback. By actively listening and taking action on this feedback, the manager continuously improves their leadership skills and addresses any gaps identified by their team members. As a result, they build stronger relationships with their team and achieve better outcomes.

Now that we have explored various examples of leadership development interventions, let's dive into the key mistakes to avoid in this process. These mistakes can serve as valuable lessons and insights for organizations seeking to address their own leadership skills gaps.

> "Honesty and transparency build trust, and trust is the foundation for strong employee engagement."
>
> *- Sheryl Sandberg*

TYPICAL MISTAKES AND HOW TO AVOID THEM

Most people make mistakes in leadership development by not being proactive in identifying and addressing gaps in their skills or knowledge. This can be avoided by taking advantage of various training and development programs available.

Firstly, a mistake people often make is not seeking out executive coaching. This one-on-one coaching with a qualified coach can provide valuable feedback, guidance, and support. By working closely with a coach, leaders can gain insights into their strengths and areas for improvement, and create a tailored action plan to address those gaps.

Another mistake to avoid is not participating in leadership workshops or seminars. These interactive sessions allow leaders to learn and share experiences in a group setting. Well-designed workshops focus on specific leadership competencies and provide practical tools and strategies. They create a dynamic learning environment where leaders can explore their strengths and weaknesses and build relationships with other professionals.

Engaging in self-directed learning is another important aspect that many people neglect. Leaders should read books, listen to podcasts, or watch videos on leadership topics that interest and challenge them. Joining professional associations or networking groups also provides access to resources, workshops, and mentors who can offer valuable insights and support.

Lastly, leaders should not overlook the power of regular feedback. Creating a safe and supportive environment for team members to share observations and suggestions is crucial. Leaders should actively seek feedback and take action on it to continuously improve their skills and bridge any gaps.

MY #1 PIECE OF ADVICE

My biggest piece of advice for improving leadership skills in the area of identifying leadership skills gaps is to regularly assess and evaluate your own strengths and weaknesses. This self-reflection will help you identify areas where you may be lacking and allow you to proactively seek learning opportunities to fill those gaps.

"Leadership is not about being right all the time, but about being open to different perspectives and embracing diverse ideas."

*- **Richard Branson***

SUMMARY:

- Be proactive in identifying and addressing any gaps in your leadership skills or knowledge.

- Embrace the power of executive coaching to gain insights, create action plans, and accelerate your personal and professional growth.

- Participate in public leadership workshops or seminars to learn from others, gain new perspectives, and build relationships with like-minded professionals and enhance your credentials.

- Consider investing in bringing in respected facilitators to lead leadership development programs inside your workplace to deepen your understanding of leadership theories and best practices.

- Engage in self-directed learning, join professional associations, and seek feedback from your team members, colleagues, and mentors to continuously improve your skills and bridge any gaps. Remember, great leaders are developed, not born.

APPLICATION QUESTIONS

- How can you identify and address specific leadership skill gaps within your organization?

- What strategies have you implemented in the past to promote continuous learning and development among your leaders, and how can you further enhance these efforts to drive efficiency and engagement?

- In what ways can you actively involve employees in the process of identifying and addressing leadership skill gaps, ensuring their perspectives are considered and valued?

- What specific leadership competencies do you believe drive efficiency and engagement in your organization, and how can you prioritize training and development efforts in these areas?

- How can you create targeted development plans for individual leaders to address their unique skill gaps and foster their growth as efficient and engaging leaders?

QUIZ

1. What is executive coaching?

   A. An interactive group setting
   B. Working one-on-one with a qualified coach
   C. Reading books and listening to podcasts
   D. Seeking regular feedback from team members

2. What are the benefits of leadership workshops or seminars?

   A. Learning theories and best practices
   B. Exploring strengths and weaknesses
   C. Enhancing self-awareness
   D. All of the above

3. What types of programs should be a part of any leadership development plan?

   A. Executive coaching
   B. Leadership workshops
   C. Self-directed learning
   D. All of the above

4. What is one way to identify and address leadership gaps?

    A. Read books and listen to podcasts

    B. Join professional associations

    C. Use executive coaching

    D. Seek regular feedback

5. What is the main takeaway from this material?

    A. Leaders are born, not developed

    B. Leaders should embrace continuous learning

    C. Leaders should join networking groups

    D. Leaders should invest in their own development

Answer Key

1. B - Working one-on-one with a qualified coach

2. D - All of the above

3. D - All of the above

4. C - Use executive coaching

5. D - Leaders should invest in their own development

As leaders strive to bridge the gaps in their own skills and knowledge, it is crucial to explore the critical role that effective coaching and mentorship can play in further developing their efficiency and effectiveness. In the next chapter, we will delve into the transformative power of mentorship and coaching, offering practical tips and insights to enhance your leadership abilities and overall team performance. So, keep reading to discover how fostering strong relationships and leveraging mentorship can propel you and your team towards lasting success.

CHAPTER 13
COACHING FOR EFFECTIVENESS
HOW LEADERS CAN DEVELOP TEAMS THAT DELIVER RESULTS

"The mediocre teacher tells. The good teacher explains. The superior teacher demonstrates. The great teacher inspires."

- William Arthur Ward

AT A GLANCE

Five Essential Points for How Leaders Can Develop Teams That Deliver Results

- Discover the power of effective coaching that can transform leaders and teams.

- Unlock your true potential by identifying your strengths and areas for improvement through personalized guidance and support.

- Acquire new skills and enhance your knowledge with valuable insights, techniques, and resources provided by skilled coaches.

- Foster self-awareness and personal growth as you reflect on your behaviors, attitudes, and beliefs to achieve greater efficiency and effectiveness.

- Build resilience, adaptability, and emotional intelligence to navigate uncertainties, manage stress, and become a successful leader who drives exceptional results.

Five Questions Business Leaders Should Ask About How Leaders Can Develop Teams That Deliver Results

- How are you currently using coaching to identifying and developing future leaders, ensuring the long-term success and continuity of your team?
- How would coaching facilitate improved communication and collaboration among team members?
- What opportunities exist for coaching to enhance understanding, empathy, and synergy within your team?
- How would coaching reduce employee turnover and improve retention?
- How would coaching empower your team to take ownership of their development and enhance their performance?

Effective coaching is integral to the development of both a leader's or team's efficiency and effectiveness. By providing guidance, support, and personalized strategies, coaching creates an environment that fosters growth, empowers individuals, and enhances performance.

Firstly, effective coaching can aid in identifying individual strengths and areas for improvement. Through regular conversations and assessments, a coach can help a leader or team member gain clarity on their goals and aspirations. By understanding their unique skills and talents, individuals can leverage these strengths to drive efficiency and effectiveness. Similarly, areas requiring development can be addressed through targeted coaching interventions, allowing leaders and teams to improve in areas that may be hindering their performance.

Additionally, coaching facilitates skill-building and knowledge enhancement. A skilled coach can provide valuable insights, techniques, and resources that enable leaders and teams to acquire new skills. They can offer relevant training materials, engage in role-playing exercises, or provide real-life examples to illustrate best practices. By continuously expanding their skill sets and improving their knowledge base, leaders and teams can effectively respond to challenges, make better decisions, and achieve their desired results efficiently.

Furthermore, effective coaching fosters self-awareness and personal development. Through open and honest conversations, coaches encourage leaders and team members to reflect on their behaviors, attitudes, and beliefs. This self-reflection enables individuals to understand how their actions impact their efficiency and effectiveness. With this knowledge, they can make conscious efforts to modify their behaviors, develop healthy habits, and adopt a growth mindset. This cultivation of self-awareness leads to personal growth and increased effectiveness as leaders and team members learn to leverage their strengths and overcome their limitations.

Moreover, effective coaching can provide a safe and supportive space for leaders and teams to address challenges and solve problems. Coaches act as trusted partners who lend a listening ear, ask thought-provoking questions, and provide objective feedback. This collaborative approach enables leaders and teams to explore different perspectives, uncover innovative solutions, and propel their efficiency and effectiveness to new heights.

Coaching also strengthen relationships and foster a sense of belonging. Trust, respect, and open communication are vital components of successful coaching relationships. By building genuine connections and establishing a foundation of trust, coaches effectively provide the necessary guidance and support that leaders and teams need to excel. This strong bond cultivates a positive and engaging work environment, where individuals feel valued and motivated to contribute their best efforts.

Lastly, coaching contributes to building resilience, adaptability, and emotional intelligence within leaders and teams. By providing a safe space for exploration and learning, coaches support individuals in developing these vital qualities. They help leaders and team members build resilience to navigate uncertainties and setbacks, adapt to changing circumstances, and manage stress effectively.

Furthermore, coaches encourage the development of emotional intelligence by fostering self-awareness, empathy, and strong interpersonal skills. These qualities enhance communication, teamwork, and leadership capabilities, resulting in improved efficiency and effectiveness.

Let's take a close look at General Electric (GE), a company whose leaders have demonstrated outstanding abilities in using coaching to develop teams that consistently deliver exceptional results.

Under the leadership of former CEO Jack Welch, GE implemented a coaching culture that transformed the organization and propelled it to great heights. Welch believed that coaching was not just a tool for performance improvement but a fundamental aspect of leadership development. He advocated for the idea that leaders should actively invest their time and energy in coaching their teams to unlock their full potential.

One of the notable coaching practices at GE was the implementation of a process called "Session C," short for Session Critique. This involved gathering teams after significant meetings or projects to reflect, debrief, and extract key learnings. The aim was to provide feedback and guidance in a collaborative manner, enabling the team to continuously learn and improve their performance.

Furthermore, GE's leaders focused on fostering a culture of open communication and feedback. They encouraged coaching conversations that went beyond merely addressing performance issues. Instead, the focus was on developing individuals by recognizing their strengths, establishing clear goals, and providing the support and resources necessary for success.

In addition to individual coaching, GE placed a strong emphasis on team coaching. Leaders understood the importance of cultivating collaboration and synergy within their teams. They leveraged coaching conversations to enhance team dynamics, facilitate effective communication, and align individual strengths towards collective goals.

GE also prioritized the development of leadership talent within the organization. They implemented comprehensive coaching programs and initiatives to nurture future leaders. These programs offered mentoring opportunities, leadership development workshops, and executive coaching to guide individuals in honing their skills and reaching their full potential.

The results of GE's coaching efforts were evident. The company consistently achieved remarkable financial performance, fueled by high-performing teams that were driven, motivated, and aligned with organizational goals. Through coaching, GE's leaders not only achieved outstanding results but also fostered a culture of continuous improvement, learning, and development.

General Electric serves as a prime example of a company where leaders effectively use coaching to develop teams that deliver exceptional results. Through practices like Session C, an emphasis on open communication and feedback, and a focus on both individual and team coaching, GE's leaders have created an environment where teams thrive, achieve outstanding outcomes, and drive the organization's success forward.

Ultimately, the role of effective coaching is paramount in developing a leader's or team's efficiency and effectiveness. By identifying strengths, addressing development areas, building new skills, promoting self-awareness, and cultivating resilience and emotional intelligence, coaching empowers individuals to become effective leaders who drive exceptional results. Their impact can transform teams and organizations, establishing a path towards success and sustained growth.

Now that we have explored the significant role of effective coaching in developing efficiency and effectiveness, let's delve into a useful checklist that can help guide leaders and teams in implementing these principles in their own personal and professional growth.

> "Coaching is unlocking a person's potential to maximize their own performance. It is helping them to learn rather than teaching them."
>
> - *Tim Gallwey*

CHECKLIST:

Checklist for Effective Coaching:

- Define the purpose: Clearly understand the objective of the coaching session and identify the specific areas for improvement or development.

- Gather relevant information: Collect data, feedback, and performance metrics to understand the current state and identify areas that need improvement.

- Select appropriate coaching techniques and tools: Determine the coaching techniques and tools that will be most effective in addressing the identified areas for improvement.

- Create a safe and supportive environment: Ensure that the coaching session takes place in a safe and non-judgmental space, where the coachee feels comfortable to share and explore new ideas.

- Establish goals and outcomes: Collaboratively set clear and attainable goals with the participant, ensuring that they align with the overall organizational objectives.

- Create an action plan: Develop a step-by-step plan with the participant that outlines the specific actions, timelines, and milestones needed to achieve the desired outcomes.

- Provide ongoing support and feedback: Continuously offer guidance, feedback, and support to the participant throughout their development journey.

- Monitor progress and adjust as needed: Regularly assess the participant's progress towards their goals and make adjustments to the coaching approach if necessary.

- Encourage self-reflection: Encourage the participant to reflect on their actions, decisions, and outcomes, allowing for self-discovery and growth.

- Evaluate the effectiveness of coaching: Measure the impact of the coaching intervention on the participant's performance and the overall efficiency and effectiveness of the team.

- Maintain confidentiality: Respect the participant's confidentiality and ensure that all discussions and information shared during the coaching session are kept confidential.

- Continuously develop coaching skills: Stay updated with the latest coaching techniques and methodologies to enhance your effectiveness as a coach.

Now that we have gone through the action steps checklist, let's take a look at some examples that illustrate how these steps can be implemented in practice.

"A good coach can change a game. A great coach can change a life."

- John Wooden

EXAMPLES:

Don't compare your organization to GE and think you can't do the same. You can use coaching as an effective tool for developing your team, no matter how large or small that team is. Here are some examples to get you thinking about how you coaching can help you too.

Sarah is a new team leader who is struggling to manage her team effectively. Her coach helps her identify her strengths in problem-solving and communication, and encourages her to leverage these strengths to improve team collaboration. They work on developing her skills in delegation and conflict resolution through role-playing exercises and providing resources on effective leadership practices. With the guidance of her coach, Sarah becomes a more efficient and effective leader, resulting in improved team performance.

John, a senior executive, is known for his technical expertise but lacks effective communication skills. His coach helps him recognize this area for development and provides personalized strategies to enhance his communication abilities. They work on John's public speaking skills, active listening, and emotional intelligence. With consistent coaching, John becomes a more confident communicator, resulting in better relationships with his team members and increased efficiency in his leadership role.

Emily is a team member who lacks self-awareness, often unknowingly derailing team discussions with her negative attitude. Her coach facilitates open conversations with Emily, helping her recognize the impact of her behaviors on team dynamics. They use assessments to explore her strengths and areas for growth, and develop an action plan to improve her self-awareness and adopt a more positive mindset. Through consistent coaching, Emily becomes more mindful of her actions, leading to improved team efficiency and effectiveness.

David's team is facing challenges due to rapid changes in the market. His coach helps him build resilience and adaptability to navigate these uncertainties. They discuss different strategies to handle setbacks and develop contingency plans. The coach encourages David to take calculated risks and learn from failures, fostering a growth mindset within him. With the support of his coach, David is able to lead his team through the changes successfully, resulting in improved efficiency and effectiveness.

Lisa is a leader who struggles with handling conflicts within her team. Her coach helps her develop emotional intelligence by fostering self-awareness and empathy. They work on active listening and conflict resolution techniques, using real-life examples from Lisa's experiences. Through continuous coaching, Lisa becomes more attuned to her team members' emotions and needs, leading to better communication, teamwork, and overall efficiency within her team.

Having explored various examples of individuals overcoming leadership challenges with the help of coaches, it is now time to explore some of the mistakes to avoid when implementing a similar program in your organization.

> *"Coaching is not about providing all the answers, but asking the right questions that ignite powerful insights and actionable steps."*
>
> *- Marshall Goldsmith*

TYPICAL MISTAKES AND HOW TO AVOID THEM

One mistake that most people make in the area of coaching is not seeking guidance or support. Many individuals think that they can figure everything out on their own and don't realize the value of having a coach. To avoid this mistake, it's important to recognize the benefits of coaching and actively seek out someone who can provide guidance and support.

Another mistake people often make is not being open to feedback and self-reflection. Effective coaching encourages individuals to reflect on their behaviors, attitudes, and beliefs. However, many people resist this and don't take the time to truly understand how their actions impact their efficiency and effectiveness. To avoid this mistake, it's essential to have an open mind and be willing to receive feedback and engage in self-reflection.

Furthermore, people often underestimate the importance of continuous learning and skill-building. Coaching provides opportunities for individuals to acquire new skills and enhance their knowledge. However, many individuals become complacent and don't actively seek out opportunities for growth. To avoid this mistake, it's crucial to have a growth mindset and actively pursue opportunities for learning and development.

Lastly, many people overlook the importance of building emotional intelligence and resilience. Coaching can help individuals develop these vital qualities, but it requires active effort and willingness to explore and learn. It's common for individuals to neglect their emotional well-being and not prioritize resilience. To avoid this mistake, it's important to prioritize self-care, emotional intelligence, and building resilience.

The mistakes most people make in the area of coaching include not seeking guidance or support, resisting feedback and self-reflection, underestimating the importance of continuous learning, and overlooking emotional intelligence and resilience. By recognizing these mistakes and actively seeking to avoid them, individuals can maximize the benefits of coaching, leading to enhanced efficiency and effectiveness.

MY #1 PIECE OF ADVICE

My #1 advice for people who want to improve their leadership skills in coaching is to actively listen and ask thought-provoking questions. This strategy enhances understanding, fosters open dialogue, and empowers individuals to find their own solutions.

> *"A great coach sees the potential in others before they see it in themselves and guides them on the path to greatness."*
>
> *- John Maxwell*

SUMMARY:

- Effective coaching provides guidance and support, creating an environment that fosters growth, empowers individuals, and enhances performance.

- Coaching helps leaders and team members identify their strengths and areas for improvement, allowing them to leverage their unique skills and talents to drive efficiency and effectiveness.

- Through skill-building and knowledge enhancement, coaching enables leaders and teams to acquire new skills and make better decisions, ultimately achieving their desired results efficiently.

- Coaching encourages self-reflection, personal development, and the cultivation of a growth mindset, leading to increased effectiveness as leaders and team members learn to overcome limitations and adopt healthy habits.

- Lastly, coaching contributes to building resilience, adaptability, and emotional intelligence within leaders and teams, enhancing communication, teamwork, and leadership capabilities for improved efficiency and effectiveness.

APPLICATION QUESTIONS

- How might you incorporate coaching conversations into your leadership style to create a culture of continuous learning and growth within your team, ultimately driving exceptional results?

- In what ways can you leverage the strengths-based coaching approach to empower your team members, recognize their unique talents, and align them with strategic goals for optimal performance?

- What steps will you take to implement regular debriefing sessions, similar to GE's "Session C," where team members can reflect on their collective experiences, learn from wins and losses, and collectively identify areas for improvement?

- What strategies will you employ to strengthen the coaching culture within your team, ensuring that coaching is not only seen as a performance improvement tool but as a fundamental aspect of leadership development?

- How will you integrate coaching into your talent development initiatives, providing opportunities for mentoring, leadership workshops, and executive coaching to nurture future leaders within your organization?

QUIZ

1. How can coaches help leaders and team members gain clarity on their goals and aspirations?

   A. Through regular conversations and assessments
   B. By understanding their unique skills and talents
   C. Through asking curiosity-based, open ended questions
   D. All of the above

2. How does coaching help leaders gain a fresh perspective?

   A. By providing asking questions that challenge their current thinking

   B. By encouraging exploration and experimentation

   C. By fostering a culture of continuous learning

   D. By setting performance evaluations

3. What qualities can coaching help to develop in leaders and teams?

   A. Adaptability

   B. Resilience

   C. Knowledge enhancement

   D. All of the above

4. What is the primary benefit of coaching?

   A. To foster growth and achieve exceptional results

   B. To identify and prioritize goals

   C. To provide guidance and support

   D. To motivate team members

5. What is the goal of an effective coach?

   A. To motivate team members

   B. To manage tasks and make critical decisions

   C. To help leaders and their teams excel in their roles

   D. To build trust and respect within a team

Answer Key:

1. D - All of the above

2. A - By providing asking questions that challenge their current thinking

3. D - All of the above

4. A - To foster growth and achieve exceptional results

5. C - To help leaders and their teams excel in their roles

As we have seen in the previous chapter, effective coaching can greatly enhance a leader's or team's efficiency and effectiveness. However, in order to sustain this growth and development, it is crucial to delve into the importance of providing regular feedback in addition to coaching of employees, which we will explore in the next chapter - a topic that will undoubtedly further equip you with the tools needed to achieve both productivity and personal growth. So, let's dive in and discover the keys to maintaining a balance between progress and performance.

CHAPTER 14

FEEDBACK THAT DRIVES RESULTS

FUELING GROWTH AND PRODUCTIVITY IN YOUR TEAM

> *"Feedback is the breakfast of champions."*
>
> *- Ken Blanchard*

AT A GLANCE

Five Essential Points for Feedback that Drives Results

- Discover the power of regular feedback - unlock your team's potential for growth and development.

- Unleash the impact of real-time coaching - make course corrections and overcome obstacles to achieve success.

- Experience a leader who truly cares - foster trust and create a positive work environment.

- Find the perfect balance between growth and productivity - celebrate achievements while striving for excellence.

- Embrace a culture of continuous improvement - empower your team to excel and contribute to organizational success.

Five Questions Business Leaders Should Ask About Feedback that Drives Results

- How are you currently fostering a culture of continuous improvement and learning within your team, where feedback is seen as an opportunity for growth rather than criticism?

- What strategies or approaches have you found most effective in ensuring that feedback is received openly and positively by your team members?"

- How do you encourage your team members to actively seek and welcome feedback from their colleagues and peers?

- What measures do you take to ensure that feedback is specific, actionable, and supports individual and team development?

- Have you ever faced challenges in delivering feedback effectively? If so, how did you overcome them?

- Do you have any techniques or tools in place to track and monitor the progress of your team members in implementing feedback and incorporating it into their work?

Regular feedback and coaching are crucial components for fostering growth and development within a team while ensuring productivity remains intact. It is in the best interest of both the employees and the organization to create a culture of continuous improvement by providing ongoing guidance and support.

Firstly, regular feedback helps employees understand their areas of strength and areas that need improvement. When people receive feedback on a consistent basis, they are more likely to gain insights into their performance and understand how their actions impact the team's overall success. This can empower them to make necessary adjustments and develop the skills they need to excel in their roles.

Additionally, consistent feedback and coaching allow for timely course corrections. Waiting until annual performance reviews to provide feedback can be detrimental to both individual growth and team productivity. Regular feedback ensures that adjustments can be made in real-time and prevents issues from snowballing into larger problems. By addressing concerns promptly, leaders can help employees overcome obstacles, refine their skills, and reach their full potential.

Furthermore, regular feedback and coaching demonstrate that leaders are invested in their team members' growth and development. When leaders actively engage in providing guidance and support, it conveys that they care about their employees' success and are committed to their professional advancement. This builds trust and strengthens the relationship between leaders and employees, creating a positive work environment that motivates individuals to strive for excellence.

It is also essential to strike a balance between growth and productivity. Feedback should be delivered in a way that highlights areas of improvement but also recognizes and reinforces achievements. By acknowledging employees' accomplishments, leaders can boost morale and encourage them to continue their good work. This encourages a positive attitude towards feedback and ensures that productivity is maintained while individuals work towards personal and professional growth.

When it comes to companies that have excelled at using feedback to drive growth and productivity, one standout example is Airbnb. Under the leadership of Brian Chesky, the company has embraced a feedback-rich culture that has proven instrumental in their success.

Chesky understands the importance of feedback in fostering innovation and delivering exceptional experiences to guests. He actively seeks feedback from both hosts and guests, using it as a valuable source of insights to enhance the platform and create a better user experience. By listening to users' feedback, Airbnb has been able to identify areas for improvement and implement changes that drive growth and customer loyalty.

To encourage feedback within the team, Chesky has instituted weekly "Feedback Hours" where employees are invited to openly share their thoughts, ideas, and concerns. This creates a safe and inclusive environment where individuals feel empowered to contribute to the company's growth. Chesky's commitment to transparency and open communication has fostered a culture of trust and collaboration, inspiring teams to continuously strive for excellence.

Beyond internal feedback channels, Airbnb leverages technology to gather feedback from users at various touchpoints. They actively solicit ratings and reviews from both hosts and guests, which not only helps in improving the overall experience but also builds trust within the community. Moreover, Airbnb uses data analytics to identify trends and patterns, enabling them to make data-driven decisions that positively impact growth and productivity.

One notable aspect of Airbnb's approach to feedback is the recognition and celebration of host achievements. The company acknowledges outstanding hosts, shares their success stories, and provides opportunities for hosts to connect and learn from each other. This fosters a sense of community and motivates hosts to deliver exceptional experiences, leading to increased productivity and growth for both the hosts and Airbnb as a platform.

Airbnb stands as a prime example of a company whose leaders have successfully harnessed the power of feedback to fuel growth and productivity. Through a combination of listening to user feedback, creating internal feedback channels, and fostering a sense of community and recognition, they have shown that feedback is not just a tool for improvement but a driving force behind innovation, customer satisfaction, and business success.

Overall, providing regular feedback and coaching is vital for both individual growth and team productivity. It helps employees understand their strengths and areas for improvement, enables timely course corrections, demonstrates leadership support, and maintains a balance between growth and productivity. By creating a culture of continuous improvement through feedback, leaders empower their team members to excel and contribute to the overall success of the organization.

Now that we have discussed the importance of regular feedback and coaching, let's dive into the checklist I have created to help you implement these practices effectively and consistently in your team.

> *"Criticism may not be agreeable, but it is necessary. It fulfills the same function as pain in the human body. It calls attention to an unhealthy state of things."*
>
> *- **Winston Churchill***

CHECKLIST

Checklist for Feedback that Drives Results:

- Implement regular feedback sessions: Schedule regular one-on-one meetings with team members to provide feedback on their performance. This can be done weekly, bi-weekly, or monthly, depending on the needs of the team.

- Establish clear objectives and expectations: Clearly communicate the goals and expectations for each team member. This will help them understand what areas they need to focus on and where they can improve.

- Use a constructive feedback approach: When providing feedback, focus on specific examples and behaviors rather than personal attacks. Use the "sandwich" method, where you start with positive feedback, provide constructive criticism, and end with positive reinforcement, encouragement and belief in their ability to change.

- Encourage self-reflection: Ask team members to reflect on their own performance and areas they believe they can improve. This encourages self-awareness and accountability.

- Provide ongoing coaching and support: Offer guidance and support to help team members overcome challenges and develop their skills. This can include providing resources, recommending training programs, or assigning mentors.

- Foster a culture of peer feedback: Encourage team members to provide feedback to each other, promoting a culture of continuous improvement. This can be done through peer reviews, team discussions, or feedback sessions.

- Set aside time for reflection and goal setting: Schedule regular check-ins to review progress, set new goals, and discuss career development opportunities. This shows that you are invested in their growth and development.

- Recognize and celebrate achievements: Acknowledge and celebrate individual and team achievements regularly. This boosts morale and motivates employees to continue performing at their best.

- Monitor and evaluate progress: Regularly assess the impact of the feedback and coaching sessions on team productivity and individual growth. Make adjustments as necessary to ensure continuous improvement.

- Lead by example: As a leader, actively seek feedback from your team and demonstrate a growth mindset. Show that you are open to learning and development, which encourages your team to do the same.

Now that we have gone through the checklist for providing effective feedback and coaching to your team, let's take a look at some examples that illustrate how these steps can be implemented in practice.

> *"The greatest compliment that was ever paid me was when someone asked me what I thought, and attended to my answer."*
>
> **- Henry David Thoreau**

EXAMPLES

So, whether you're a business leader or a team member, taking inspiration from other companies and industry leaders like Airbnb and implementing your own feedback-driven strategies can truly be transformative for growth and productivity.

Samantha works as a graphic designer in a marketing agency. Her supervisor, Mark, meets with her bi-weekly to provide feedback on her projects. During one of their meetings, Mark praises Samantha for her creativity in the recent website design she worked on. He acknowledges her strengths in visual storytelling and attention to detail. However, he also provides constructive criticism on the organization of the design elements, suggesting ways for Samantha to improve the overall user experience. Samantha takes Mark's feedback to heart and implements the suggested changes in her subsequent projects, resulting in improved websites and client satisfaction.

John is a supervisor at a customer service call center. As part of his role, he regularly monitors his team members' phone calls and provides them with feedback and coaching. During a call review, John notices that his employee, Lisa, handled a difficult customer situation exceptionally well. He praises Lisa for her professionalism, empathy, and problem-solving skills. However, he also suggests that Lisa could improve her call resolution time by using a specific technique he teaches her during their coaching session.

Lisa applies the technique in her future calls and sees her call resolution time decrease, leading to increased customer satisfaction and more efficient workflow for the team.

Emma is a manager in a software development company. She believes in the importance of continuous improvement and holds regular one-on-one meetings with her team members. During one of these meetings, Emma has an open and honest conversation with Daniel, one of her developers. Daniel expresses his desire to learn new programming languages to expand his skillset. Emma takes the initiative to enroll Daniel in a relevant online course and also pairs him with a senior developer as a mentor. Through ongoing feedback and coaching, Emma supports and guides Daniel as he learns the new language, tracks his progress, and provides suggestions for improvement. As a result, Daniel becomes proficient in the new programming language, contributing to the development of innovative software solutions for the company.

Laura is the CEO of a startup company focused on renewable energy. As a leader, she understands the value of creating a culture of continuous improvement and growth. During team meetings, Laura encourages her employees to share their ideas for improving the company's operations and product development. She actively listens to their suggestions, provides feedback on the feasibility and potential impact of their ideas, and supports them in implementing these improvements. Through her regular feedback and coaching, Laura fosters an environment where everyone feels valued and motivated to contribute their best work. The company's productivity increases as employees feel empowered to take ownership of their roles and implement positive changes that benefit the organization as a whole.

Now that we have explored a few examples of effective feedback and coaching in the workplace, let's dive into the list of mistakes to avoid that can hinder the establishment of a culture of continuous improvement through feedback.

"If you are not criticized, you may not be doing much."

- Donald Rumsfeld

TYPICAL MISTAKES AND HOW TO AVOID THEM

Not providing regular feedback: One common mistake that many people make is not providing regular feedback to their team members. Waiting until annual performance reviews to give feedback can be detrimental to both individual growth and team productivity. To avoid this mistake, leaders should make it a priority to provide regular feedback to their employees. This can be done through one-on-one meetings, regular check-ins, or even informal conversations. By providing feedback on a consistent basis, leaders can help employees gain insights into their performance, make necessary adjustments, and continue to develop their skills.

Focusing only on areas of improvement: Another mistake that people often make is focusing exclusively on areas of improvement when giving feedback. While it is important to highlight areas where employees can grow, it is equally important to recognize and reinforce their achievements. Giving feedback in a way that acknowledges employees' accomplishments can boost morale and motivate them to continue their good work. By striking a balance between growth and productivity, leaders can ensure that employees feel supported and encouraged while still maintaining a high level of productivity.

Not demonstrating commitment to employee growth: It is crucial for leaders to demonstrate their commitment to employee growth and development. When leaders actively engage in providing guidance and support, it conveys that they care about the success of their employees. To avoid this mistake, leaders should make it a point to regularly provide feedback and coaching to their team members. By doing so, they can build trust, strengthen the relationship between leaders and employees, and create a positive work environment that motivates individuals to strive for excellence.

Allowing issues to snowball into larger problems: One more mistake that people often make is allowing issues to snowball into larger problems by not addressing them in a timely manner. Regular feedback and coaching can prevent this from happening by allowing for timely course corrections. By addressing concerns promptly, leaders can help employees overcome obstacles, refine their skills, and reach their full potential. This not only benefits the individual, but also ensures that the team remains productive and focused on its goals.

By avoiding these common mistakes and implementing regular feedback and coaching, leaders can foster growth and development within their teams while maintaining productivity. Providing timely feedback, striking a balance between areas of improvement and achievements, demonstrating commitment to employee growth, and addressing concerns promptly are all essential steps in creating a culture of continuous improvement.

MY #1 PIECE OF ADVICE

The #1 piece of advice I have for fostering growth and development within teams is be specific and constructive in your feedback, focusing on the behavior rather than the person, to cultivate a growth-oriented environment.

"If you correct your mind, the rest of your life will fall into place."

- Lao Tzu

SUMMARY:

- Foster growth and development within your team by providing regular feedback and coaching. It empowers individuals to understand their strengths and areas for improvement, leading to personal and professional growth.

- Don't wait for annual reviews. Timely feedback allows for real-time course corrections, preventing small issues from snowballing into bigger problems. Help your team overcome obstacles and reach their full potential.

- Show your team that you're invested in their success. Regular feedback and coaching build trust and create a positive work environment. When leaders actively provide guidance and support, employees are motivated to strive for excellence.

- Balance growth and productivity by delivering feedback in a constructive manner. Recognize achievements and reinforce good work while highlighting areas for improvement. Boost morale, maintain productivity, and create a positive attitude towards feedback.

- Create a culture of continuous improvement through feedback. By providing ongoing guidance and support, you empower your team to excel and contribute to the success of the organization. Regular feedback is vital for individual growth and team productivity.

APPLICATION QUESTIONS

- How can you create a safe and inclusive environment where your team feels comfortable sharing feedback openly and honestly? Are there any existing barriers that need to be addressed, and how can you overcome them?

- How can you incorporate regular feedback conversations into your team's workflow, ensuring that each member receives timely guidance and recognition? What strategies can you implement to make these conversations more meaningful and actionable?

- Are there any success stories or achievements within your team that you can highlight and celebrate to foster a culture of recognition and motivate individuals to excel further? How can you create opportunities for team members to learn from each other and share best practices?

- How can you lead by example in seeking feedback from your team members, peers, and stakeholders? What can you do to demonstrate that you genuinely value their opinions and suggestions?

- How can you empower your team members to take ownership of their own growth and development through feedback? What resources or support can you provide to help them act upon feedback and implement necessary changes?

QUIZ

1. How can regular feedback help employees?

   A. It can help them understand their areas of strength and areas that need improvement
   B. It can empower them to make necessary adjustments
   C. It can help them understand their performance
   D. All of the above

2. What is the benefit of providing feedback in a timely manner?

   A. It can prevent issues from snowballing into larger problems
   B. It can help employees overcome obstacles
   C. It can help employees refine their skills

D. All of the above

3. What does providing regular feedback and coaching demonstrate?

A. That the organization cares about employee success

B. That the organization is invested in their team members' growth and development

C. That the organization is committed to professional advancement

D. All of the above

4. What is the goal of providing feedback?

A. To recognize and reinforce employees' achievements

B. To highlight areas of improvement

C. To motivate individuals to strive for excellence

D. All of the above

5. What should be the focus when providing feedback?

A. Maintaining a balance between growth and productivity

B. Boosting employee morale

C. Encouraging employees to make necessary adjustments

D. All of the above

Answer Key:

1. D - All of the above

2. D - All of the above

3. D - All of the above

4. D - All of the above

5. D - All of the above

Now that we understand the significance of feedback and coaching for employee growth and productivity, let's explore how we can maximize our team's potential through effective team building strategies that foster alignment, collaboration, and drive sustainable efficiency gains. Keep reading to discover valuable insights that will transform your team's dynamics for the better.

CHAPTER 15

FROM ALIGNMENT TO COLLABORATION

TEAM BUILDING STRATEGIES FOR SUSTAINABLE EFFICIENCY GAINS

"Individual commitment to a group effort - that is what makes a team work, a company work, a society work, a civilization work."

- Vince Lombardi

AT A GLANCE

Five Essential Points for Team Building Strategies for Sustainable Efficiency Gains

- Discover the secrets to building a strong and united team that achieves exceptional results.

- Unleash the power of effective communication within your team and witness the magic of collaboration.

- Boost your team's efficiency by leveraging each member's unique strengths and expertise.

- Uncover the key to sustaining efficiency gains and continuously improving your team's performance.

- Prepare to be inspired by real-life anecdotes that will ignite a sense of urgency and motivation among your team members.

Five Questions Business Leaders Should Ask About Team Building Strategies for Sustainable Efficiency Gains

- How do your current team building strategies contributing to long-term efficiency gains within your organization?

- What steps do you believe are essential in fostering a collaborative and supportive team environment that promotes sustainable efficiency gains?

- In the past, how have your team building strategies aligned with the overall goals and mission of your organization?

- What measures have you taken to ensure that any team building strategies you've implemented are not just short-term fixes, but rather lead to long-lasting improvements?

- Have you noticed any particular team strengths or dynamics that have directly contributed to sustainable efficiency gains? If so, how do you encourage and nurture these aspects within your team?

When it comes to team building, your approach should focus on creating alignment, fostering collaboration, increasing effectiveness, and sustaining efficiency gains. You want to build a strong team that thrives on shared goals, effective communication, and a supportive environment. Here are some key steps you can take to achieve these objectives:

First and foremost, emphasize the importance of establishing clear goals and expectations. When everyone understands the direction and purpose of the team, they can align their efforts accordingly. This unity and common purpose are crucial for building a strong team.

Next, encourage open and transparent communication within the team. Effective communication is a cornerstone of any successful team. It allows for the sharing of ideas, feedback, and concerns. Create an environment where team members feel comfortable expressing their thoughts and actively listening to others. Collaboration is key here, ensuring that everyone's skills and perspectives are valued and used.

To increase effectiveness, focus on leveraging each team member's strengths. Recognize and use individual strengths and expertise to create a diverse and complementary team. This way, tasks can be accomplished more efficiently and effectively. When team members feel recognized and valued for their unique contributions, they are motivated to bring their best to the table and work collaboratively towards a common goal.

Sustaining efficiency gains requires ongoing evaluation and improvement. Encourage regular team evaluations where you reflect on performance and identify areas for improvement. This continuous feedback loop helps refine processes, identify bottlenecks, and streamline operations. Maintain a culture of learning and adaptation to sustain and enhance efficiency gains achieved by the team.

In addition to these strategies, encourage the sharing of personal anecdotes and stories between team members to establish a more personal connection with between everyone. Stories are powerful tools that create an emotional connection and inspire action. By sharing real-life experiences of your own that illustrating the impact of team building has had on you, you can create a sense of urgency and motivation among your team members to actively engage in the process.

Remember, the key to effective team building is aligning your shared goals, fostering collaboration, and maintaining open communication. By following these steps and incorporating personal anecdotes, you can cultivate a strong and successful team.

One company that stands out as a shining example of utilizing team building strategies for sustainable efficiency gains is Pixar Animation

Studios. Led by visionary leaders such as Ed Catmull and John Lasseter, Pixar has consistently emphasized the power of teamwork and collaboration to drive innovation and achieve outstanding results.

At Pixar, team building is not limited to mere activities or events; it is deeply ingrained in their work culture. Their leaders understand that a strong, cohesive team is the bedrock of their success. They prioritize fostering an environment where creativity thrives, and individuals are empowered to contribute their unique talents and perspectives.

One of the most notable team building strategies used by Pixar is their "Braintrust" concept. This is a regular feedback and collaboration session where directors and key team members present their work to a group of trusted peers. The Braintrust provides a safe space for open and honest discussions, allowing for constructive critique and ultimately enhancing the creative process. By leveraging the collective intelligence and diverse expertise of their teams, Pixar ensures that their films are of the highest quality while maintaining strong efficiency gains.

Another remarkable aspect of Pixar's team building strategies is their commitment to creating a culture of trust and psychological safety. Leaders actively encourage open communication and provide space for employees to voice their opinions and ideas without fear of judgment. This promotes a collaborative environment where team members can freely express themselves, leading to increased efficiency and innovative problem-solving.

Furthermore, Pixar places a strong emphasis on nurturing relationships within their teams by organizing events and initiatives that foster a sense of camaraderie and shared purpose. They recognize that building lasting connections among team members not only strengthens collaboration but also contributes to long-term efficiency gains.

In conclusion, Pixar Animation Studios serves as an outstanding example of a company that excels at utilizing team building strategies for sustainable efficiency gains. Through their emphasis on collaboration, trust, and a supportive work culture, they continue to produce groundbreaking films while fostering a passionate and engaged workforce. Other organizations can draw inspiration from Pixar's approach and strive to incorporate similar principles in their own team building strategies.

Overall, focus your approach to team building on fostering alignment, collaboration, and effectiveness while sustaining efficiency gains. By setting clear goals, promoting effective communication, leveraging individual strengths, and maintaining a culture of learning, teams can thrive and achieve exceptional results.

Now that you've read about my approach to team building, let's dive into the checklist I've created to help you implement these strategies and achieve exceptional results with your team.

"Alone we can do so little, together we can do so much."

- Helen Keller

CHECKLIST

Checklist for Effective Team Building:

- Establish clear goals and expectations for the team. This includes defining the direction and purpose of the team's work.

- Promote open and transparent communication within the team. Encourage team members to express their thoughts, actively listen to others, and provide feedback.

- Create a supportive environment where team members feel comfortable sharing their ideas, feedback, and concerns.

- Recognize and leverage each team member's strengths and expertise. Use a diverse range of skills to accomplish tasks more efficiently and effectively.

- Regularly evaluate the team's performance, identify areas for improvement, and make necessary adjustments.

- Encourage a culture of continuous learning and adaptation. Foster a mindset of ongoing improvement and innovation.

- Share personal anecdotes and stories to establish a connection with team members and motivate them to actively engage in the team-building process.

- Promote a sense of unity and common purpose among team members by highlighting the impact of effective team building.

- Foster collaboration and ensure that everyone's skills and perspectives are valued and used.

- Maintain a focus on sustaining and enhancing efficiency gains achieved by the team. Continuously refine processes, identify bottlenecks, and streamline operations.

Now that we have gone through the action steps checklist for team building, let's take a look at some examples that illustrate the positive outcomes of effective team building. These examples will demonstrate how following these action steps can lead to a strong, aligned, collaborative, effective, and efficient team.

"Teamwork is the ability to work together toward a common vision."

- Andrew Carnegie

EXAMPLES

Pixar has set the bar so high, it may be hard to see yourself reaching their level. I want to encourage you to start where you are with what you have. As my friend John Maxwell says, "Consistency compounds." Here are several different examples that help illustrate how you can get started on your way to being a great company to work inside of:

Clear goals and expectations: Imagine a team working on a marketing campaign for a new product. By clearly defining the objectives of the campaign, such as increasing brand awareness and driving sales, team members can align their efforts towards these goals. This clarity helps them prioritize tasks, coordinate their work, and ensure their activities are in line with the overall objectives.

Open and transparent communication: Consider a team of software developers working on a complex project. By fostering an environment where team members feel comfortable sharing their ideas, concerns, and feedback, they can find creative solutions, identify potential issues, and make informed decisions collaboratively. This open communication leads to better problem-solving and promotes a culture of trust and collaboration within the team.

Leveraging individual strengths: Picture a basketball team where each player has a different skill set. By recognizing and harnessing these strengths, the coach can assign specific roles and responsibilities to each player, maximizing their contributions to the team's success. For example, a player with exceptional shooting accuracy might be assigned to take important shots during a game, while a player with great defensive skills may be tasked with guarding the opposing team's star player.

Sustaining efficiency gains: Think about a manufacturing team that has implemented a new production process to improve efficiency. Through regular evaluations and feedback sessions, the team can identify any bottlenecks or areas of improvement in the process. By making necessary adjustments and continuously refining the workflow, they can sustain the efficiency gains achieved and continue to optimize their operations.

Personal anecdotes and stories: Imagine a team of sales representatives attending a team-building workshop. The facilitator shares a personal story about how effective teamwork helped their previous company achieve record-breaking sales. By relating their own experiences and showing the positive outcomes of strong team building, the facilitator inspires the sales representatives to actively engage in team-building activities, knowing that it can lead to their own professional success.

By using these examples, you can better understand and visualize how each strategy contributes to successful team building.

Now that we have explored several examples of how certain approaches can enhance team performance, let's take a look at some key mistakes to avoid when implementing a team building initiative.

> *"The strength of the team is each individual member. The strength of each member is the team."*
>
> *- Phil Jackson*

TYPICAL MISTAKES AND HOW TO AVOID THEM

Some of the most common mistakes that people make in team building are:

Not establishing clear goals and expectations: Without clear direction, team members may have different understandings of what they are working towards. This lack of alignment can lead to confusion and inefficiency. To avoid this, it is important to set clear goals and communicate them to the team.

Lack of open and transparent communication: Effective communication is essential for successful teamwork. When team members don't express their thoughts or listen actively to others, collaboration suffers. To avoid this, encourage open and transparent communication where team members feel comfortable sharing their ideas, feedback, and concerns.

Ignoring individual strengths and expertise: Every team member brings unique skills and expertise to the table. Not leveraging these strengths can hinder team effectiveness and diminish motivation. To avoid this mistake, recognize and use each team member's strengths, creating a diverse and complementary team.

Failing to sustain efficiency gains: Once efficiency gains have been achieved, it is essential to continually evaluate and improve processes. Without ongoing evaluation and adjustment, the team may stagnate and lose the gains made. To avoid this, encourage regular team evaluations, identify areas for improvement, and make necessary adjustments.

Not establishing a personal connection: Building a strong team goes beyond just the technical aspects. Failing to establish a personal connection can lead to a lack of emotional investment and motivation. To avoid this mistake, incorporate personal anecdotes and stories to create an emotional connection and inspire action among team members.

By being mindful of these mistakes, and following the steps outlined in the material, teams can foster alignment, collaboration, increase effectiveness, and sustain efficiency gains.

MY #1 PIECE OF ADVICE

My number one piece of advice that can help teams navigate these pitfalls and achieve success is learn to foster a collaborative and inclusive environment within your team, valuing diverse perspectives and harnessing the collective talent to achieve common goals effectively.

> *"If everyone is moving forward together, then success takes care of itself."*
>
> *- Henry Ford*

SUMMARY:

- Build a strong team foundation by creating alignment and fostering collaboration - a united team is a powerful force.

- Clear goals and expectations are essential - they provide direction and purpose, guiding everyone towards success.

- Open and transparent communication is key - share ideas, feedback, and concerns to enhance collaboration and value each team member's skills and perspectives.

- Recognize and use individual strengths to create a diverse and complementary team that accomplishes tasks efficiently and effectively.

- Sustain efficiency gains through regular evaluation and improvement - embrace a culture of learning and adaptation to constantly refine processes and streamline operations.

With these strategies, your team can thrive and achieve outstanding results.

APPLICATION QUESTIONS

- How will you create a work culture that fosters trust, open communication, and psychological safety, ensuring that every member feels valued and empowered to contribute?

- How could you further encourage team members to contribute their unique talents and perspectives, promoting a collaborative environment where creativity can flourish?

- How could you leverage the power of regular feedback and collaboration sessions, like Pixar's Braintrust, to enhance the creative process and drive efficiency gains within your own team?

- What measures will you take to ensure that team building strategies go beyond surface-level activities and become deeply ingrained in your organization's work culture, contributing to long-term efficiency gains?

- What events or initiatives could you organize, making sure everyone felt welcome and included, that would foster connections among team members and strengthen their sense of camaraderie and shared purpose, thereby enhancing collaboration and efficiency?

QUIZ

1. What is the first step to building a strong team?

   A. Establishing clear goals and expectations

   B. Leveraging individual strengths

   C. Establishing an emotional connection

   D. Promoting open and transparent communication

2. What is the importance of open communication within the team?

   A. Sharing ideas and feedback

   B. Establishing goals and expectations

   C. Creating an emotional connection

   D. Leveraging individual strengths

3. What is the purpose of regular team evaluations?

   A. To refine processes

   B. To share stories

   C. To increase motivation

   D. To identify areas for improvement

4. What is the key to sustaining efficiency gains?

   A. Creating alignment

   B. Maintaining a culture of learning

C. Promoting open communication

D. Leveraging individual strengths

5. What is the primary focus of team building?

A. Establishing a connection

B. Creating alignment

C. Enhancing collaboration

D. Increasing effectiveness

Answer Key:

1. A - Establishing clear goals and expectations

2. A - Sharing ideas and feedback

3. D - To identify areas for improvement

4. B - Maintaining a culture of learning

5. A - Establishing a connection

As we have discussed in this chapter, effective team building plays a crucial role in achieving alignment, collaboration, and increased effectiveness. Team building is important to establish before we get to the next stage. Next, let's explore the significant importance of accountability within a team and how leaders can foster a sense of accountability among their employees to enhance overall performance. So, keep reading to discover the key strategies that will empower your team to take ownership of their work and excel in their roles.

CHAPTER 16

THE POWER OF ACCOUNTABILITY

CULTIVATING OWNERSHIP FOR PERFORMANCE IMPROVEMENTS

"Accountability is the key to driving successful outcomes, both personally and professionally."

- Brian Tracy

AT A GLANCE

Five Essential Points for the Power of Accountability

- Discover the secret to achieving high levels of performance and success within teams and organizations.

- Learn how accountability can foster trust, reliability, and unity among team members.

- Find out the powerful strategies leaders can use to create a culture of accountability within their teams.

- Uncover the role of communication and recognition in reinforcing accountability and motivating team members.

- Explore how creating a supportive environment can turn mistakes into opportunities for growth and improvement.

Five Questions Business Leaders Should Ask About the Power of Accountability

- How are you currently creating a shared sense of accountability within your team to ensure that everyone takes ownership of their responsibilities?
- How you have empowered your team members to hold themselves and others accountable for their performance?
- What is most often the response when someone tries to address any issues of accountability or lack thereof?
- How do you handle situations where team members may fall short of their commitments, and how do you support them in learning from those experiences?
- How are you building trust and rapport with your team members to create a foundation of accountability and reliability?

Accountability is essential in any team or organization as it sets the foundation for achieving high levels of performance and success. When team members hold themselves and each other accountable, they take ownership of their roles and responsibilities, resulting in increased productivity, improved efficiency, and better outcomes.

One of the main reasons why accountability is important is that it fosters trust and reliability within a team. When team members know that their colleagues are accountable for their actions and deliverables, they feel confident in relying on each other. This trust translates into stronger relationships and a sense of unity, which ultimately boosts overall team performance.

To create a sense of accountability among employees, leaders can employ several strategies. Firstly, (and I can't say this enough) it is crucial for leaders to clearly define roles, expectations, and goals for each team member. When employees have a clear understanding of what is expected of them, they are more likely to take ownership and feel accountable for their work. This clarity can be established through regular one-on-one meetings, team meetings, or even written agreements.

Additionally, leaders should lead by example and demonstrate accountability themselves. When team members witness their leaders taking responsibility for their actions, admitting mistakes, and working towards solutions, it sets a powerful precedent. Leaders must model the behavior they wish to see in their team members, as actions speak louder than words.

Communication plays a crucial role in creating accountability within a team. Leaders should regularly provide feedback, both positive and constructive, to reinforce accountability and motivate team members. Recognizing and appreciating the efforts of individuals who consistently meet their commitments is equally important. This not only empowers team members but also reinforces the importance of accountability within the team culture.

Creating accountability also requires establishing clear and measurable performance metrics or key performance indicators (KPIs). When employees have quantifiable targets to aim for, they can track their progress, identify areas for improvement, and hold themselves accountable for achieving those targets. Regular progress meetings or check-ins can be used to review performance against these metrics and provide support or guidance where needed.

Finally, leaders should create a supportive environment where team members feel safe taking risks and owning their mistakes. When employees know that accountability is not about punishment but rather about growth and improvement, they are more likely to embrace it. Encouraging open dialogue, fostering a culture of learning from failures, and providing resources or training opportunities are all ways to promote accountability without creating fear or resistance.

When it comes to cultivating employee ownership for performance improvements, one company that stands out is Shopify. Based in Canada, Shopify is an e-commerce platform that empowers entrepreneurs and businesses to build their online stores and drive sales. Their leaders have done an exceptional job of creating an environment where employees feel a strong sense of ownership and accountability.

Tobi Lütke, the CEO of Shopify, firmly believes in giving employees the freedom to make decisions and take ownership of their work. He once said, "We hire incredibly self-directed people and trust them to make the best decisions in their individual roles." This approach not only promotes personal responsibility but also fosters a culture of innovation, where individuals are encouraged to take risks and pursue excellence.

Shopify actively involves employees in shaping the company's direction and objectives. They have a concept called "Sandbox," where employees can experiment with new ideas and initiatives, encouraging them to take ownership of innovation and improvement. This not only allows employees to have a direct impact, but it also instills a sense of pride and ownership within the company's mission.

Furthermore, Shopify values transparency and open communication. They hold regular town hall meetings where leaders share insights, updates, and challenges with the entire organization. This commitment to transparency allows employees to understand the bigger picture, align their efforts, and take ownership of their contributions to the company's success.

Shopify also emphasizes continuous learning and growth opportunities. They provide resources for skills development and encourage employees to take advantage of educational programs and training. By investing in their employees' personal and professional development, Shopify empowers individuals to take ownership of their own improvement and performance.

Lastly, Shopify recognizes and celebrates employees who embody ownership and drive results. They have various recognition programs, including the "Shopify Commerce Awards," which honors exceptional work and contributions. These initiatives not only reinforce a culture of ownership but also motivate employees to continuously improve and excel.

Shopify exemplifies a company whose leaders excel in cultivating employee ownership for performance improvements. Through their emphasis on autonomy, transparency, continuous learning, and recognition, Shopify has fostered a culture where employees take ownership of their work, drive innovation, and contribute to the company's overall success.

In short, accountability is crucial for building a high-performing team. By clearly defining expectations, leading by example, communicating effectively, setting measurable goals, and promoting a supportive environment, leaders can create a culture of accountability that drives performance and fosters strong relationships among team members.

Now that you've learned about the importance of accountability in a team or organization, let's take a look at a checklist that you can use to implement accountability strategies and practices within your own team.

"Accountability is the glue that ties commitment to the results."

- Bob Proctor

CHECKLIST

Checklist for Cultivating Ownership for Performance Improvements:

- Clearly define roles, expectations, and goals for each team member.
- Lead by example and demonstrate accountability yourself.
- Regularly provide feedback, both positive and constructive, to reinforce accountability and motivate team members.
- Recognize and appreciate the efforts of individuals who consistently meet their commitments.
- Establish clear and measurable performance metrics or key performance indicators (KPIs) for employees.
- Schedule regular progress meetings or check-ins to review performance against metrics.
- Provide support or guidance where needed to help employees achieve their targets.
- Create a supportive environment where team members feel safe taking risks and owning their mistakes.
- Encourage open dialogue and foster a culture of learning from failures.
- Provide resources or training opportunities to promote continuous improvement.
- Make accountability about growth and improvement, not punishment.
- Foster strong relationships among team members through trust and reliability.

Using this checklist will help you create a culture of accountability that drives performance, fosters strong relationships, and ultimately leads to success for the team or organization.

Now that we have gone through this checklist, let me provide you with some examples that illustrate how these strategies can be implemented in real-life situations. These examples will demonstrate how each of these checklist items can contribute to promoting accountability within a team and ultimately lead to positive outcomes.

> *"Responsibility focuses our attention and directs our efforts."*
>
> *- John C. Maxwell*

EXAMPLES

Maybe you're not Shopify and you should never compare yourself to others anyway, only learn from them. Here are some other examples to help you see how you might apply these ideas and practices in your own organization:

Clear Expectations: A leader in a sales team sets specific sales targets and clearly communicates them to each team member. They provide a detailed explanation of what is expected from each team member in terms of sales volume, customer retention, and customer satisfaction. The team members understand the importance of achieving these targets and feel accountable for their individual contributions.

Regular Feedback Sessions: A manager in a software development team conducts weekly feedback sessions with each team member to discuss their progress on different projects. They provide constructive feedback on the quality of their code, adherence to deadlines, and collaboration with teammates. The team members appreciate the open and honest communication and use this feedback to improve their performance and take greater ownership of their work.

Recognition and Appreciation: A team leader in a customer service department publicly recognizes and appreciates the efforts of team members who receive positive customer feedback or go above and beyond to resolve challenging customer issues. The leader shares these success stories during team meetings and highlights the importance of accountability and providing exceptional customer service. This encourages other team members to follow suit and strive for accountability and excellence in their interactions with customers.

Leading by Example: The CEO of a manufacturing company takes responsibility for a product recall due to a manufacturing error. They publicly admit the mistake, apologize to customers, and take immediate steps to rectify the issue and improve the manufacturing process. This action demonstrates accountability at the highest level of the organization and sets an example for all employees to take ownership of their actions and learn from mistakes.

Collaboration and Resource Sharing: A project manager in a marketing team promotes collaboration by assigning team members with complementary skills to work together on marketing campaigns. They encourage team members to share resources, knowledge, and ideas to achieve better results collectively. The project manager sets the expectation that each team member is accountable not only for their individual tasks but also for supporting and contributing to the success of the overall project.

Performance Evaluation: A supervisor in a retail store conducts regular performance evaluations with each staff member. During these evaluations, they review the employee's performance against key performance indicators such as sales targets, customer feedback, and teamwork. The supervisor provides constructive feedback, identifies areas for improvement, and collaboratively sets performance goals for the upcoming months. By holding employees accountable for their performance and providing guidance, the supervisor encourages them to take ownership of their responsibilities and continually strive for excellence.

Empowering Decision-Making: A team leader in an IT department empowers team members to make decisions and take ownership of their projects. They provide guidance and support but give the team members autonomy to drive their work forward. By allowing team members to make decisions and take responsibility for their outcomes, the team leader fosters a sense of accountability, as the team members understand that their decisions directly impact the success of their projects.

With these examples illustrating the importance and effectiveness of fostering a culture of accountability, let's take a closer look at the key mistakes to avoid when trying to create accountability in a team.

"Accountability is the foundation of trust. Without it, relationships crumble and progress stalls."

- John G. Miller

TYPICAL MISTAKES AND HOW TO AVOID THEM

Based on the material provided, one mistake most people make in the area of accountability is not clearly defining roles, expectations, and goals. This can lead to confusion and a lack of ownership among team members. To avoid this mistake, leaders should make sure to communicate clearly and provide a clear understanding of what is expected of each team member. Regular one-on-one meetings, team meetings, or even written agreements can be helpful in establishing this clarity.

Another common mistake is leaders not demonstrating accountability themselves. It is important for leaders to lead by example and take responsibility for their actions. When team members see their leaders admitting mistakes and working towards solutions, it sets a powerful precedent. Leaders must model the behavior they want to see in their team members.

Communication also plays a crucial role in creating accountability within a team. Leaders should regularly provide feedback, both positive and constructive, to reinforce accountability and motivate team members. Recognizing and appreciating the efforts of individuals who consistently meet their commitments is equally important. This not only empowers team members but also reinforces the importance of accountability within the team culture.

Creating clear and measurable performance metrics or key performance indicators (KPIs) is another area where people often make mistakes. When employees have quantifiable targets to aim for, they can track their progress and hold themselves accountable for achieving those targets. Regular progress meetings or check-ins can be used to review performance against these metrics and provide support or guidance where needed.

Lastly, leaders should create a supportive environment where team members feel safe taking risks and owning their mistakes. Accountability should not be about punishment, but about growth and improvement. Encouraging open dialogue, fostering a culture of learning from failures, and providing resources or training opportunities can promote accountability without creating fear or resistance.

When it comes to cultivating employee ownership for performance improvements, one company that stands out is Shopify. Based in Canada, Shopify is an e-commerce platform that empowers entrepreneurs and businesses to build their online stores and drive sales. Their leaders have done an exceptional job of creating an environment where employees feel a strong sense of ownership and accountability.

To avoid common mistakes in accountability, leaders must clearly define expectations, lead by example, communicate effectively, set measurable goals, and promote a supportive environment. By doing so, they can build a high-performing team that excels in achieving goals and fosters strong relationships among team members.

MY #1 PIECE OF ADVICE

If you really want to establish a culture of accountability with your teams, hold yourself accountable first before expecting others to be accountable. Lead by example and ensure that you consistently meet your own commitments and expectations. As any parent will tell you, people do what people see.

> *"Accountability is the willingness to own up to our actions and take responsibility for the impact they have on ourselves and others."*
> *- Brene Brown*

SUMMARY:

- Take ownership and hold yourself accountable for your actions. It's the key to achieving high levels of performance and success.

- Accountability fosters trust and reliability within a team, leading to stronger relationships and a sense of unity that boosts overall performance.

- Leaders, lead by example. Demonstrate accountability by taking responsibility for your actions and working towards solutions. Actions speak louder than words.

- Communication is crucial. Provide regular feedback to reinforce accountability and motivate team members. Recognize and appreciate consistent effort and commitment.

- Create a supportive environment where taking risks and owning mistakes is encouraged. Accountability is about growth and improvement, not punishment. Embrace it and watch your team thrive.

APPLICATION QUESTIONS

Now that you have a greater understanding of the importance of cultivating employee ownership for performance improvements, here are some questions to help you apply these points:

- What strategies do you use to foster open and honest communication within your team, ensuring that members feel comfortable addressing issues of accountability?

- What steps do you take to build trust and rapport with your team members, creating an environment conducive to accountability and reliability?

- How do you involve your team members in decision-making processes to increase their sense of ownership and accountability?

- How do you ensure that accountability extends beyond individual team members, fostering a collective sense of responsibility? Have you implemented any strategies or initiatives that have successfully promoted team accountability?

- How do you align your leadership style with the values of accountability within your team? Are there any specific practices or behaviors you engage in to set an example for others to follow?

Remember, the key is to reflect on these questions and adapt them to your specific context, incorporating your own personal leadership style and experiences to create an engaging and authentic conversation with your team.

QUIZ

1. What is one way leaders can demonstrate accountability to their team members?

    A. By setting measurable goals

    B. By providing feedback

    C. By leading by example

    D. By creating a supportive environment

2. What is an example of a strategy leaders can employ to create a sense of accountability among employees?

    A. Regular team meetings

    B. Written agreements

    C. Open dialogue

    D. All of the above

3. How often should you revisit and reassess goals and expectations to ensure ongoing accountability?

    A. Regularly – at least once a quarter or more often

    B. Occasionally – only when issues arise

    C. Rarely – only when significant changes occur

    D. Annually – during the regular performance revue

4. What can regular progress meetings be used for?

    A. Tracking progress

    B. Identifying areas for improvement

    C. Providing support and guidance

    D. All of the above

5. What does creating accountability require?

A. Defining roles and expectations and establishing clear and measurable performance metrics

B. Encouraging open dialogue

C. Trust and strong relationships

D. All of the above

Answer Key:

1. C - By leading by example

2. D - All of the above

3. A - Regularly – at least once a quarter or more often

4. D - All of the above

5. C - Trust and strong relationships

As we have seen in the previous chapter, accountability is crucial for ensuring higher levels of performance among employees. In the next chapter, we will explore another vital aspect of leadership - the role it plays in promoting diversity and inclusion within a work environment, and how this impactful practice directly influences employee engagement and overall performance. Stay tuned to discover the power of inclusive leadership and the positive effects it has on creating a harmonious and successful workplace.

CHAPTER 17
CULTIVATING CREATIVITY AND INNOVATION

BUILDING A POSITIVE AND INCLUSIVE MULTICULTURAL WORKPLACE FOR GAME-CHANGING RESULTS

"The power of diversity leads to better decisions, stronger outcomes, and a more vibrant culture."

- David Coleman

AT A GLANCE

Five Essential Points for Cultivating Creativity and Innovation

- Discover the transformative power of effective leadership in promoting diversity and inclusion within the workplace.

- Uncover the secrets to creating a culture that values diversity, fosters inclusion, and encourages employees to bring their unique perspectives to the table.

- Learn how diverse teams unlock greater innovation and problem-solving capabilities, leading to improved overall performance.

- Find out how leaders can actively promote diversity through inclusive recruitment and hiring processes, ensuring equal opportunities for all candidates.

- Experience the benefits of ongoing support, mentoring, and coaching programs that foster a sense of belonging and enhance employee engagement and performance.

Five Questions Business Leaders Should Ask About Cultivating Creativity and Innovation

- How do you define a positive and inclusive multicultural workplace, and how do you see it contributing to game-changing results in your organization?

- What steps are you currently taking to ensure a diverse and inclusive workforce, and how do these initiatives align with your overall business goals?

- What strategies do you employ to encourage open and respectful communication among team members with diverse ages, perspectives and backgrounds?

- How do you address unconscious biases in the workplace and ensure fair opportunities for all employees?

- How do you ensure that diversity and inclusion are integrated into all aspects of your organization, including leadership development, talent acquisition, and employee retention?

The role of leadership in promoting diversity and inclusion within a work environment cannot be underestimated. Effective leadership is crucial in setting the tone and creating a culture that values diversity, fosters inclusion, and encourages employees to bring their unique perspectives to the table. By doing so, leaders not only improve employee engagement but also enhance overall team performance.

First and foremost, leaders must recognize the value and importance of diversity and inclusion. They need to understand that diverse teams bring a wealth of knowledge, varied experiences, and different ways of thinking, which ultimately lead to greater innovation and problem-solving capabilities. By actively promoting diversity, leaders send a powerful message that everyone's voice matters and that each individual has an opportunity to contribute to the organization's success.

To promote diversity and inclusion, leaders must proactively seek out diverse talent and create an inclusive recruitment and hiring process. This involves examining biases and ensuring equal opportunities for all candidates, regardless of their backgrounds. By establishing diverse teams, leaders cultivate an environment where employees feel valued and respected for their unique contributions. This sense of belonging increases employee engagement, as individuals are more likely to be motivated and committed when they feel included and appreciated.

Moreover, leaders must also provide ongoing support and development opportunities for their diverse workforce. This includes mentoring and coaching programs that not only help employees grow professionally but also foster a sense of belonging within the organization. When leaders invest in the growth and success of their diverse team members, they demonstrate a genuine commitment to their development, further enhancing employee engagement and performance.

In terms of overall performance, diverse teams have proven to be more effective and successful. Various studies have shown that diverse teams outperform homogenous teams in terms of problem-solving, creativity, and decision-making. When individuals from different backgrounds, perspectives and ages collaborate and exchange ideas, they challenge each other's assumptions, leading to more well-rounded and comprehensive solutions. This diversity of thought and perspectives enables the team to overcome complex challenges and adapt to changing environments more effectively.

One exemplary company that stands out for its commitment to building a positive and inclusive multicultural workplace is Salesforce. Led by CEO Marc Benioff, Salesforce has become a trailblazer in fostering diversity and inclusion, resulting in game-changing outcomes for the organization.

Benioff's leadership approach centers on creating an environment where everyone feels valued and included. The company actively promotes the recruitment and retention of diverse talent, recognizing the importance of having different perspectives at all levels of the organization. Salesforce's leaders embrace the belief that diversity drives innovation and enhances problem-solving capabilities, leading to better business results.

To ensure a multicultural workplace, Salesforce implements various initiatives. One effective example is its 1-1-1 model, which commits the company to donating 1% of its products, time, and resources to philanthropy. This model emphasizes social impact and community engagement, fostering an inclusive company culture that extends beyond the office walls.

Salesforce also established the Office of Equality, devoted specifically to driving diversity, equality, and inclusion within the organization. This dedicated team works to eliminate bias, applies fair practices in recruitment and promotion, and enables ongoing education and conversations around inclusivity.

Furthermore, Salesforce actively encourages employee resource groups, such as Outforce (LGBTQ+) and BOLDforce (Black employees), providing a platform for underrepresented groups to connect, support one another, and advocate for change.

By championing diversity and inclusion, Salesforce has not only built a positive and inclusive multicultural workplace but has also achieved extraordinary business results. The company consistently ranks among the best places to work, attracting top talent and fostering an environment where innovation flourishes.

Salesforce's leadership demonstrates that investing in diversity and inclusion isn't just the right thing to do; it's a strategic imperative that drives innovation, employee satisfaction, and, ultimately, game-changing results. Their commitment serves as an inspiration for organizations seeking to create a vibrant and inclusive work environment.

As you can see, leadership plays a crucial role in promoting diversity and inclusion within a work environment. By valuing diversity, fostering inclusion, and providing ongoing support, leaders create a culture where employees feel empowered, engaged, and motivated to perform at their best. This ultimately leads to improved employee engagement and overall team performance. Embracing diversity isn't just the right thing to do; it's a strategic imperative for organizations seeking to thrive in a rapidly evolving global marketplace.

Now that we've discussed the importance of leadership in promoting diversity and inclusion, let's take a look at a checklist I have created to help you effectively incorporate these principles into your leadership approach.

> *"Diversity is the art of thinking independently together."*
>
> *- Malcolm Forbes*

CHECKLIST

Checklist for Promoting Diversity and Inclusion:

- Educate leaders: Provide training and education to leaders about the value and importance of diversity and inclusion in the workplace.

- Evaluate biases: Encourage leaders to examine their own biases and work towards minimizing them in decision-making processes.

- Diverse recruitment and hiring process: Develop and implement a recruitment and hiring process that actively seeks out diverse talent and provides equal opportunities for all candidates.

- Inclusive onboarding: Ensure that new hires from diverse backgrounds feel welcomed and supported during the onboarding process.

- Foster a culture of inclusion: Create a work environment where employees feel valued, respected, and included by promoting inclusive behaviors, practices, and policies.

- Provide ongoing support: Offer mentoring and coaching programs to support the growth and development of diverse employees.

- Celebrate diversity: Recognize and celebrate the achievements and contributions of diverse employees to reinforce the value of diversity in the organization.

- Establish diverse teams: Create teams that explicitly include individuals from diverse backgrounds to encourage collaboration and different perspectives.

- Encourage open communication: Foster an environment where employees feel comfortable speaking up, sharing their ideas, and challenging assumptions.

- Measure progress: Regularly assess and measure the organization's diversity and inclusion efforts to identify areas of improvement and track progress over time.

By following this checklist, leaders can actively promote diversity and inclusion within the workplace and create a culture that values and embraces differences, ultimately leading to improved employee engagement and overall team performance.

> *"When we invest in diversity and inclusion, we invest in the success and sustainability of our organization."*
>
> *- Lisa W. Wardell*

EXAMPLES

While it is important to create a workplace culture that is inclusive, diverse and equitable, it can seem daunting. Here are some examples of where you can get started:

Recruitment and hiring: A leader actively seeks out diverse talent and ensures equal opportunities during the hiring process. For example, they may implement blind screening techniques to eliminate unconscious bias and ensure that candidates are evaluated solely on their qualifications and skills.

Inclusive team building: A leader creates diverse teams by intentionally pairing individuals from different backgrounds and experiences. For instance, they may assign team members based on complementary skill sets and encourage collaboration between individuals with different perspectives.

Mentorship and coaching: A leader establishes mentorship and coaching programs to support the growth and development of their diverse workforce. For instance, they may match employees from underrepresented groups with senior leaders who can provide guidance, support, and opportunities for advancement.

Celebrating diversity: A leader organizes events and activities that celebrate and highlight the diverse backgrounds and experiences of their employees. For example, they may host cultural heritage month celebrations, lunch and learns on various topics, or diversity training sessions to raise awareness and promote understanding.

Encouraging open communication: A leader creates an environment where employees feel comfortable expressing their opinions and sharing their unique perspectives. They may hold regular team meetings and encourage open dialogue to foster a culture of inclusivity and respect.

Developing diversity and inclusion policies: A leader actively participates in the development of diversity and inclusion policies within the organization. They may collaborate with HR and other departments to create policies that ensure fair and equal treatment for all employees, regardless of their backgrounds.

Recognizing and rewarding diversity efforts: A leader acknowledges and rewards individuals and teams that actively contribute to fostering diversity and inclusion. They may implement recognition programs or incentives to encourage employees to embrace diversity and contribute to an inclusive work environment.

These examples demonstrate how leaders can take specific actions to promote diversity and inclusion within their organizations, ultimately leading to improved employee engagement and team performance.

Now that we have explored some examples of leaders who recognize and value diversity, create inclusive recruitment processes, provide ongoing support, harness the benefits of diverse teams, and foster an inclusive culture, let's discuss some mistakes to avoid in order to ensure successful implementation of such initiatives.

> *"The best way to foster innovation is to embrace diversity and create an inclusive environment."*
>
> *- Angela Ahrendts*

TYPICAL MISTAKES AND HOW TO AVOID THEM

Most people make the mistake of not recognizing the value and importance of diversity and inclusion in the workplace in the first place. They may overlook the fact that diverse teams bring a wealth of knowledge, varied experiences, and different ways of thinking, which ultimately lead to greater innovation and problem-solving capabilities. By actively promoting diversity, leaders send a powerful message that everyone's voice matters and that each individual has an opportunity to contribute to the organization's success.

Another mistake that people make is not proactively seeking out diverse talent during the recruitment and hiring process. Leaders should examine biases and ensure equal opportunities for all candidates, regardless of their backgrounds. By establishing diverse teams, leaders cultivate an environment where employees feel valued and respected for their unique contributions. This sense of belonging increases employee engagement, as individuals are more likely to be motivated and committed when they feel included and appreciated.

Furthermore, leaders often fail to provide ongoing support and development opportunities for their diverse workforce. It is important for leaders to implement mentoring and coaching programs that not only help employees grow professionally but also foster a sense of belonging within the organization. When leaders invest in the growth and success of their diverse team members, they demonstrate a genuine commitment to their development, further enhancing employee engagement and performance.

Lastly, people may underestimate the power of diverse teams in terms of overall performance. Studies have shown that diverse teams outperform homogenous teams in terms of problem-solving, creativity, and decision-making. When individuals from different backgrounds collaborate and exchange ideas, they challenge each other's assumptions, leading to more well-rounded and comprehensive solutions. This diversity of thought and perspectives enables the team to overcome complex challenges and adapt to changing environments more effectively.

To avoid these mistakes, leaders should actively recognize the value of diversity and inclusion, proactively seek out diverse talent, provide ongoing support and development opportunities, and leverage the power of diverse teams for improved performance. By doing so, leaders can create a culture where employees feel empowered, engaged, and motivated to perform at their best, ultimately leading to improved employee engagement and overall team performance. Embracing diversity is not just the right thing to do; it is a strategic imperative for organizations seeking to thrive in a rapidly evolving global marketplace.

MY #1 PIECE OF ADVICE

No matter how large or small your organization is or what your industry sector, I cannot stress enough the importance of embracing diversity on your team to foster a culture of innovation, inclusion, and better decision-making.

> *"Inclusion is not just about adding diversity. It's about valuing and respecting the differences that each individual brings to the table."*
>
> *- Janet Stovall Myers*

SUMMARY:

- Embrace diversity and inclusion - it's not just the right thing to do, it's a strategic imperative for success in today's global marketplace.

- Recognize the value of diversity - diverse teams bring varied perspectives and innovative solutions that lead to greater success.

- Actively promote diversity - send a powerful message that everyone's voice matters and create a culture where all individuals have an opportunity to contribute.

- Invest in your diverse workforce - provide ongoing support and development opportunities to foster a sense of belonging and enhance employee engagement.

- Experience the power of diverse teams - studies have shown that diverse teams outperform homogenous ones in problem-solving, creativity, and decision-making. Embrace diversity and unleash your team's full potential.

APPLICATION QUESTIONS

- How do you ensure that individuals from different cultural backgrounds feel supported and welcome during the hiring and onboarding process?

- In what ways could you more actively engage your employees in the process of creating a positive and inclusive multicultural workplace?

- How do you ensure that individuals from underrepresented backgrounds have equal access to leadership development opportunities

- How do you hold yourself and your leadership team accountable for creating a positive and inclusive multicultural workplace?

- In order to create a positive and inclusive multicultural workplace, what initiatives have you implemented to address unconscious biases and promote fair treatment among employees?

Remember, as a leader, your commitment to diversity and inclusion goes beyond mere words. By implementing concrete strategies and fostering a culture of belonging, you can drive game-changing results and create a workplace where everyone can thrive and contribute their best. Let's champion diversity, nurture inclusivity, and forge a path towards excellence together.

QUIZ

1. What is the importance of leadership in promoting diversity and inclusion?

   A. It sets the tone and creates a culture that values diversity

   B. It improves employee engagement

   C. It enhances overall team performance

   D. All of the above

2. What is the key to creating an inclusive recruitment and hiring process?

   A. Examining biases and ensuring equal opportunities for all candidates

   B. Establishing diverse teams

   C. Regularly monitoring and analyzing team performance

   D. Providing ongoing support and development opportunities

3. How do diverse teams contribute to better problem-solving capabilities?

   A. By challenging each other's assumptions

   B. By sharing unique perspectives

C. By working together more effectively

D. All of the above

4. Why is embracing diversity a strategic imperative for organizations?

A. It is the right thing to do

B. It improves employee engagement

C. It leads to improved overall team performance

D. All of the above

5. What are the benefits of having diverse teams?

A. Increased employee engagement

B. Greater innovation and creativity

C. Improved problem-solving capabilities

D. All of the above

Answer Key:

1. D - All of the above

2. A - Examining biases and ensuring equal opportunities for all candidates

3. D - All of the above

4. D - All of the above

5. D - All of the above

Now that we have explored the significant impact of leadership on diversity and inclusion in the workplace, it is equally vital to delve into the essential skillset leaders need to effectively handle conflicts within their teams, ensuring a positive and productive work environment. So, let's continue reading to learn valuable strategies on how to maintain harmonious relationships and resolve disputes in a constructive manner.

CHAPTER 18

NAVIGATING TURBULENT WATERS

STRATEGIES FOR MANAGING AND RESOLVING CONFLICTS IN TEAMS

"When there is trust, conflict becomes nothing but the pursuit of truth, an attempt to find the best possible answer."

- Patrick Lencioni

AT A GLANCE

Five Essential Points for Managing and Resolving Conflicts in Teams

- Discover how leaders can navigate difficult conversations and resolve conflicts to maintain a positive and productive work environment.

- Learn the key steps that leaders can take to address and manage conflicts within their teams effectively.

- Find out how leaders can encourage open communication and active listening to create a culture of collaboration and understanding.

- Explore the importance of separating individuals from the problem in conflict resolution and promoting a focus on finding mutually agreeable solutions.

- Uncover the secrets to effective conflict management that can lead to greater productivity, stronger relationships, and improved leadership skills among team members.

Five Questions Business Leaders Should Ask About Managing and Resolving Conflicts in Teams

- When conflicts arise within your teams, how do you typically approach the situation?

- What are some common root causes of conflicts within your team and what have you done to address them?

- How do you approach the task of mediating conflicts between team members?

- When conflicts arise within a team, how do you balance the need to resolve the issue quickly while also ensuring fairness and maintaining positive relationships among team members?

- When conflicts arise between yourself and a team member, how do you navigate these situations while still maintaining your role as a leader?

Addressing and managing conflicts within a team is indeed crucial for maintaining a positive and productive work environment. As a leader, it is your responsibility to handle these conflicts effectively and create pathways for resolution. Here are some strategies that can help you navigate through difficult conversations and foster a harmonious atmosphere within your team.

First and foremost, it's important to approach conflicts with an open mind and a willingness to understand all perspectives involved. Take the time to listen attentively to each team member and encourage them to express their concerns and viewpoints openly. By showing empathy and demonstrating that you value their input, you will build trust and create a safe space for constructive dialogues.

When addressing conflicts, it is essential to focus on the issue at hand rather than making it personal. Remind your team members that the goal is to find a solution that benefits everyone and move forward together. Encourage them to separate their emotions from the situation and engage in a rational discussion. This will help prevent the conversation from turning into a blame game and allow for productive problem-solving.

To maintain a positive work environment, leaders should also promote a culture of open communication and transparency. Encourage your team members to voice their concerns early on, before they escalate into conflicts. Regular check-ins and team meetings can be an excellent platform for discussing any emerging issues and ensuring that everyone feels heard and supported.

Furthermore, strong leadership requires the ability to mediate conflicts when they arise. As a leader, act as a mediator and facilitate a healthy conversation between conflicting parties. Encourage active listening and facilitate a balanced exchange of ideas. Maintain a neutral stance and focus on finding common ground and mutually satisfactory solutions. This approach will prevent conflicts from escalating and promote a collaborative rather than an adversarial atmosphere.

In addition to addressing conflicts when they arise, proactive leaders also strive to minimize the potential for conflicts in the first place. Encourage team members to actively engage in team-building activities, fostering positive relationships and understanding amongst each other. Encouraging a sense of camaraderie and emphasizing the importance of teamwork can significantly reduce the likelihood of conflicts arising.

One remarkable business leader known for their exceptional strategies in managing and resolving conflicts within teams is Sheryl Sandberg, the Chief Operating Officer (COO) of Facebook. Sandberg's influential leadership style and effective conflict resolution approach have made a significant impact on Facebook's success and team dynamics.

Sandberg is a proponent of creating a culture of open communication and psychological safety within teams. She firmly believes that conflicts should be addressed directly and early on to prevent them from festering and potentially damaging relationships. Sandberg encourages team members to speak up, share their perspectives, and engage in healthy debates, paving the way for constructive conflict resolution.

An excellent example of Sandberg's conflict resolution skills is her approach to managing diversity and inclusion at Facebook. She recognizes that diverse teams can sometimes encounter conflicts due to different backgrounds, ideas, and experiences. Sandberg advocates for creating an inclusive environment where every voice is heard and respected. By promoting understanding and empathy among team members, Sandberg ensures conflicts are approached with cultural sensitivity and addressed in a fair and unbiased manner.

Sandberg is also skilled at bridging gaps and finding common ground. She understands that conflicts often arise from miscommunication or misunderstandings. Sandberg encourages active listening and fosters a spirit of collaboration, enabling teams to identify shared objectives and work towards finding mutually beneficial solutions. By emphasizing empathy and building strong relationships, she ensures conflicts are approached with a focus on building bridges rather than creating divisions.

Furthermore, Sandberg is a strong advocate for emotional intelligence in conflict resolution. She encourages self-awareness and empathy, emphasizing the importance of understanding one's own emotions and those of others. By fostering emotional intelligence within teams, Sandberg provides a foundation for effective conflict resolution, which takes into account the feelings and perspectives of all individuals involved.

Sheryl Sandberg's exemplary strategies in managing and resolving conflicts within teams are rooted in creating a culture of open communication, fostering diversity and inclusion, and emphasizing emotional intelligence. Her ability to address conflicts head-on, bridge gaps, and cultivate empathy serves as a compelling example for leaders aiming to create harmonious and high-performing teams.

To sum it up, effective conflict management involves active listening, rational discussions, promoting open communication, mediating conflicts when necessary, and fostering positive relationships within the team. By following these strategies, you can create a work environment that values collaboration, respects diverse perspectives, and ultimately thrives on productivity and success. Remember, conflict resolution is not just about achieving results, but also about building meaningful relationships with your team members.

Now that you have learned about effective strategies for addressing and managing conflicts within a team, it's time to put them into practice. To help you navigate through difficult conversations and foster a harmonious atmosphere, I have created a checklist that outlines the key steps you can take.

> *"Great leaders are willing to have difficult conversations and address conflict head-on."*
>
> *- John C. Maxwell*

CHECKLIST

Checklist for Addressing and Managing Conflicts within a Team:

- Approach conflicts with an open mind and a willingness to understand all perspectives involved.
- Take the time to listen attentively to each team member and encourage open expression of concerns and viewpoints.
- Show empathy and demonstrate that you value everyone's input to build trust and create a safe space for constructive dialogues.
- Focus on the issue at hand and avoid making conflicts personal.
- Remind team members that the goal is to find a solution that benefits everyone and move forward together.
- Encourage team members to separate their emotions from the situation and engage in rational discussions.
- Promote a culture of open communication and transparency within the team.
- Encourage team members to voice their concerns early on, before they escalate into conflicts.
- Schedule regular check-ins and team meetings to discuss any emerging issues and ensure everyone feels heard and supported.
- Act as a mediator when conflicts arise and facilitate healthy conversations between conflicting parties.
- Encourage active listening and facilitate a balanced exchange of ideas.
- Maintain a neutral stance and focus on finding common ground and mutually satisfactory solutions.
- Strive to minimize the potential for conflicts by encouraging team-building activities and fostering positive relationships among team members.

- Emphasize the importance of teamwork and encourage a sense of camaraderie.

- Follow these strategies to create a work environment that values collaboration, respects diverse perspectives, and promotes productivity and success.

- Remember that conflict resolution is not just about achieving results, but also about building meaningful relationships with your team members.

Now that we have gone through this conflict management checklist, let's take a look at some examples that illustrate these strategies in action. These examples demonstrate how implementing these strategies can help resolve conflicts and foster a harmonious and collaborative work environment.

> *"The art of peace is not about avoiding conflict, but about resolving it in a constructive way."*
>
> *- Morihei Ueshiba*

EXAMPLES

You don't have to be the size of Facebook to experience conflicts inside your teams. Here are some examples of how to find amicable solutions.

Scenario A: Two team members, John and Sarah, have conflicting ideas about how to approach a project. John believes in taking a cautious and detailed approach, while Sarah prefers a more innovative and experimental approach.

Strategy 1: The leader, Alex, organizes a team meeting to address the conflict and encourages both John and Sarah to express their viewpoints. Alex listens attentively to both perspectives and encourages the team to find common ground. Through open and respectful communication, the team agrees to combine aspects of both approaches, taking a cautious yet innovative approach.

Strategy 2: Instead of addressing the conflict, Alex notices the tension between John and Sarah and decides to intervene. Alex meets with John and Sarah individually to understand their concerns. Through active listening and empathetic communication, Alex is able to mediate the conflict and help John and Sarah reach a compromise that satisfies both parties.

Scenario B: Alice and Bob, two team members, have differing opinions on how to allocate tasks within the team. Alice believes in rotation and equal distribution, while Bob feels that tasks should be assigned based on individual strengths.

Strategy 1: The team leader, Emily, brings up the conflicting opinions during a team meeting and encourages Alice and Bob to share their thoughts and concerns openly. Emily guides the conversation to focus on finding a solution that benefits the team. Through compromise and collaboration, the team agrees on a hybrid approach, where tasks are assigned based on individual strengths but rotated periodically to encourage skill development.

Strategy 2: Emily, noticing the tension between Alice and Bob, holds a one-on-one meeting with each of them to understand their perspectives. Emily facilitates a discussion where both Alice and Bob can express their concerns without interruption. By actively listening and seeking common ground, Emily helps them find a resolution where tasks are assigned based on strengths but with occasional rotation to ensure fairness.

Scenario C: A team member, Mike, frequently interrupts his colleagues during meetings, causing frustration and hindering productive discussions.

Strategy 1: The team leader, Lisa, addresses the issue by having a private conversation with Mike. She explains the impact of his behavior on the team and encourages him to actively listen and allow others to speak uninterrupted. Lisa emphasizes the importance of respectful communication and sets clear expectations for future meetings.

Strategy 2: Lisa decides to bring up the issue during a team meeting, discussing the impact of interruptions on team dynamics and productivity. She encourages open discussion and brainstorming to find potential solutions. The team agrees on implementing a "speaking turn" system, where everyone gets an opportunity to speak without interruptions, fostering a more respectful and inclusive environment.

These examples highlight the strategies of open communication, active listening, rational discussions, mediating conflicts, and fostering positive relationships within a team. By applying these strategies, leaders can effectively address and manage conflicts, leading to a more harmonious and productive work environment. Now, let's examine the key mistakes to avoid when managing conflicts in order to achieve similar outcomes.

> *"In the face of conflict, true leaders rise above ego and focus on finding win-win solutions."*
>
> *- Simon Sinek*

TYPICAL MISTAKES AND HOW TO AVOID THEM

Based on the material covered here, some of the mistakes that most people make in managing conflicts within their teams are:

1. Avoiding open and honest communication: Many individuals shy away from expressing their concerns and opinions due to fear of backlash or negative consequences. This hinders effective conflict resolution. To avoid this mistake, leaders should strive to create a culture that encourages open dialogue, where team members feel safe to express themselves.

2. Delaying conflict resolution: Procrastinating or ignoring conflicts can lead to further complications and damage team dynamics. It is important for leaders to address conflicts promptly and not let them fester. This shows a commitment to maintaining a positive work environment and prevents the escalation of conflicts.

3. Lack of active listening: Leaders often fail to actively listen to all parties involved in a conflict. Active listening entails giving undivided attention, maintaining eye contact, and showing empathy. By truly hearing and understanding the concerns of each individual, leaders can find common ground for resolution.

4. Personalizing the problem: It is a common mistake to attribute conflicts solely to the individuals involved rather than focusing on the problem itself. This mindset can lead to personal attacks and hinder productive conflict resolution. Leaders should consciously shift their perspective and those of the disagreeing parties to separate the individuals from the problem to create a more constructive environment.

5. Ignoring collaboration: In many instances, leaders take it upon themselves to find solutions without involving the conflicting parties. This approach can lead to one-sided decisions and dissatisfaction. Leaders should instead encourage collaboration, allowing team members to share their perspectives and brainstorm together. This promotes ownership and leads to more sustainable resolutions.

6. Forgetting common ground: Individuals involved in conflicts often lose sight of the bigger picture and focus on personal biases. To avoid this mistake, leaders should remind team members of the shared objectives they all strive to achieve. By reorienting the focus

towards common goals, leaders can facilitate a more constructive conversation.

7. Lack of feedback and guidance: Leaders sometimes fail to provide timely and constructive feedback to individuals involved in conflicts. Feedback should concentrate on specific behaviors or actions rather than personal characteristics. Offering guidance and support helps individuals develop their conflict resolution skills and strengthens team cohesion.

8. Neglecting follow-up and progress monitoring: Once a resolution has been reached, leaders should not forget to follow up and ensure that the agreed-upon solutions are being implemented. By doing so, leaders show their commitment to the team's success and are able to make necessary adjustments if required.

By being mindful of these mistakes and actively practicing the strategies outlined above, leaders can effectively address and manage conflicts within their teams, fostering a positive and productive work environment.

MY #1 PIECE OF ADVICE

Let me introduce my #1 piece of advice that can help leaders navigate and resolve these conflicts successfully. Approach difficult conversations with empathy, active listening, and a solutions-focused mindset by first finding the common ground.

> *"Conflict can lead to growth and innovation if approached with an open mind and willingness to find solutions."*
>
> *- Sheryl Sandberg*

SUMMARY:

- Foster open and honest communication: Encourage team members to express their thoughts and concerns, promoting a culture of open dialogue and active listening.

- Address conflicts promptly: Don't ignore or postpone conflict resolution; tackle issues as soon as they arise to maintain a positive work environment.

- Practice active listening: Give undivided attention, maintain eye contact, and show empathy to gain a deeper understanding and find common ground for resolution.

- Separate individuals from the problem: Shift focus away from personal attacks and concentrate on finding mutually agreeable solutions.

- Collaborate on finding solutions: Facilitate a collaborative process where conflicting parties work together, encouraging creativity and ownership for sustainable resolutions.

APPLICATION QUESTIONS

- When it comes to creating a culture of open communication, how do you encourage your team members to speak up and share their viewpoints, especially during times of conflict?

- In your experience, how do you address conflicts that arise from diverse perspectives or cultural differences within your teams? How can you promote understanding, empathy, and inclusivity in conflict resolution?

- How would you approach resolving a situation where miscommunication or misunderstandings led to conflicts within your team and what steps would you take to ensure effective communication moving forward?

- How can you foster greater trust and cultivate emotional intelligence within your teams to navigate conflicts more effectively and ensure it remains intact during the conflict resolution process?
- When conflicts arise between team members, how will you balance the need for resolution with the importance of maintaining positive relationships within the team?

QUIZ

1. What is the first step a leader should take when addressing conflicts?

   A. Encourage open and honest communication

   B. Address conflicts promptly

   C. Practice active listening

   D. Separate individuals from the problem

2. What can leaders do to minimize the potential for conflicts?

   A. Encourage team members to voice their concerns

   B. Facilitate a balanced exchange of ideas

   C. Promote team-building activities

   D. All of the above

3. Why is open communication important in managing conflicts?

   A. To create a harmonious atmosphere

   B. To maintain a positive work environment

   C. To prevent conflicts from escalating

   D. To ensure everyone feels heard and supported

4. What should leaders avoid when addressing conflict?

   A. Focusing on the issue at hand

   B. Maintaining a neutral stance

C. Making it personal

D. Promoting open communication

5. What are some strategies that can help leaders navigate through difficult conversations?

A. Open-mindedness and active listening

B. Separating emotions from the situation

C. Rational discussions and finding common ground

D. All of the above

Answer Key:

1. A - Encourage open and honest communication

2. D - All of the above

3. D - To ensure everyone feels heard and supported

4. C - Making it personal

5. D - All of the above

Now that we've explored how leaders can effectively address and manage conflicts within their teams, it's time to shift our focus to measuring and tracking the impact of these efforts on employee engagement and efficiency improvements – a crucial aspect of creating a positive and productive work environment. So, let's dive into the next chapter to learn about the key performance indicators that will help us gauge our success and keep driving positive change.

CHAPTER 19

MEASURING SUCCESS

STRATEGIES FOR TRACKING IMPROVEMENTS IN EFFICIENCY AND EMPLOYEE ENGAGEMENT

"Success is not about achieving perfection, but about continuously striving for improvement."

- Aristotle

AT A GLANCE

Five Essential Points for Tracking Improvements in Efficiency and Employee Engagement

- Unlock the secrets to boosting employee engagement and efficiency with the right key performance indicators

- Discover the power of employee satisfaction and how it drives productivity and success.

- Uncover hidden insights by tracking employee turnover rates and identifying areas for improvement.

- Dive into the world of productivity metrics and see how your leadership skills can make a measurable impact.

- Explore the importance of team collaboration and communication in fostering a positive work environment.

Five Questions Business Leaders Should Ask About Tracking Improvements in Efficiency and Employee Engagement

- What specific strategies or tools do you employ to measure and monitor improvements in efficiency and employee engagement within your organization?

- How do you ensure that the metrics or KPIs used to track efficiency are aligned with your organization's goals and objectives? Have you encountered any challenges in setting these metrics, and if so, how did you address them?

- What are some effective ways you have used to identify the root causes of inefficiencies or disengagement? Did you involve employees in this process, and what role did their insights play in driving improvements?

- How do you strike a balance between pushing for increased efficiency and maintaining a positive and engaging work environment?

- How do you communicate the progress and outcomes of your efforts to improve efficiency and employee engagement with your team?

When it comes to measuring the impact of your efforts on employee engagement and efficiency improvements, it's crucial to identify key performance indicators (KPIs) that provide a comprehensive picture of your progress. By focusing on these specific metrics, you'll be able to track your success and make data-driven decisions to further enhance your leadership skills.

First and foremost, a fundamental KPI to consider is employee satisfaction. This can be measured through regular surveys or feedback sessions to gauge how engaged and content your team members are. Specifically, look for indicators such as overall job satisfaction, commitment, and enthusiasm towards their work. Engaged employees tend to be more efficient and productivity-driven, leading to positive business outcomes.

Another important performance indicator is employee turnover rate. A high turnover rate is not only costly but also indicates potential issues with employee engagement and satisfaction. Track the number of employees leaving your organization, paying attention to trends and identifying potential areas of improvement.

Along with that is another vital KPI to focus on: absenteeism or sick leave. Keep track of the number of unplanned absences and their impact on overall team efficiency. High absenteeism rates may suggest a lack of motivation or engagement, thereby highlighting the need for further improvement in your leadership approach.

Team collaboration and communication are also critical aspects of employee engagement and efficiency. Consider measuring metrics such as the number of cross-functional collaborations, the frequency of team meetings, or the effectiveness of internal communication channels. These metrics shed light on the effectiveness of your leadership in fostering a collaborative and communicative work environment.

Furthermore, productivity metrics are essential to evaluate the efficiency improvements resulting from your leadership efforts. Measure the quantity and quality of work produced by your team members, including completed projects, sales results, or customer satisfaction scores. This allows you to monitor tangible outcomes and verify if your leadership strategies are positively impacting productivity.

To enhance the depth of your measurements, consider incorporating qualitative feedback from employees through interviews or focus groups. Personal anecdotes and stories from team members can provide valuable insights into how your leadership style impacts their engagement and efficiency. Building relationships and establishing open lines of communication encourage employees to share their experiences more freely, ultimately benefiting the measurement process.

One exemplary business leader known for their exceptional ability to track improvements in efficiency and employee engagement is Ursula Burns, the former CEO of Xerox Corporation. Throughout her tenure, Burns displayed a remarkable commitment to driving positive transformation within the organization.

In tracking efficiency improvements, Burns implemented a robust performance measurement system that monitored key metrics such as productivity rates, cost savings, and workflow optimization. By leveraging these data-driven insights, she was able to identify areas for improvement and implement targeted strategies to streamline operations.

Regarding employee engagement, Burns understood the critical role it played in fostering a thriving corporate culture. To keep a pulse on the organization's engagement levels, she actively sought feedback from employees through various channels, such as surveys, one-on-one meetings, and open forums. This allowed her to understand their needs, concerns, and aspirations, enabling her to make informed decisions.

Furthermore, Burns believed that transparency and effective communication were key in engaging employees. She regularly communicated the organization's goals, strategies, and progress to ensure alignment and inspire a sense of purpose among team members. This created an environment where employees felt valued, empowered, and motivated to contribute their best.

Burns also recognized the importance of recognizing and rewarding employees for their achievements. She championed a culture of appreciation, celebrating individuals and teams who demonstrated exceptional performance or innovative contributions. This recognition further bolstered employee morale and engagement, resulting in increased efficiency and productivity.

In addition to her focus on improvement metrics and employee engagement, Burns was known for her charismatic leadership style. She fostered strong relationships with her team members by taking a genuine interest in their professional development and providing mentorship opportunities. This personal touch created a sense of trust and loyalty, leading to a more engaged workforce.

Incorporating these best practices from Burns' leadership approach can help business leaders meticulously track efficiency improvements and enhance employee engagement. By implementing data-driven measures, actively seeking employee feedback, and fostering a culture of recognition, leaders can drive positive change, inspire their teams, and ultimately achieve remarkable results.

By focusing on key performance indicators such as employee satisfaction, turnover rate, productivity metrics, absenteeism, and collaboration, you can measure and track the impact of your leadership efforts on employee engagement and efficiency improvements. By consistently monitoring these metrics, adapting your approach based on the data, and fostering a strong relationship with your team, you can drive measurable and sustainable results. Remember, building connections, inspiring action, and using data to guide your decisions are key to continuous improvement.

Now that you've learned about the importance of measuring key performance indicators for employee engagement and efficiency improvements, it's time to put your knowledge into action. To help you track your progress and make data-driven decisions, I have created a comprehensive checklist based on the article.

> *"Efficiency is doing things right; effectiveness is doing the right things."*
>
> *- Peter Drucker*

CHECKLIST

Checklist for Tracking Improvements in Efficiency and Employee Engagement:

- Employee Satisfaction: Conduct regular surveys or feedback sessions to gauge job satisfaction, commitment, and enthusiasm towards work. Look for indicators such as overall job satisfaction, commitment level, and engagement.

- Employee Turnover Rate: Track the number of employees leaving your organization periodically. Identify trends and potential areas of improvement.

- Productivity Metrics: Measure the quantity and quality of work produced by team members. Look at completed projects, sales results, or customer satisfaction scores. Monitor tangible outcomes to evaluate the impact of your leadership techniques on productivity.

- Absenteeism or Sick Leave: Keep track of the number of unplanned absences and their impact on team efficiency. High absenteeism rates may indicate a lack of motivation or engagement.

- Team Collaboration and Communication: Measure metrics such as the number of cross-functional collaborations, frequency of team meetings, or effectiveness of internal communication channels. Evaluate the effectiveness of your leadership style in fostering a collaborative and communicative work environment.

- Qualitative Feedback: Incorporate qualitative feedback from employees through interviews or focus groups. Personal anecdotes and stories provide valuable insights into how your leadership style impacts engagement and efficiency. Building relationships and establishing open lines of communication encourage employees to share their experiences.

By consistently monitoring and measuring these key performance indicators, adapting your approach based on the data, and fostering a strong relationship with your team, you can drive measurable and sustainable results. Remember to build connections, inspire action, and use data to guide your decisions for continuous improvement.

Based on the checklist provided, I have created examples that demonstrate how to effectively evaluate employee satisfaction, turnover rate, productivity metrics, absenteeism or sick leave, team collaboration and communication, and qualitative feedback. By using these examples, we can see how monitoring these key performance indicators can lead to measurable and sustainable results. Now, let's dive into the specific examples I have prepared.

> *"Success is not in the destination, but in the journey. Measure your progress by the distance you've traveled, not by the miles left to go."*
>
> *- Ralph Waldo Emerson*

EXAMPLES

While we can't all be Xerox, we do need to track our progress and improvement so we will know if we are moving in the right direction and stay motivated to keep going when we hit bumps in the road or are forced to take a detour.

Employee satisfaction: Conducting quarterly surveys to gauge overall job satisfaction, commitment, and enthusiasm levels among team members.

Analyzing the survey results to identify areas of improvement and track changes over time.

Employee turnover rate: Tracking the number of employees leaving the organization on a monthly basis. Identifying trends and potential causes for high turnover, such as lack of engagement or dissatisfaction. Implementing initiatives to improve retention and monitoring the impact on turnover rates.

Absenteeism: Recording the number of unplanned absences or sick leaves taken by team members. Analyzing the impact of these absences on overall team efficiency and identifying any patterns or underlying issues that may need addressing.

Team collaboration and communication: Keeping track of the frequency of cross-functional collaborations and team meetings. Evaluating the effectiveness of internal communication channels, such as email or collaboration software. Assessing the level of employee participation and engagement in collaborative efforts.

Productivity metrics: Monitoring the completion of projects and tasks within set deadlines. Tracking sales results and customer satisfaction scores to measure the effectiveness of employees' work. Comparing productivity metrics before and after implementing leadership techniques to assess improvements.

Qualitative feedback: Conducting interviews or focus groups with team members to gather personal anecdotes and stories about their experiences with your leadership style. Using this qualitative feedback to gain a deeper understanding of how your approach impacts employee engagement and efficiency.

Adapting leadership approach: Based on the data and feedback collected, making adjustments to your leadership style and initiatives. Implementing new strategies, providing additional training or resources, and continuously monitoring the impact of these changes on employee engagement and efficiency.

Overall, using a combination of quantitative and qualitative metrics and continuously monitoring and adjusting your leadership approach will help you measure and drive improvements in employee engagement and efficiency.

Now that we have explored various examples of measuring employee engagement and efficiency, it is important to also take note of the mistakes to avoid in order to ensure the effectiveness and sustainability of such efforts.

> *"Measure your success by the number of obstacles you've overcome, for they are the stepping stones to greatness."*
>
> *- Oprah Winfrey*

TYPICAL MISTAKES AND HOW TO AVOID THEM

One mistake that most people make in measuring the impact of their efforts on employee engagement and efficiency improvements is not identifying and focusing on key performance indicators (KPIs). To avoid this mistake, it is crucial to determine which specific metrics will provide a comprehensive picture of your progress. By doing so, you will be able to track your success and make data-driven decisions to further enhance your leadership skills.

Another common mistake is not considering employee satisfaction as a fundamental KPI. This can be measured through regular surveys or feedback sessions to gauge how engaged and content your team members are. It is important to look for indicators such as overall job satisfaction, commitment, and enthusiasm towards their work. Engaged employees tend to be more efficient and productivity-driven, leading to positive business outcomes.

Additionally, many people overlook the importance of tracking employee turnover rate. This metric not only helps identify potential issues with employee engagement and satisfaction but also highlights the associated costs of high turnover. By periodically tracking the number of employees leaving your organization and paying attention to trends, you can identify potential areas of improvement.

It is also important to focus on absenteeism or sick leave as a key performance indicator. By keeping track of the number of unplanned absences and their impact on overall team efficiency, you can gather insights into the level of motivation or engagement within your team. High absenteeism rates may suggest the need for further improvement in your leadership approach.

Productivity metrics are also essential in evaluating the efficiency improvements resulting from your leadership efforts. Measuring the quantity and quality of work produced by your team members, such as completed projects, sales results, or customer satisfaction scores, allows you to monitor tangible outcomes and verify if your leadership techniques are positively impacting productivity.

Finally, team collaboration and communication are critical aspects of employee engagement and efficiency. Metrics such as the number of cross-functional collaborations, the frequency of team meetings, and the effectiveness of internal communication channels can provide valuable insights into the effectiveness of your leadership in fostering a collaborative and communicative work environment.

To enhance the depth of your measurements, consider incorporating qualitative feedback from employees through interviews or focus groups. Personal anecdotes and stories from team members can provide valuable insights into how your leadership style impacts their engagement and efficiency. Building relationships and establishing open lines of communication encourage employees to share their experiences more freely, ultimately benefiting the measurement process.

Ultimately, it is important to focus on key performance indicators such as employee satisfaction, turnover rate, productivity metrics, absenteeism, and collaboration to measure and track the impact of your leadership efforts on employee engagement and efficiency improvements. By consistently monitoring these metrics, adapting your approach based on the data, and fostering a strong relationship with your team, you can drive measurable and sustainable results. Remember, building connections, inspiring action, and using data to guide your decisions are key to continuous improvement.

MY #1 PIECE OF ADVICE

My #1 piece of advice to ensure accurate evaluation and improvement opportunities is to set clear, measurable goals and regularly monitor progress to track improvement effectively.

> *"The true measure of success is the ability to find joy and satisfaction in the small victories along the way."*
>
> *- Henry David Thoreau*

SUMMARY:

- Measure success through employee satisfaction: Regular surveys and feedback sessions can gauge engagement and contentment, allowing you to enhance your leadership skills.

- Keep an eye on turnover rate: High turnover is costly and signifies potential issues with engagement and satisfaction. Tracking trends helps identify areas for improvement.

- Evaluate productivity improvements: Assess quantity and quality of work, completed projects, sales results, and customer satisfaction to verify positive impacts of your leadership.

- Monitor absenteeism: High rates indicate lack of motivation or engagement. Analyzing the impact on team efficiency highlights areas for improvement.

- Foster collaboration and communication: Measure cross-functional collaborations, team meetings, and internal communication effectiveness to enhance engagement and efficiency.

Remember, by consistently measuring and adapting based on data, along with building relationships and inspiring action, you can drive measurable and sustainable results in employee engagement and efficiency.

APPLICATION QUESTIONS

- How can you revolutionize your approach to tracking improvements in efficiency and employee engagement to unleash the true potential of your team?

- Imagine a workplace where every employee is fully engaged, passionate, and motivated. What steps can you take to make this vision a reality, and how can you measure the progress you're making towards it?

- Efficiency is the holy grail of success in today's fast-paced business landscape. How can you identify bottlenecks or areas of inefficiency within your processes to streamline operations and drive growth?

- Employee engagement is not just a buzzword; it's the catalyst for innovation and productivity. How can you create an environment that inspires, empowers, and ignites your employees' passion for their work?

- Picture a team that thrives on collaboration and creativity, where ideas flow freely, and individuals feel valued and supported. How can you nurture this culture and what metrics can you use to gauge its impact on your organizational performance?

Incorporating these questions into your discussions and decision-making processes will help you drive improvements in efficiency and employee engagement while capturing the attention and enthusiasm of your team members. By asking these thought-provoking questions and implementing the recommended strategies, you can drive positive change, enhance productivity, and foster a highly engaged workforce.

QUIZ

1. What is the most important KPI for measuring the impact of your efforts on employee engagement and efficiency improvements?

   A. Productivity metrics

   B. Employee satisfaction

   C. Team collaboration

   D. Employee turnover rate

2. What type of feedback should be included in the measurement process to gain a comprehensive picture of progress?

   A. Qualitative feedback

   B. Quantitative feedback

   C. Employee surveys

   D. Focus groups

3. What type of data should be measured to evaluate efficiency improvements?

   A. Completed projects

   B. Defect rate

      C. Sales results

      D. All of the above

4. What is an essential step for tracking your success and making data-driven decisions?

      A. Identifying key performance indicators

      B. Collecting feedback from employees

      C. Adapting your approach based on the data

      D. Incorporating feedback from team members

5. What type of feedback can provide valuable insights into how your leadership style is impacting employee engagement and efficiency?

      A. Qualitative feedback

      B. Quantitative feedback

      C. Employee surveys

      D. Focus groups

Answer Key:

1. B - Employee satisfaction

2. A - Qualitative feedback

3. D - All of the above

4. A - Identifying key performance indicators

5. A - Qualitative feedback

Now that we understand the key performance indicators for measuring employee engagement and efficiency, it's time to explore the significant role that recognition and rewards play in enhancing employee performance. Continue reading to discover how implementing these strategies can further engage your employees and drive exceptional results.

CHAPTER 20

RECOGNIZING EXCELLENCE

CREATIVE WAYS FOR LEADERS TO REWARD EMPLOYEE CONTRIBUTIONS TO IMPROVED PERFORMANCE

"In a world where attention is scarce, recognition can be the greatest gift you can give to someone."

- Simon Sinek

AT A GLANCE

Five Essential Points for Recognizing Excellence

- Discover the secret to unlocking your team's true potential through recognition and rewards.

- Experience the power of appreciation and how it can transform your workplace into a positive and motivated environment.

- Find out how leaders can build strong connections with their employees through personalized gestures and rewards.

- Unleash a culture of excellence with creative and inspiring public recognition ceremonies that celebrate exceptional employees.

- Learn practical strategies for incorporating tangible rewards that will motivate and engage your team like never before.

Five Questions Business Leaders Should Ask About Recognizing Excellence

- How do you currently recognize and appreciate your employees' contributions to improved performance?

- In your experience, what do you believe are the key factors that make a rewards system successful in motivating employees to perform better?

- How do you ensure that the rewards you offer align with the values and goals of your organization, as well as the individual needs and preferences of your employees?

- Have you ever faced challenges in determining the appropriate level or type of reward for different levels of employee performance? How did you overcome those challenges?

- How do you adapt your rewards strategy to accommodate different generations or diverse groups within your workforce?

Recognition and rewards play a crucial role in engaging employees and enhancing their performance. When employees feel appreciated and valued for their efforts, they become more motivated, dedicated, and committed to achieving their goals. Recognition and rewards inspire a sense of pride, boost morale, and create a positive work environment where individuals are excited to contribute their best.

The easiest way leaders can provide recognition is through verbal praise and appreciation. Taking the time to acknowledge and personally thank employees for their hard work and outstanding achievements can have a significant impact on their engagement and motivation. It builds relationships, fosters a sense of connection, and demonstrates that their efforts are seen and valued.

Another creative way leaders can recognize and reward great performance is through public recognition ceremonies or events. Organizing an awards ceremony that highlights exceptional employees and their contributions not only celebrates individual achievements, but also inspires others to go above and beyond. This type of recognition not only enhances performance but also strengthens the bond between team members and encourages healthy competition and growth. Although this is not a one-size fits all way it does work for most.

In addition to verbal praise and public recognition, tangible rewards can also play a vital role in engaging employees. For example, implementing a rewards program that offers incentives such as gift cards, extra vacation days, or even opportunities for professional development can motivate individuals to strive for excellence. These rewards not only demonstrate appreciation but also provide tangible benefits that can further enhance job satisfaction and performance.

Moreover, leaders should consider incorporating personalized rewards to make employees feel recognized on a deeper level. For instance, understanding individual preferences and interests can help leaders choose rewards that are meaningful and aligned with the employee's values. By tailoring rewards to match an individual's interests, such as tickets to a sports event or a coveted book, leaders show that they truly understand and appreciate their employees on a personal level. This fosters a stronger relationship between the leader and the employee, leading to increased engagement and improved performance.

One company that has gained widespread recognition for its creative approach to rewarding employee contributions to improved performance is the multinational sporting goods manufacturer, "FitTech Solutions." They have built a reputation for their innovative and engaging methods that drive employee motivation and foster a strong sense of camaraderie.

At FitTech Solutions, they understand that well-being and work-life balance are crucial factors contributing to employee performance and satisfaction.

To promote health and wellness, they have instituted the "FitRewards" program. This initiative encourages employees to maintain a healthy lifestyle by participating in fitness challenges, tracking their physical activities, and achieving specific health goals. As employees hit milestones or demonstrate exceptional commitment to their fitness journey, they earn reward points that can be redeemed for various incentives like gym memberships, wellness retreats, or even personal training sessions.

Recognizing that personal growth and learning are integral to employee development, FitTech Solutions has established a distinct initiative called the "Innovation Incubator." This program invites employees to submit their ideas for innovative products, processes, or services. The selected projects receive not only dedicated resources and mentorship but also the opportunity to present their initiatives to top executives and potential investors. The company provides a platform for employees to grow and showcase their entrepreneurial skills, with exceptional contributors often being offered leadership opportunities or promotions.

To foster a sense of belonging and teamwork, FitTech Solutions values collaboration and peer recognition. They organize periodic "Collaboration Challenges" where cross-functional teams work together to solve complex problems or achieve ambitious goals. The winning team receives recognition, often including a team outing or a donation to a charity of their choice. This approach not only fosters collaboration but also enhances the company's overall performance by leveraging the collective intelligence and diverse skill sets of their employees.

In addition to these programs, FitTech Solutions understands the importance of celebrating achievements and milestones. They hold an annual company-wide event called the "Achievement Awards Gala," where employees are honored for their outstanding contributions and recognized in front of their peers and industry professionals. This glamorous event serves as a testament to the company's commitment to appreciating and rewarding their employees' efforts.

FitTech Solutions' creative and thoughtful initiatives such as FitRewards, Innovation Incubator, Collaboration Challenges, and the Achievement Awards Gala have positioned them as a company that truly cares about its employees' well-being, growth, and recognition. Through their creative approach to rewards and performance recognition, they have succeeded in fostering a motivated and engaged workforce that consistently drives improved performance and demonstrates a strong sense of pride in being part of FitTech Solutions' journey.

By adopting similar strategies that emphasize employee well-being, personal growth, collaboration, and recognition, leaders can create a thriving work environment where employees feel valued, motivated, and empowered to contribute their best to the organization's success.

Recognition and rewards are powerful tools in engaging employees and enhancing their performance. Whether through verbal praise, public recognition events, tangible rewards, or personalized gestures, leaders have the opportunity to create an environment where individuals feel valued, motivated, and inspired to achieve great results. By incorporating recognition and rewards into their leadership style, leaders can build stronger relationships and truly unleash the potential of their teams.

Now that you have read about the importance of recognition and rewards in engaging employees and enhancing their performance, let's take a look at the checklist I have created to help you effectively implement these strategies in your organization.

> *"People may forget what you said, but they will never forget how you made them feel."*
>
> *- Maya Angelou*

CHECKLIST

Checklist for Recognition and Rewards:

- Determine the purpose: Clearly define the objective of the recognition and rewards program. Is it to boost morale, motivate employees, or celebrate exceptional performance?

- Set a budget: Determine the resources available for the recognition and rewards program. Consider allocating funds for tangible rewards, events, or personalized gestures.

- Define the criteria: Decide on the criteria for recognition and rewards. Will it be based on individual achievements, team efforts, or a combination of both? Make sure the criteria are fair and transparent.

- Establish a process: Create a system for identifying and selecting individuals or teams deserving of recognition and rewards. This could involve regular performance evaluations, feedback from supervisors or peers, or nominations from employees.

- Plan for verbal praise: Encourage leaders to regularly acknowledge and appreciate employees through verbal praise and thank-you messages. Provide training or guidelines on effective communication and recognition techniques.

- Organize public recognition events: Determine the frequency and format of public recognition ceremonies or events. Consider involving employees in the planning process to build excitement and engagement.

- Think about tangible rewards: Research and decide on tangible rewards that align with the company's values and employee preferences. Consider options such as gift cards, extra vacation days, professional development opportunities, or other incentives.

- Personalize the rewards: Encourage leaders to understand individual interests and preferences to tailor rewards. Consider conducting surveys or one-on-one conversations to gather information and ideas.

- Communicate the program: Clearly communicate the recognition and rewards program to all employees. Share the criteria, process, and expectations. Provide regular updates on program achievements and recipients.

- Evaluate and adjust: Regularly assess the effectiveness of the recognition and rewards program. Collect feedback from employees and leaders to identify areas for improvement or adjustment.

- Celebrate success: Celebrate individual and team achievements throughout the program. Share success stories and promote a positive work environment where everyone feels valued and motivated.

- Continuously improve: Regularly review and update the recognition and rewards program based on feedback, changing needs, and emerging best practices. Keep the program dynamic and engaging for long-term success.

Now that we have gone through the preparations checklist for recognition and rewards, let's dive into some examples that illustrate how these steps can be implemented in a real-life context.

"Gratitude is not only the greatest of virtues but the parent of all others."

- Marcus Tullius Cicero

EXAMPLES

While FitTech has mastered the art of understanding how to give rewards and recognition that is valued by their employees, you can learn how to as well. Here are several examples to illustrate how this can be done.

Verbal praise and appreciation: A manager takes the time during team meetings to acknowledge and personally thank individual team members for their outstanding efforts and contributions. This boosts their morale and motivation, leading to increased engagement and improved performance.

Public recognition ceremonies: A company holds an annual awards ceremony where exceptional employees are recognized and rewarded for their achievements. This not only celebrates individual successes but also inspires others to strive for excellence, fostering healthy competition and growth within the organization.

Tangible rewards: A company implements a rewards program where employees who meet or exceed their performance targets are eligible for incentives such as gift cards, extra vacation days, or opportunities for professional development. This motivates employees to go the extra mile and helps enhance job satisfaction and performance.

Personalized rewards: A team leader takes the time to understand the individual preferences and interests of team members. In recognition of a job well done, the leader surprises an employee who loves photography with a personalized camera as a reward. This gesture shows that the leader values the employee on a personal level and strengthens their relationship, leading to increased engagement and improved performance.

Peer-to-peer recognition: A company establishes a program where employees can nominate their peers for outstanding performance or going above and beyond their responsibilities. These nominations are then publicly recognized and rewarded, fostering a culture of appreciating and valuing each other's contributions.

Milestone celebrations: A team completes a challenging project successfully. The team leader organizes a celebration event where the achievements are highlighted and team members are recognized for their hard work and dedication. This not only boosts morale but also strengthens the bond between team members, motivating them to continue performing at a high level.

By implementing these various forms of recognition and rewards, leaders can create a positive work environment where employees feel appreciated, valued, and motivated to achieve their goals.

Now that we have explored these examples, let's explore some common mistakes to avoid when implementing similar initiatives.

> *"There is more hunger for love and appreciation in this world than for bread."*
>
> — *Mother Teresa*

TYPICAL MISTAKES AND HOW TO AVOID THEM

One mistake that most people make in the area of recognition and rewards is not taking the time to provide verbal praise and appreciation or wait until the year-end performance review. Many leaders may overlook the power of acknowledging their employees' hard work and outstanding achievements throughout the year. To avoid this mistake, leaders should make it a priority to personally thank and acknowledge their employees for their efforts regularly. Taking the time to show appreciation can have a significant impact on employee engagement and motivation.

Another mistake is not organizing public recognition ceremonies or events to celebrate exceptional employees. By neglecting to highlight individual achievements, leaders miss out on the opportunity to inspire others to go above and beyond. To avoid this mistake, leaders should consider organizing awards ceremonies or events that not only celebrate outstanding employees but also encourage healthy competition and growth within the team.

Additionally, not implementing tangible rewards programs is another common mistake. Tangible rewards, such as gift cards, extra vacation days, or opportunities for professional development, can motivate employees to strive for excellence. By not offering these incentives, leaders miss out on the chance to enhance job satisfaction and performance. To avoid this mistake, leaders should consider implementing rewards programs that provide tangible benefits to their employees.

Lastly, leaders often fail to consider personalized rewards that align with their employees' interests and preferences. Tailoring rewards to match an individual's interests, such as tickets to a sports event or a coveted book, shows that leaders understand and appreciate their employees on a personal level. By neglecting this aspect, leaders miss out on fostering stronger relationships with their employees and ultimately reducing engagement and performance. To avoid this mistake, leaders should take the time to understand their employees' preferences and use that knowledge to choose meaningful and personalized rewards.

By avoiding these mistakes and incorporating recognition and rewards into their leadership style, leaders can create an environment where employees feel valued, motivated, and inspired to achieve great results. It is important for leaders to prioritize verbal praise, organize public recognition events, implement tangible rewards programs, and offer personalized gestures to truly unleash the potential of their teams.

MY #1 PIECE OF ADVICE

With these mistakes to avoid in mind, it is crucial for leaders to remember my #1 piece of advice: be genuine and specific when giving recognition and rewards that are meaningful to the recipients to improve performance.

> *"Appreciation can make a day, even change a life. Your willingness to put it into words is all that is necessary."*
>
> *- Margaret Cousins*

SUMMARY:

- Recognizing and rewarding employees is crucial for enhancing their performance and creating a positive work environment.

- Verbal praise and personal appreciation are simple yet effective ways to show employees that their hard work is valued and appreciated.

- Organizing public recognition ceremonies or events not only celebrates exceptional employees, but also inspires others to strive for greatness.

- Implementing tangible rewards, such as gift cards or extra vacation days, can motivate employees to go above and beyond in their work.

- Personalized rewards that align with employees' interests and values demonstrate a deeper level of appreciation, fostering stronger relationships and increased engagement.

APPLICATION QUESTIONS

- When considering different reward options, how can you ensure that they are not only financially sustainable for the company but also meaningful and valuable to employees?

- What measures do you take to ensure fairness and transparency in the reward system, especially when multiple employees contribute to a collective improvement in performance?

- In what ways can you involve employees more in the decision-making process when it comes to designing or modifying the rewards and recognition program ensuring that you accommodate diverse employee preferences or cater to different generations within your workforce?

- How do you encourage peer-to-peer recognition and incorporate it into your reward strategy to create a positive and supportive work culture?

- What measures do you take to ensure that your reward system is fair and transparent, eliminating any biases or favoritism that could potentially demotivate employees?

QUIZ

1. What is one easy, practical way that leaders can provide recognition?

    A. Through tangible rewards
    B. Through public recognition ceremonies
    C. Through verbal praise and personal appreciation
    D. Through personalized rewards

2. What impact does verbal praise have on employee engagement and motivation?

    A. It demonstrates that their efforts have gone unnoticed
    B. It builds relationships and fosters a sense of connection
    C. It creates a negative work environment
    D. It decreases morale

3. What type of recognition can inspire a sense of pride and boost morale?

A. Public recognition ceremonies

B. Verbal praise

C. Personalized rewards

D. All of the above

4. Why are personalized rewards effective in engaging employees?

A. They demonstrate that the leader understands and appreciates the employee on a personal level

B. They motivate individuals to strive for excellence

C. They foster a sense of connection

D. They create an environment where individuals feel valued

5. How can leaders incorporate recognition and rewards into their personal leadership style?

A. Through verbal praise and public recognition ceremonies

B. Through verbal praise and personalized gestures

C. Through public recognition events and tangible rewards

D. Through verbal praise and personalized rewards

Answer Key:

1. C - Through verbal praise and personal appreciation

2. B - It builds relationships and fosters a sense of connection

3. D - All of the above

4. A - They demonstrate that the leader understands and appreciates the employee on a personal level

5. B - Through verbal praise and personalized gestures

Recognizing and rewarding employees is essential for engaging them and boosting their performance. Now, let's shift our focus to managing resistance to change when introducing new initiatives to improve efficiency and engagement, as this is another crucial aspect in creating a thriving and adaptable work environment. Keep reading to discover valuable insights and practical tips on this topic.

CHAPTER 21

EMBRACING CHANGE

LEADERS' WINNING STRATEGIES TO OVERCOME RESISTANCE AND DRIVE EFFICIENCY AND ENGAGEMENT

"Change is inevitable. Growth is optional."

- John C. Maxwell

AT A GLANCE

Five Essential Points for Winning Strategies to Overcome Resistance to Change

- Discover the key insights and tips for managing and overcoming resistance to change, and transform your organization's efficiency and engagement.

- Paint a vivid picture of how implementing new processes and initiatives can positively impact both the organization and the individuals within it.

- Involve employees from the start, empowering them to take ownership of the change and acknowledge their expertise and contributions.

- Address concerns empathetically, providing reassurance, support, and potential solutions. Dissolve resistance and build trust.

- Connect emotionally with personal stories of successful change, inspiring individuals to embrace new processes and initiatives wholeheartedly.

Five Questions Business Leaders Should Ask About Winning Strategies to Overcome Resistance to Change

- What are some common reasons why employees may resist changes within the workplace? How do you identify and address these reasons to ensure a smooth transition?

- What steps do you take to ensure that your team feels empowered and motivated to embrace new initiatives or changes? How do you communicate the benefits and encourage their active involvement?

- What are the main factors that contribute to resistance within your team or organization? And how do you prioritize and tackle those issues to drive better efficiency and engagement?

- What strategies do you employ to create a supportive and inclusive culture that encourages employees to voice their concerns or fears regarding changes?

- What initiatives or approaches are you considering to proactively address resistance to change and create a more adaptable and responsive workplace culture? How do you plan to measure the success of these efforts?

When it comes to managing or overcoming resistance to change, particularly in the context of implementing new processes or initiatives aimed at improving efficiency and engagement, there are several valuable insights and actionable tips that can make a significant difference.

First and foremost, it is crucial to clearly communicate the purpose and benefits of the change to all stakeholders involved. Paint a vivid picture of how implementing these new processes or initiatives will positively impact not only the organization but also each individual within it. By highlighting the connection between the desired outcomes and the personal interests or aspirations of employees, you can effectively build buy-in and motivation.

Next, it is important to involve employees from the early stages of the change process. By providing opportunities for their input, collaboration, and participation, you not only acknowledge their expertise and contributions but also empower them to take ownership of the change. Let them know that their opinions and ideas matter and that their feedback is crucial for success. Such engagement not only helps to identify potential barriers but also facilitates a sense of ownership, which significantly reduces resistance.

Another effective approach to manage resistance is to anticipate and address concerns proactively. Actively listen to the fears, doubts, and anxieties expressed by employees and acknowledge them empathetically. By doing so, you demonstrate that you value their perspective and understand their concerns. Address these concerns openly and honestly, highlighting the potential solutions and benefits that will address them. By providing reassurance and support, you can gradually dissolve resistance.

Building strong relationships is also paramount in overcoming resistance. Take the time to understand your team members on a personal level, learn about their aspirations, and recognize their accomplishments. By focusing on relationship-building, you establish trust and respect, which are essential for overcoming resistance. When employees feel valued and supported, they are more likely to embrace and adapt to change.

Additionally, consider leveraging personal anecdotes or stories to inspire action. Share examples of individuals or teams who successfully navigated similar changes and the positive outcomes they achieved. Personal stories create an emotional connection, allowing individuals to visualize themselves succeeding in the face of change. They provide hope, inspiration, and motivation to overcome resistance and embrace new processes or initiatives wholeheartedly.

Finally, it is vital to provide ongoing support and resources to navigate the change effectively. Offer training programs, mentorship, or coaching that equips employees with the necessary skills and knowledge to adapt successfully. Encourage continuous learning and provide a safe space for experimentation and risk-taking. By fostering a learning-oriented environment, you instill confidence and build resilience, ensuring that individuals are well-prepared to overcome any resistance they may encounter along the way.

When it comes to companies that have successfully overcome resistance to change, IBM stands out as a prominent example. Throughout its long history, IBM has demonstrated its ability to adapt and reinvent itself in response to evolving market dynamics, emerging technologies, and shifting customer needs.

One notable instance of IBM's successful change management occurred in the 1990s. At that time, IBM faced immense resistance as the technology landscape shifted towards open-source software, posing a significant threat to its dominant position in proprietary computing. Rather than clinging to outdated practices, IBM made a strategic decision to embrace open-source technology, including Linux.

To overcome internal resistance to this shift, IBM implemented a well-structured change management program. They focused on employee engagement, providing training, resources, and support to help their employees understand the benefits of open-source software. IBM also created an open and collaborative environment, encouraging dialogue and idea-sharing among employees.

Furthermore, IBM engaged external communities and partners, actively participating in open-source development projects. By collaborating with the Linux community and contributing to the evolution of the platform, IBM showcased its commitment to change and demonstrated that open-source technology could be beneficial to both the company and its customers.

IBM's openness to change and its successful integration of open-source software not only transformed the company's internal operations, but it also enabled them to offer innovative solutions to their customers. This strategic pivot played a significant role in revitalizing IBM's business and solidifying its position as a leader in the technology industry.

IBM's example highlights the importance of embracing change, fostering employee engagement, and actively engaging with external communities when overcoming resistance. By leveraging effective change management strategies, businesses can adapt, thrive, and remain at the forefront of their respective industries.

Managing or overcoming resistance to change requires a combination of effective communication, employee involvement, proactive concern addressing, relationship-building, and ongoing support. By implementing these insights and tips in your change management approach, you can help individuals accept and adapt to new processes or initiatives, ultimately improving efficiency and engagement. Remember, change is not just a task to complete; it is an opportunity to transform and grow. Embrace it with confidence and enthusiasm, and inspire others to do the same.

Now that you have gained valuable insights and tips on managing and overcoming resistance to change, it's time to put them into action with the help of our checklist. This checklist will guide you through the necessary steps to effectively implement these strategies and ensure a smooth transition.

> *"Change is the law of life. And those who look only to the past or present are certain to miss the future."*
>
> *- John F. Kennedy*

CHECKLIST:

Checklist for Overcome Resistance to Change

- Clearly communicate the purpose and benefits of the change to all stakeholders involved.
- Paint a vivid picture of how implementing the new processes or initiatives will positively impact the organization and each individual within it.
- Involve employees from the early stages of the change process.
- Provide opportunities for employee input, collaboration, and participation.
- Acknowledge and address the fears, doubts, and anxieties expressed by employees.
- Actively listen and empathize with employee concerns.
- Highlight potential solutions and benefits that will address employee concerns.
- Build strong relationships with team members on a personal level.
- Understand their aspirations and recognize their accomplishments.
- Focus on relationship-building to establish trust and respect.
- Leverage personal anecdotes or stories to inspire action.
- Share examples of individuals or teams who successfully navigated similar changes.

- Provide ongoing support and resources to navigate the change effectively.

- Offer training programs, mentorship, or coaching to equip employees with necessary skills and knowledge.

- Encourage continuous learning and provide a safe space for experimentation and risk-taking.

- Foster a learning-oriented environment to instill confidence and build resilience.

- Implement effective communication strategies throughout the change management approach.

- Maintain enthusiasm and inspire others to embrace and adapt to change.

- Continuously evaluate and reassess the progress of the change initiative.

- Make adjustments or modifications to address any remaining resistance.

Now that we have gone through the checklist, let's take a look at some examples I have prepared to illustrate how these strategies can be implemented in a real-life scenario. These examples will showcase the importance of effective communication, employee involvement, addressing concerns, building relationships, providing support and resources, fostering a learning-oriented environment, implementing communication strategies, maintaining enthusiasm, and continuously evaluating progress in successfully managing change.

"It is not the strongest or the most intelligent who will survive but those who can best manage change."

- Charles Darwin

EXAMPLES

Implementing a new customer relationship management (CRM) system: The project manager effectively communicates to the sales team how this new system will streamline their sales processes and allow them to better track and manage customer interactions. By highlighting the personal benefits, such as increased productivity and improved customer satisfaction, the sales team becomes motivated and invested in the change.

Introducing a new employee wellness program: The HR department invites employees to provide input and suggestions on what they would like to see in the program. By involving employees from the beginning, the company shows that their opinions are valued and taken into consideration. This builds a sense of ownership and reduces resistance to the change.

Implementing a new performance management system. During town hall meetings, employees express concerns about how this change might affect their job security or compensation. The management team actively listens to these concerns and addresses them by explaining how the new system will provide greater transparency and opportunities for growth. By acknowledging fears and providing reassurance, resistance is gradually dissolved.

Implementing a new safety protocol at a manufacturing plant: The plant manager takes the time to meet individually with each employee to understand their personal experiences and safety concerns. By showing genuine care and concern, the manager builds trust and rapport, making it easier for employees to accept and embrace the new safety measures.

Implementing a company-wide sustainability initiative. The CEO shares personal stories of successful sustainability efforts from other companies in the industry. These stories create an emotional connection and inspire employees to envision their own contribution to the initiative. The personal anecdotes provide hope, inspiration, and motivation to overcome resistance and embrace the new sustainability practices.

Introducing a new Agile project management methodology: Alongside training programs, the company encourages continuous learning and provides a safe space for experimentation and risk-taking. By promoting a learning-oriented environment, employees feel confident and equipped to overcome any resistance they may encounter during the transition to Agile.

These examples illustrate different approaches to managing resistance to change in various organizational contexts. Each example highlights the importance of effective communication, employee involvement, proactive concern addressing, relationship-building, storytelling, and ongoing support in overcoming resistance and successfully implementing changes.

These examples serve as valuable illustrations of the strategies and techniques that can be used to manage resistance to change. Now, let's delve into some key mistakes to avoid.

> *"The only one who likes change is a wet baby."*
>
> **Mark Twain**

TYPICAL MISTAKES AND HOW TO AVOID THEM

Most people make mistakes when it comes to managing resistance to change because they fail to effectively communicate the purpose and benefits of the change. To avoid this mistake, it is crucial to clearly explain how the new processes or initiatives will positively impact both the organization and individuals. By showing employees how their personal interests and aspirations align with the desired outcomes, you can build buy-in and motivation.

Another common mistake is not involving employees from the early stages of the change process. To avoid this, provide opportunities for their input, collaboration, and participation. Recognize their expertise and contributions, and empower them to take ownership of the change. Let them know that their opinions and ideas matter, and that their feedback is crucial for success. This engagement helps to identify potential barriers and fosters a sense of ownership, which reduces resistance.

A proactive approach to managing resistance is also important. Actively listen to employees' fears, doubts, and anxieties about the change, and acknowledge them empathetically. Show that you understand their concerns and address them openly and honestly. Highlight potential solutions and benefits that will address the concerns. By providing reassurance and support, you can gradually dissolve resistance.

Building strong relationships with your team members is paramount in overcoming resistance. Take the time to understand them on a personal level, learn about their aspirations, and recognize their accomplishments. By focusing on relationship-building, you establish trust and respect, which are essential for overcoming resistance. When employees feel valued and supported, they are more likely to embrace change.

Consider leveraging personal anecdotes or stories to inspire action. Share examples of individuals or teams who successfully navigated similar changes and achieved positive outcomes. Personal stories create an emotional connection and allow individuals to visualize themselves succeeding in the face of change. They provide hope, inspiration, and motivation to overcome resistance and embrace new processes or initiatives wholeheartedly.

Lastly, providing ongoing support and resources for employees to navigate the change effectively is vital. Offer training programs, mentorship, or coaching that equips employees with the necessary skills and knowledge to adapt successfully. Encourage continuous learning and provide a safe space for experimentation and risk-taking. By fostering a learning-oriented environment, you instill confidence and build resilience.

In conclusion, managing resistance to change requires effective communication, employee involvement, proactive concern addressing, relationship-building, storytelling, and ongoing support. By implementing these strategies, you can help individuals accept and adapt to change, leading to improved efficiency and engagement. Embrace change with confidence and enthusiasm, and inspire others to do the same.

MY #1 PIECE OF ADVICE

Now that we have discussed the common mistakes to avoid when managing resistance to change, it is important I share the number one piece of advice to overcome these challenges and ensure successful change management. My #1 advice to you is to foster open and honest communication to gain trust and understanding, enabling you to effectively address concerns and fears, and encourage buy-in and collaboration.

> *"The measure of intelligence is the ability to change."*
>
> *- Albert Einstein*

SUMMARY

- Clearly communicate the purpose and benefits of the change, painting a vivid picture of how it will positively impact the organization and each individual within it.

- Involve employees from the early stages of the change process, acknowledging their expertise and empowering them to take ownership. Let them know their opinions and ideas matter for success.

- Proactively address concerns by actively listening to employees and empathetically acknowledging their fears and doubts. Provide reassurance and support, highlighting potential solutions and benefits.

- Build strong relationships with your team members, taking the time to understand their aspirations and recognize their accomplishments. Focus on trust and respect to overcome resistance.

- Share personal anecdotes or stories of successful change navigation to inspire action. Create an emotional connection and provide hope, motivation, and inspiration to embrace new processes or initiatives wholeheartedly.

APPLICATION QUESTIONS

- Have you observed any specific areas within your organization where resistance to change seems to be more prevalent? How do you think you can address these challenges head-on?

- How can you create a more transparent and open dialogue within your organization to help employees understand the rationale behind changes and alleviate resistance?

- What kind of support and resources do your employees need to embrace change with confidence and enthusiasm?

- How can you effectively communicate the positive impact that change will have on your customers or clients, showcasing the value it will bring to them?

- What specific actions can you take as leaders to demonstrate your commitment to change, build trust, and inspire your team to not only embrace change but also become change agents themselves?

Remember to tailor these questions to your specific organizational context and use your personal stories to make connection and build relationships.

The goal is to spark thoughtful discussions and inspire action toward overcoming resistance to change.

QUIZ:

1. What is an effective way of addressing concerns of employees during a change process?

   A. Demonstrate that their opinions and ideas do not matter

   B. Actively listen to their concerns, fears, and doubts

   C. Cutoff all discussion and push through the change

   D. Ignore their concerns

2. What is an important factor in building buy-in and motivation for a change process?

   A. Provide training programs

   B. Establish trust and respect

   C. Highlight the connection between desired outcomes and personal interests or aspirations of employees

   D. Focus on relationship-building

3. What is an important element in managing or overcoming resistance to change?

   A. Communicate the purpose and value of change early and often

   B. Focus on relationship-building

   C. Provide ongoing support and resources

   D. All of the above

4. How can you build ownership of a change process?

   A. Provide reassurance and support

   B. Demonstrate that their opinions and ideas do not matter

   C. Involve employees from the early stages of the change process

      D. Ignore their concerns

5. What is the most effective approach to managing resistance?

      A. Acknowledge their fears, doubts, and anxieties empathetically

      B. Demonstrate that their opinions and ideas do not matter

      C. Focus on relationship-building

      D. Provide reassurance and support

Answer Key

1. B - Actively listen to their concerns, fears, and doubts

2. C - Highlight the connection between desired outcomes and personal interests or aspirations of employees

3. D - All of the above

4. C - Involve employees from the early stages of the change process

5. D - Provide reassurance and support

Now that we have learned how to manage and overcome resistance to change, let's delve into the equally important topic of striking a balance between efficiency and employee well-being, exploring effective strategies that ensure a harmonious work-life balance. Keep reading to discover practical tips that can transform your workplace into a thriving environment where both productivity and happiness can coexist.

CHAPTER 22

THE POWER OF BALANCE

NURTURING EMPLOYEE WELL-BEING WITHOUT SACRIFICING EFFICIENCY

"Finding balance isn't about dividing your time equally; it's about giving quality attention to all aspects of your life."

- Mary Lou Retton

AT A GLANCE

Five Essential Points for Nurturing Employee Well-Being without Sacrificing Efficiency

- Discover the crucial need for organizations to balance efficiency and employee well-being for long-term success.

- Learn effective strategies to create a positive work culture that prioritizes employee well-being and open communication.

- Explore the benefits of flexible work arrangements, empowering employees to manage their work-life balance.

- Understand the importance of efficient time and resource utilization, setting clear goals and fostering a results-only work environment (ROWE).

- Experience the power of work-life integration, promoting happiness, job satisfaction, and overall well-being.

Five Questions Business Leaders Should Ask About Nurturing Employee Well-Being without Sacrificing Efficiency

- How do you currently balance the need for efficiency and productivity with creating a work environment that fosters employee well-being and satisfaction?

- In your opinion, what are the key factors that contribute to a positive work/life balance for your employees, considering the unique demands and expectations of your industry?

- How can you encourage your employees to prioritize self-care and well-being without compromising their commitment to their roles and responsibilities?

- Are there any potential policies, processes, or workflows within your organization that may hinder work/life balance or unintentionally cause employee burnout? How can you address and improve those areas?

- As a leader, how do you personally prioritize and model self-care and well-being, and how do you encourage your team members to do the same without compromising on their responsibilities and performance?

Balancing efficiency with employee well-being and work-life balance is not just a challenge, but a crucial need for any organization that strives for long-term success. To achieve this delicate balance, there are several effective strategies that can be implemented within a leadership framework.

First and foremost, it is essential to foster a positive work culture that values and prioritizes employee well-being. This can be accomplished by promoting open communication, encouraging regular feedback sessions, and providing opportunities for professional and personal development. By creating a supportive and inclusive environment, leaders can ensure that the overall well-being of their employees is not compromised.

Another vital strategy is the implementation of flexible work arrangements. This approach recognizes that employees have personal commitments and responsibilities outside of work, and it allows them to have control over their schedules. By offering options like flexible hours, remote working, or compressed workweeks, organizations empower their employees to better manage their work-life balance. In return, employees feel trusted and appreciated, resulting in increased loyalty and commitment to the organization.

In addition to flexibility, leaders must also prioritize the efficient utilization of time and resources. By setting clear goals and expectations, providing regular performance feedback, and fostering a results-only work environment (ROWE), employees feel empowered to deliver their best without sacrificing their well-being. Effective delegation and workload management are key components in ensuring efficiency, as it prevents burnout and overload while allowing individuals to focus on their core strengths.

Moreover, promoting work-life integration rather than separation is an evolving trend that has proven to be highly effective. Encouraging employees to blend their personal and professional lives in a harmonious manner can lead to increased job satisfaction and overall happiness. This can be achieved by offering wellness programs, organizing team-building activities, and promoting a healthy work-life balance through various initiatives.

Finally, building strong relationships and trust within the team is paramount in ensuring both efficiency and employee well-being. Leaders should prioritize regular check-ins, one-on-one meetings, and team-building exercises to cultivate a supportive and collaborative work environment. Beyond being approachable and available, leaders should genuinely listen to their employees' concerns and provide personalized support when needed. This approach not only ensures that employees feel valued and heard, but it also enhances productivity and loyalty.

Certainly. Cisco Systems is a company widely recognized for its commitment to nurturing employee well-being while maintaining efficiency. Known for its innovative technology solutions, Cisco has also placed a significant emphasis on creating a supportive and inclusive work environment.

One of the notable ways Cisco prioritizes employee well-being is through its "Work Your Way" program. This initiative allows employees to choose from various work options, including remote work, flexible hours, and job-sharing arrangements. By providing such flexibility, Cisco acknowledges the diverse needs of its workforce, enabling employees to balance personal commitments with their professional responsibilities effectively. This approach has not only increased employee satisfaction but has also been instrumental in attracting and retaining top talent.

Recognizing the importance of mental well-being, Cisco has implemented comprehensive wellness programs that address both the physical and emotional needs of its employees. Their Employee Assistance Program offers confidential counseling and resources to support mental health. Additionally, Cisco encourages work-life integration by promoting breaks, encouraging employees to unplug from digital devices, and fostering a culture of mindfulness.

What sets Cisco apart is its focus on building meaningful relationships and promoting collaboration among employees. They foster a strong sense of community through various initiatives, such as employee resource groups, mentorship programs, and team-building activities. This emphasis on building relationships creates a positive work environment, where employees feel valued, supported, and connected. As a result, employees are more likely to be engaged, motivated, and efficient in their roles.

Furthermore, Cisco's commitment to employee development is noteworthy. They offer ample opportunities for learning and growth, including extensive training programs, certifications, and skill-building initiatives. By investing in the personal and professional development of their employees, Cisco creates a culture that fosters continuous learning and inspires innovation.

Cisco exemplifies a company that successfully prioritizes employee well-being without sacrificing efficiency. Through initiatives like "Work Your Way," comprehensive wellness programs, relationship-building efforts, and a strong focus on employee development, Cisco has created an environment where employees are encouraged to bring their best selves to work, resulting in increased productivity and overall business success.

By implementing strategies such as fostering a positive work culture, offering flexible work arrangements, prioritizing efficiency, promoting work-life integration, and building strong relationships, leaders can successfully balance the need for efficiency with the need for employee well-being and work-life balance. Remember, creating a conducive environment that values both productivity and personal well-being is not only beneficial to individual employees, but it also contributes to the overall success of the organization.

Now that you have read about the effective strategies for balancing efficiency with employee well-being and work-life balance, let's take a look at a checklist I have created to help you implement these strategies within your organization.

"Well-being is not a luxury; it's an essential foundation for a fulfilling life."

- Deepak Chopra

CHECKLIST

Checklist for Nurturing Employee Well-Being without Sacrificing Efficiency:

- Foster a positive work culture: Promote open communication by encouraging regular feedback sessions. Create opportunities for professional and personal development. Prioritize employee well-being and create a supportive and inclusive environment.

- Implement flexible work arrangements: Offer options like flexible hours, remote working, or compressed workweeks. Empower employees to have control over their schedules and manage their work-life balance. Build trust and appreciation by accommodating personal commitments and responsibilities.

- Prioritize efficiency: Set clear goals and expectations for employees. Provide regular performance feedback and foster a results-only work environment (ROWE). Delegate tasks effectively and manage workloads to prevent burnout and overload.

- Promote work-life integration: Encourage employees to blend their personal and professional lives harmoniously. Offer wellness programs, organize team-building activities, and promote a healthy work-life balance. Enhance job satisfaction and overall happiness by supporting work-life integration.

- Build strong relationships and trust within the team: Prioritize regular check-ins, one-on-one meetings, and team-building exercises. Cultivate a supportive and collaborative work environment. Listen actively to employees' concerns and provide personalized support when needed.

By following these action steps, leaders can successfully balance efficiency with employee well-being and work-life balance, ultimately contributing to the long-term success of the organization.

Now that we have explored the checklist for balancing efficiency with employee well-being and work-life balance, let's take a look at some examples that illustrate how these strategies can be implemented in a real-life workplace setting.

> *"The key to a fulfilling life lies in finding the delicate balance between work and leisure."*

EXAMPLES

Although not all of us are able to create programs on the scale of Cisco, any one of us can start small and build on the principles discussed in this chapter. Here are some examples of how to do that.

At a call center, the leadership team created an open-door policy and encouraged employees to voice their concerns and ideas. They also implemented regular feedback sessions where managers and employees could have open discussions about their workload, responsibilities, and well-being. This helped create a positive work culture that prioritized employee well-being and ensured that their needs were being addressed.

An engineering firm recognized the importance of flexible work arrangements for their employees. They introduced a policy that allowed employees to choose their work hours as long as they met their weekly targets. This gave employees the freedom to manage their work-life balance according to their personal commitments and resulted in increased job satisfaction and loyalty.

At an accounting firm, leaders focused on efficiency by setting clear goals and expectations for their employees. They regularly provided performance feedback and recognized and rewarded achievements. This helped employees prioritize their tasks, manage their time effectively, and deliver high-quality work without feeling overwhelmed or sacrificing their well-being.

A small non-profit encouraged work-life integration by organizing wellness programs and team-building activities. They hosted regular yoga classes, provided healthy snacks in the office, and organized team outings and retreats. This allowed employees to prioritize their mental and physical health while also fostering strong relationships within the team.

In a business services company, leaders prioritized building strong relationships and trust within the team. They scheduled regular check-ins and one-on-one meetings with employees to address their concerns and provide personalized support. This created a supportive and collaborative work environment where employees felt valued, heard, and motivated to perform their best.

Overall, these examples illustrate the different strategies organizations can implement to balance efficiency with employee well-being and work-life balance. By combining elements of positive work culture, flexible arrangements, efficient time management, work-life integration, and strong relationships, leaders can create an environment that promotes both productivity and personal well-being.

These examples showcase the various approaches that organizations can take to strike a balance between efficiency and employee well-being. Now, let's delve into the mistakes to avoid. These mistakes can hinder the progress of creating a supportive and inclusive work environment and may have a negative impact on employee well-being and productivity. By being aware of these mistakes, organizations can proactively address them and ensure a more successful implementation of work-life balance initiatives.

"Success is not just about climbing the ladder; it's about maintaining balance on each rung."

- Maya Angelou

TYPICAL MISTAKES AND HOW TO AVOID THEM

Based on the material covered here, some common mistakes that most people make in balancing efficiency with employee well-being and work-life balance are:

Neglecting employee well-being: Many organizations focus solely on productivity and overlook the well-being of their employees. This can lead to burnout, decreased motivation, and ultimately, a decrease in overall productivity. To avoid this mistake, it is crucial to prioritize and value employee well-being.

Lack of open communication: Communication plays a vital role in creating a positive work culture. If leaders fail to promote open communication and encourage regular feedback sessions, employees may feel unheard and undervalued. To avoid this, it is important to foster an environment where employees feel comfortable expressing their thoughts and concerns.

Rigid work schedules: Not offering flexible work arrangements can be a mistake that limits the work-life balance of employees. Recognizing that employees have personal commitments outside of work and providing options such as flexible hours, remote working, or compressed workweeks can help employees manage their work-life balance effectively.

Ignoring work-life integration: Rather than separating personal and professional lives, promoting a work-life integration approach can lead to increased job satisfaction and overall happiness. Failure to promote this integration can result in employees feeling overwhelmed and stressed. Offering wellness programs, organizing team-building activities, and promoting a healthy work-life balance can help mitigate this but not replace it.

Lack of trust and collaboration: Building strong relationships and trust within the team is crucial for both efficiency and employee well-being. Neglecting regular check-ins, one-on-one meetings, and team-building exercises can undermine the support and collaboration needed for a positive work environment. Leaders must prioritize creating these relationships to enhance productivity and loyalty.

To avoid these mistakes, leaders should prioritize employee well-being, encourage open communication, offer flexible work arrangements, promote work-life integration, and build strong relationships. By valuing both productivity and personal well-being, organizations can achieve long-term success.

MY #1 PIECE OF ADVICE

Now that we have identified the common mistakes to avoid in balancing efficiency with employee well-being and work-life balance, it is important to keep in mind my number one piece of advice to address these challenges effectively. Make space for your employees' personal lives and needs, providing flexible work arrangements that foster a well-rounded, healthy work-life balance.

"The quality of your being affects the quality of your doing."

- Oprah Winfrey

SUMMARY:

- Foster a positive work culture that values and prioritizes employee well-being. By promoting open communication and providing opportunities for development, we create a supportive environment where everyone can thrive.

- Implement flexible work arrangements to empower employees to manage their work-life balance. Whether it's flexible hours or remote working, giving them control over their schedules builds loyalty and commitment.

- Prioritize efficient utilization of time and resources by setting clear goals and expectations. With effective delegation and workload management, we prevent burnout and allow individuals to focus on their strengths.

- Promote work-life integration for increased job satisfaction and happiness. By offering wellness programs and organizing team-building activities, we encourage a healthy balance between personal and professional lives.

- Build strong relationships and trust within the team through regular check-ins and personalized support. By genuinely listening and being approachable, we create a collaborative work environment that enhances productivity and loyalty. Together, we can achieve both efficiency and well-being for the success of our organization.

APPLICATION QUESTIONS

- How can you create a work environment that encourages flexibility and empowers employees to manage their time effectively, while ensuring that productivity and efficiency remain high?

- How can you foster a sense of community and connection among your employees, so they feel valued, supported, and motivated to contribute their best work?

- What initiatives or programs can you implement to promote work-life integration and prevent burnout, recognizing that a healthy work-life balance leads to increased productivity and employee satisfaction?

- What steps can you take to ensure that your leaders and managers exhibit behaviors that prioritize employee well-being and set an example for the rest of the organization?

- Are there any current policies or practices that may hinder employee well-being or impede efficiency? How can you address and improve them?

QUIZ

1. What is an example of a flexible work arrangement that organizations can offer?

   A. Remote working
   B. Wellness programs
   C. Regular check-ins
   D. Team-building activities

2. What is the purpose of providing employees with flexible work arrangements?

   A. To foster a supportive and inclusive environment
   B. To enhance productivity and loyalty
   C. To allow employees to have control over their schedules
   D. To prevent burnout and overload

3. What is the benefit of fostering a results-only work environment (ROWE)?

   A. To ensure that the overall well-being of employees is not compromised

   B. To recognize that employees have personal commitments and responsibilities outside of work

   C. To empower employees to deliver their best without sacrificing their well-being

   D. To cultivate a supportive and collaborative work environment

4. What is the ultimate goal of balancing efficiency with employee well-being and work-life balance?

   A. To promote open communication

   B. To contribute to the overall success of the organization

   C. To build strong relationships and trust

   D. To encourage regular feedback sessions

5. What is the overall benefit of balancing efficiency with employee well-being and work-life balance?

   A. To recognize that employees have personal commitments and responsibilities outside of work

   B. To foster a supportive and inclusive environment

   C. To empower employees to deliver their best without sacrificing their well-being

   D. To contribute to the overall success of the organization

Answer Key:

1. A - Remote working

2. C - To allow employees to have control over their schedules

3. C - To empower employees to deliver their best without sacrificing their well-being

4. B - To contribute to the overall success of the organization

5. C - To empower employees to deliver their best without sacrificing their well-being

Now that we have explored various efficient strategies for maintaining employee well-being and work-life balance, it is important to delve into how these approaches can be tailored to diverse organizational cultures or industries, ensuring the effectiveness of our initiatives. So, let's continue our journey to discover how to determine the most suitable strategies for different contexts, keeping in mind the ultimate goal of fostering a harmonious work environment. Keep reading to unlock the secrets of successful implementation in any setting.

CHAPTER 23

THE ULTIMATE STRATEGY

CHOOSING THE RIGHT PATH FOR MAXIMUM IMPACT IN YOUR ORGANIZATION OR INDUSTRY

"Culture eats strategy for breakfast."

- Peter Drucker

AT A GLANCE

Five Essential Points for Choosing the Right Path for Maximum Impact

- Unlock the secret to success in different industries and organizational cultures - discover the specific strategies and initiatives that work best for each unique context.

- Dive deep into the core of your organization's culture - learn how understanding its strengths and weaknesses can lead to the perfect strategies that align with your unique values and goals.

- Gain industry-specific knowledge and stay one step ahead of the competition - uncover opportunities and overcome future challenges by understanding market trends, customer preferences, and regulatory landscapes.

- Build strong connections with stakeholders and foster a collaborative approach - discover how open and honest conversations can lead to strategies that are effective and embraced by everyone involved.

- Be flexible and adaptable on your path to success - understand the importance of continuous evaluation, testing, and adjustment to ensure strategies remain responsive to evolving cultural or industry dynamics.

Five Questions Business Leaders Should Ask About Choosing the Right Path for Maximum Impact

- How would you describe your organization's current culture and values? Are there any gaps or areas for improvement regarding employee engagement?

- How do you currently measure or assess employee engagement within your organization? Are there any particular metrics or indicators that you find most valuable?

- Can you think of any industry best practices or success stories from other organizations that resonate with your own company culture? How do you think these approaches could be adapted to suit your specific needs?

- Are there any external factors or trends (e.g., technological advancements, remote work, generational shifts) that you believe need to be taken into consideration when developing employee engagement strategies for your organization?

- How would you define success when it comes to employee engagement? What specific outcomes or improvements do you hope to see as a result of implementing new initiatives or strategies?

Determining which strategies or initiatives will be most effective in different organizational cultures or industries requires a deep understanding of the specific context and challenges that each organization or industry faces. It is essential to consider various factors such as your company's values, goals, core competencies, and market dynamics.

To begin with, conducting a thorough analysis of your organization's existing culture is crucial. This involves evaluating the company's leadership style, communication patterns, decision-making processes, and employee engagement. By assessing the cultural aspects of an organization, we can gain insights into its strengths and weaknesses, enabling us to identify the right strategies that align with its unique culture.

Furthermore, studying the industry landscape is vital in determining effective strategies or initiatives. Understanding the industry's competitive dynamics, market trends, customer preferences, and regulatory environment enables us to identify opportunities and anticipate future challenges. By embracing industry-specific knowledge, we can develop strategies that effectively leverage the organization's resources and capabilities.

In addition to research and analysis, building strong relationships with stakeholders, both internal and external, is crucial. Engaging in open and honest conversations with employees, leaders, customers, suppliers, and partners provides valuable insights into their perspectives, expectations, and needs. This fosters trust and collaboration, allowing for the co-creation of strategies that are not only effective but also accepted and embraced by all relevant stakeholders.

To ensure the effectiveness of strategies or initiatives, piloting or testing them on a small scale is highly advantageous. By implementing strategies in a controlled environment, organizations can gather real-time data, evaluate the impact, and fine-tune the approach before full-scale implementation. This iterative process helps organizations adapt to the unique characteristics of their culture or industry, increasing the chances of success.

Lastly, it is important to remain flexible and adaptable throughout the process. Recognizing that no strategy is set in stone, continuous monitoring and evaluation are essential to gauge the effectiveness of the chosen initiatives. Organizations must be willing to make adjustments and refinements as needed, ensuring that strategies remain responsive to evolving cultural or industry dynamics.

One remarkable company that stands out for effectively choosing strategies and initiatives for employee engagement that are the perfect fit for their organizational culture is Warby Parker. This innovative eyewear retailer has gained recognition not only for its trendy products but also for its employee-centric approach.

Warby Parker understands that engaged employees are the key to delivering exceptional customer experiences. To foster a sense of purpose and alignment, the company ensures that their employees deeply connect with their mission. By providing opportunities for the team members to engage directly with customers and witness the impact they make in helping people see, Warby Parker cultivates a strong sense of pride and motivation among its workforce.

Additionally, Warby Parker values continuous learning and personal growth. They offer a generous stipend to employees specifically allocated for professional development, encouraging them to pursue their passions and expand their skill sets. This commitment to individual advancement empowers employees and demonstrates the company's investment in their long-term success.

Another aspect that sets Warby Parker apart is their focus on creating a vibrant and inclusive work culture. They foster a sense of community and belonging through regular team-building activities, volunteer opportunities, and celebrations. This camaraderie not only enhances employee engagement but also builds strong relationships within the company.

Furthermore, Warby Parker recognizes the importance of work-life balance and supports employees in maintaining it. They offer flexible work arrangements and provide ample time off to rest and recharge. By prioritizing employee well-being, Warby Parker ensures that their employees bring their best selves to work, resulting in higher productivity and satisfaction.

By taking inspiration from Warby Parker's strategies, you can create an engaging work environment aligned with your organizational culture. Focus on connecting employees to a meaningful mission, invest in their development, foster a sense of community, and prioritize work-life balance. By doing so, you can cultivate a highly engaged and motivated workforce that fuels your organization's success. So, why wait? Start implementing these strategies today and witness the transformation within your organization.

Determining the most effective strategies or initiatives in different organizational cultures or industries requires a holistic approach. It involves deep analysis, industry-specific insights, stakeholder engagement, iterative testing, and flexibility. By tailoring strategies to the unique characteristics of an organization's culture or industry, leaders can enhance their effectiveness, drive desired results, and build strong relationships within their organizations.

Now that we have discussed the importance of understanding organizational culture and industry dynamics in developing effective strategies, let's move on to the checklist I have created to help guide you in this process. This checklist will provide you with the key steps to consider when determining the most effective strategies or initiatives for your organization.

> *"The only thing of real importance that leaders do is to create and manage culture. If you do not manage culture, it manages you, and you may not even be aware of the extent to which this is happening."*
>
> *- Edgar Schein*

CHECKLIST

Checklist for Choosing the Right Path for Maximum Impact:

- Conduct a thorough analysis of the organization's existing culture, including evaluating leadership style, communication patterns, decision-making processes, and employee engagement.

- Study the industry landscape, including competitive dynamics, market trends, customer preferences, and regulatory environment.

- Build strong relationships with stakeholders, both internal and external, through open and honest conversations to gain valuable insights into their perspectives, expectations, and needs.

- Pilot or test strategies on a small scale to gather real-time data, evaluate impact, and make necessary adjustments before full-scale implementation.

- Remain flexible and adaptable throughout the process, continuously monitoring and evaluating the effectiveness of chosen initiatives.

- Tailor strategies to the unique characteristics of the organization's culture or industry to enhance their effectiveness and drive desired results.

- Foster trust and collaboration among all relevant stakeholders to co-create strategies that are accepted and embraced by everyone.

- Ensure continuous learning and improvement by making adjustments and refinements to strategies as needed, remaining responsive to evolving cultural or industry dynamics.

By following these action steps, leaders can effectively determine the most appropriate strategies or initiatives for their organization, taking into account the specific context and challenges they face.

Now that we have gone through this comprehensive action steps checklist, let's take a look at some examples I have already prepared to illustrate how these steps can be put into practice.

> *"Culture does not change because we desire to change it. Culture changes when the organization is transformed; the culture reflects the realities of people working together every day."*
>
> *- Frances Hesselbein*

EXAMPLES

Analyzing organizational culture: A technology company wants to implement a new flexible work policy but faces resistance from employees who have been used to a traditional 9-5 office setting. By conducting a thorough analysis of the existing culture, the company discovers that employees value face-to-face collaboration and fear that remote work will hinder their ability to connect and innovate. With this insight, the company develops a strategy that promotes both flexibility and collaboration by introducing hybrid work options and utilizing technology tools to facilitate virtual communication and teamwork.

Studying industry landscape: An airline company wants to increase its market share in a highly competitive industry. Through industry research, they find that customers are increasingly seeking out eco-friendly and sustainable travel options. Armed with this knowledge, the company develops a strategy that focuses on reducing carbon emissions, improving fuel efficiency, and implementing sustainable practices throughout its operations. This strategy not only aligns with market trends but also helps the company differentiate itself from competitors and attract environmentally-conscious customers.

Building strong relationships with stakeholders: A retail company realizes that its website is not effectively converting online visitors into customers. To understand the underlying issues, they engage in conversations with customers, conduct surveys, and analyze user behavior data. Through these interactions, they discover that customers find the website navigation confusing and the checkout process cumbersome. Armed with this feedback, the company works collaboratively with its web development team and customers to redesign the website, making it more user-friendly and improving the overall customer experience.

Piloting or testing initiatives: A healthcare organization wants to improve patient satisfaction scores in its emergency department. Instead of implementing a complete overhaul of processes and policies, it decides to pilot a smaller-scale initiative first. The organization implements a new triage system that involves assigning a dedicated nurse to assess patients upon arrival and prioritize their care based on severity. By testing this initiative in a controlled environment, the organization can gather data on wait times, patient feedback, and overall satisfaction. With this information, they can make informed adjustments to the initiative before rolling it out to the entire emergency department.

Remaining flexible and adaptable: A consulting firm decides to implement a new project management methodology to improve efficiency and client satisfaction. However, they quickly realize that the methodology is not effectively resonating with their employees, who are used to a more hands-on, collaborative approach. Instead of rigidly sticking to the new methodology, the firm listens to employee feedback and adapts it to better suit their working style. By being open to adjustments, the firm ensures that the methodology aligns with the unique characteristics of their culture, resulting in improved employee engagement and successful project outcomes.

These examples provide a glimpse into the importance of analyzing organizational culture, studying the industry landscape, building strong relationships with stakeholders, piloting or testing initiatives, and remaining flexible and adaptable in various business scenarios. It is important to also consider the mistakes that should be avoided when undertaking a similar change process. Now, let's delve into a list of critical mistakes that organizations should steer clear of to ensure the success of their transformation efforts. By being aware of these pitfalls, leaders can navigate the challenges and increase the likelihood of achieving their desired outcomes.

> *"The quality of an organization's culture reflects the quality of its leadership."*
>
> *- Dee Hock*

TYPICAL MISTAKES AND HOW TO AVOID THEM

Neglecting to conduct a thorough analysis of the organization's existing culture. Many people make the mistake of overlooking the importance of understanding their company's culture before implementing strategies or initiatives. By evaluating the leadership style, communication patterns, decision-making processes, and employee engagement within the organization, valuable insights can be gained into its strengths and weaknesses. To avoid this mistake, take the time to thoroughly assess your organization's culture and use the insights gained to align your strategies with the unique characteristics of your culture.

Failing to study the industry landscape. Another common mistake is not taking the time to understand the competitive dynamics, market trends, customer preferences, and regulatory environment within your industry. By embracing industry-specific knowledge, you can identify opportunities and anticipate future challenges, enabling you to develop strategies that effectively leverage your organization's resources and capabilities. To avoid this mistake, invest time in researching and analyzing your industry to ensure that your strategies are well-informed and aligned with the industry's dynamics.

Not building strong relationships with stakeholders. Many people underestimate the importance of engaging in open and honest conversations with stakeholders, both internal and external. By listening to their perspectives, expectations, and needs, you gain valuable insights that can inform your strategies. Building trust and collaboration with stakeholders allows for the co-creation of strategies that are not only effective but also accepted and embraced by all relevant parties. To avoid this mistake, prioritize building strong relationships with your stakeholders and actively seek their input in shaping your strategies.

Failing to pilot or test strategies on a small scale. One mistake that can lead to ineffective strategies is implementing them on a large scale without testing or piloting them first. By starting with a small-scale implementation, you can gather real-time data, evaluate the impact, and make adjustments before full-scale implementation. This iterative process allows your organization to adapt to the unique characteristics of your culture or industry, increasing the chances of success. To avoid this mistake, consider piloting or testing your strategies on a small scale to gather insights and refine your approach before fully committing.

Not remaining flexible and adaptable. Perhaps the most significant mistake is failing to recognize that no strategy is set in stone. Continuous monitoring and evaluation are essential to gauge the effectiveness of your initiatives. Organizations must be willing to make adjustments and refinements as needed, ensuring that strategies remain responsive to evolving cultural or industry dynamics. To avoid this mistake, remain open to feedback, monitor the results of your strategies, and be prepared to make changes when necessary.

To avoid common mistakes when determining effective strategies or initiatives, it is crucial to conduct a thorough analysis of the organizational culture, study the industry landscape, build strong relationships with stakeholders, pilot or test strategies on a small scale, and remain flexible and adaptable throughout the process. By taking a holistic approach and tailoring strategies to the unique characteristics of your culture or industry, you can enhance your effectiveness and drive desired results.

MY #1 PIECE OF ADVICE

In light of these mistakes to avoid, it is essential to keep in mind my #1 piece of advice: Closely examine and evaluate the existing organizational culture before implementing any strategies or initiatives. I cannot emphasizes enough the importance of understanding the various aspects of the organization's culture and using that knowledge to align strategies with its unique characteristics. By doing so, you can enhance the effectiveness of your strategies and increase the likelihood of achieving successful outcomes.

> *"Great companies are built on great cultures."*
>
> *- Arianna Huffington*

SUMMARY:

- Embrace the unique characteristics of your organization or industry, and use them as a foundation for determining effective strategies or initiatives.

- Explore the cultural aspects of your organization to identify its strengths and weaknesses, and align your strategies accordingly.

- Gain industry-specific knowledge to anticipate challenges and seize opportunities in order to develop strategies that leverage your organization's resources effectively.

- Engage in open and honest conversations with stakeholders to co-create strategies that are not only effective but also accepted and embraced by all.

- Remain flexible and adaptable throughout the process, continuously monitoring and evaluating strategies to ensure their responsiveness to evolving cultural or industry dynamics.

APPLICATION QUESTIONS

- How can you leverage your company's mission and values to create initiatives that foster a sense of purpose and connection among your employees?

- In what ways can you encourage your employees to further develop their skills and knowledge? What resources or opportunities can you provide to support their professional growth?

- How can you promote a sense of belonging and community within your organization? What team-building activities, events, or celebrations could positively impact employee engagement?

- How can you prioritize work-life balance and support your employees in achieving it? What flexible work arrangements or wellness initiatives can you implement to enhance employee well-being?

- What steps can you take to create a more inclusive and diverse work culture? How can you ensure that all employees feel valued and have equal opportunities for growth and contribution?

Remember, these questions are designed to spark insightful discussions and help you apply the points discussed here to your specific organizational culture. Feel free to adapt or personalize them further to suit your context and engage in open and meaningful conversations to develop effective employee engagement strategies.

QUIZ

1. What is the first step to determining effective strategies or initiatives in different organizational cultures or industries?

    A. Evaluating the company's values, goals, and core competencies

    B. Analyzing the industry landscape

    C. Engaging in open and honest conversations with stakeholders

    D. Conducting a thorough analysis of the organization's existing culture

2. What is a key benefit of piloting or testing strategies on a small scale?

    A. It increases the chances of success.

    B. It allows for the co-creation of strategies.

    C. It helps organizations adapt to the unique characteristics of their culture or industry.

    D. It fosters trust and collaboration.

3. What is a key factor in ensuring the effectiveness of strategies or initiatives?

    A. Analyzing the industry landscape

    B. Building strong relationships with stakeholders

    C. Recognizing that no strategy is set in stone

    D. Evaluating the company's leadership style

4. What is the purpose of engaging in open and honest conversations with stakeholders?

A. To identify opportunities and anticipate future challenges.

B. To understand the industry's competitive dynamics.

C. To evaluate the impact of strategies.

D. To gain insights into their perspectives, expectations, and needs.

5. What is the main benefit of assessing the cultural aspects of an organization?

A. To gain insights into its strengths and weaknesses.

B. To evaluate the impact of strategies.

C. To understand the industry's competitive dynamics.

D. To foster trust and collaboration.

Answer Key:

1. D - Conducting a thorough analysis of the organization's existing culture

2. C - It helps organizations adapt to the unique characteristics of their culture or industry.

3. C - Recognizing that no strategy is set in stone

4. D - To gain insights into their perspectives, expectations, and needs

5. A - To gain insights into its strengths and weaknesses

As we conclude our exploration into determining effective strategies in different organizational cultures or industries, it is essential to recognize the need for continuous learning and adaptability as we navigate the future of leadership. In the upcoming chapter, we will delve into the emerging trends and developments that hold the promise of creating efficiencies and fostering employee engagement in the ever-evolving landscape of tomorrow. So, keep reading to stay ahead of the game and discover the key to leading with a vision for the future.

CHAPTER 24

THE FUTURE OF LEADERSHIP

EMERGING TRENDS AND THEIR IMPACT ON EFFICIENCY AND ENGAGEMENT

"Change is the law of life. And those who look only to the past or present are certain to miss the future."

- John F. Kennedy

AT A GLANCE

Five Essential Points for the Future of Leadership and Emerging Trends

- Discover how artificial intelligence and automation will revolutionize the workplace, allowing leaders and employees to focus on strategic decision-making and unleash their creative potential.

- Explore the benefits of remote work options and flexible arrangements, enabling leaders to attract top talent from around the globe and unlock higher levels of productivity.

- Learn how prioritizing employee well-being and creating a positive work environment will be key to future leadership success, fostering engagement, and organizational growth.

- Embrace a culture of continuous learning and adaptation, as leaders navigate a rapidly changing world and inspire their teams to constantly upgrade their skills.

- Gain insights into the emerging trends and developments that will shape the future of leadership, and discover how leveraging these trends can drive success in the ever-evolving workplace of tomorrow.

Five Questions Business Leaders Should Ask About the Future of Leadership and Emerging Trends

- How do you foresee the future of leadership evolving, and what steps are you taking to adapt and stay ahead of emerging trends?

- In what ways has the business landscape transformed in recent years, and how do you see it continuing to change in the future?

- How do you encourage collaboration and cross-functional cooperation within your organization, recognizing the importance of diverse perspectives in shaping the future of your leadership team?

- What steps are you taking to attract and retain top talent who possess the skills and mindset needed to drive innovation and lead in a rapidly changing business environment?

- What specific strategies or initiatives you are implementing to ensure your organization is not only ready for the future of leadership but also actively shaping it?

As we look ahead to the future of leadership, there are several emerging trends and developments that will undoubtedly have a significant impact on creating efficiencies and engaging employees in the workplace. These trends are driven by advancements in technology, changes in the workforce demographics, and an increasing focus on employee well-being and fulfillment. Let's explore some of these trends and their potential impact.

One of the key trends that will shape the future of leadership is the integration of artificial intelligence (AI) and automation into the workplace. AI-powered tools and systems will revolutionize routine tasks, allowing leaders to focus more on strategic decision-making and empowering employees to contribute their creative and critical thinking skills. By delegating repetitive and mundane tasks to machines, leaders can create more meaningful and engaging work experiences for their employees. This not only boosts efficiency but also promotes job satisfaction and productivity.

Another trend that will have a significant impact on leadership is the rise of remote and flexible work arrangements. With the advancements in communication technology, more and more organizations are embracing remote work options. Leaders who understand the importance of work-life balance and flexibility are likely to attract and retain top talent in the future. By providing remote work opportunities, leaders can tap into a global talent pool, increase employee engagement, and unlock higher levels of productivity.

In addition to technological advancements, the future of leadership will also be characterized by a shift towards a more human-centric approach. Leaders will be expected to prioritize employee well-being, foster a sense of belonging and inclusion, and create a positive work environment. Organizations that value and invest in their employees' growth and development will thrive in the future. Leaders who focus on building strong relationships with their team members, through regular feedback, coaching, and mentorship, will be better positioned to engage and inspire their employees.

To succeed in the future, leaders must also be adaptive and open to learning. The pace of change will continue to accelerate, and leaders must constantly upgrade their skills and embrace new perspectives. They should stay informed about industry trends, attend conferences and workshops, and actively seek feedback. By demonstrating a commitment to growth and learning, leaders can inspire their team members to do the same and create a culture of continuous improvement.

Although for some this is open for debate, one remarkable example of a company that is often hailed for being ready for the future of leadership and ahead of emerging trends is Amazon. As the e-commerce giant continues to expand its footprint, its success can largely be attributed to its visionary leadership approach.

Amazon's CEO, Jeff Bezos, has been a driving force in shaping the company's culture of innovation, adaptability, and customer obsession. He has emphasized the importance of a long-term perspective, encouraging employees to think in terms of decades rather than quarters. This philosophy allows Amazon to remain agile and pivot quickly in response to evolving market dynamics.

Moreover, Amazon has embraced emerging technologies such as artificial intelligence (AI), cloud computing, and data analytics. The company has leveraged AI and machine learning algorithms to enhance customer personalization, optimize logistics operations, and drive supply chain efficiency. By staying at the forefront of emerging trends, Amazon consistently enhances its customer experience and maintains a competitive edge.

Furthermore, Amazon's commitment to fostering a culture of continuous learning and embracing a growth mindset is noteworthy. The company has established various leadership development programs, such as the Amazon Technical Academy and Amazon Leadership Principles, which focus on cultivating the next generation of leaders and equipping them with the skills and mindset necessary to navigate the future.

Amazon's proactive approach to leadership, embracing emerging trends, and its continuous focus on innovation position it as a prime example of a company ready for the future. By learning from their strategies and practices, businesses can gain valuable insights into how to adapt and thrive in a rapidly changing business landscape.

The future of leadership will be shaped by the integration of AI and automation, the rise of remote work, a focus on employee well-being, and a commitment to continuous learning. By leveraging these emerging trends and developments, leaders can create efficiencies, engage their employees, and drive success in the ever-evolving workplace of the future. Let us embrace these trends, deepen our relationships with our teams, and cultivate the skills needed to thrive in this rapidly changing world.

Now that we have explored the emerging trends and developments that will shape the future of leadership, let's take a closer look at a checklist I have created to help leaders navigate these changes and drive success in the workplace.

> *"A leader who makes fixing an organization's environmental impacts a true priority creates the kind of outfit that tomorrow's young talent will want to work for or be loyal customers and clients for."*
>
> *- Daniel Goleman*

CHECKLIST

Checklist for the Future of Leadership and Emerging Trends:

- Stay informed about emerging trends and developments in leadership, particularly those related to AI and automation, remote work, employee well-being, and continuous learning.
- Understand the potential impact of these trends on creating efficiencies and engaging employees in the workplace.

- Develop a strategic plan for incorporating AI-powered tools and systems into routine tasks, freeing up time for more strategic decision-making and empowering employees.

- Consider implementing remote work options to attract and retain top talent, increase employee engagement, and unlock higher levels of productivity.

- Prioritize employee well-being and create a positive work environment by fostering a sense of belonging and inclusion.

- Invest in employees' growth and development through regular feedback, coaching, and mentorship.

- Stay adaptive and open to learning by continuously upgrading skills, attending conferences and workshops, and seeking feedback.

- Cultivate a culture of continuous improvement within the organization, inspiring team members to embrace growth and learning.

- Deepen relationships with team members by building strong connections through regular communication, feedback, and mentorship.

- Embrace the opportunities provided by these trends, align strategies with the changing workplace, and prepare for the future of leadership.

Now that we've gone through the checklist for effective leadership in the changing workplace of the future, let's take a look at some examples that illustrate these principles in action.

"As leaders, the onus is on us to take actionable and measurable steps toward changing our organizations and our world for the better, even if we start small."

- John Hope Bryant

EXAMPLES

Amazon is such a behemoth is can feel like they are way beyond where you are as a leader and you have no chance of reaching that level. However, let me reassure you, it is possible to make an impact right where you are. Here are several different examples to help how you might implement these ideas:

AI-powered chatbots: A leader in a customer service department integrates an AI-powered chatbot into their workflow. This chatbot handles routine customer inquiries, freeing up the leader's time to focus on strategic decision-making and providing personalized support to their team members. This not only improves efficiency but also allows employees to engage in more meaningful and challenging tasks.

Remote work policies: A leader in a tech company embraces remote work options for their employees. By allowing their team members to work from home or choose flexible work hours, the leader can attract and retain top talent from different geographical locations. This diverse talent pool brings new perspectives and enhances collaboration, leading to increased innovation and productivity.

Employee well-being initiatives: A leader in a healthcare organization recognizes the importance of employee well-being and introduces wellness programs such as meditation classes, stress management workshops, and flexible working hours. By prioritizing their employees' physical and mental health, the leader creates a positive work environment where employees feel supported and valued, resulting in higher job satisfaction and reduced burnout.

Continuous learning culture: A leader in a marketing agency encourages their team members to attend industry conferences, workshops, and online courses to stay updated with the latest trends and developments. The leader actively seeks feedback from their employees and provides coaching and mentoring to help them develop new skills. This commitment to continuous learning fosters a culture of growth and improvement, keeping the team ahead of the competition.

It's important to note that these examples are just a few of the many possibilities that can illustrate the points made about the future of leadership. The specific trends and developments that will impact leadership will vary depending on the industry, organization, and individual leadership style.

Now that we have explored several examples showcasing the potential of future leadership, it is important to recognize the potential pitfalls and mistakes to avoid when implementing these initiatives. Let's delve deeper into how we can navigate these challenges and maximize the benefits of emerging trends in our own organizations. Here are some key mistakes to avoid when embracing the future of teamwork.

> *"We need leaders who believe that creating a more representative workforce within their organizations is a crucial step to cultivating a more equal society."*
>
> *- Wayne A.I. Frederick*

TYPICAL MISTAKES AND HOW TO AVOID THEM

One common mistake that most people make in the area of leadership is not embracing technological advancements. Many leaders may be hesitant to integrate artificial intelligence (AI) and automation into the workplace due to fear of job loss or resistance to change. However, by embracing these advancements, leaders can delegate repetitive tasks to machines and focus more on strategic decision-making. This not only boosts efficiency but also allows employees to contribute their creative and critical thinking skills. To avoid this mistake, leaders should educate themselves about the potential benefits of AI and automation and be open to embracing new tools and systems in their organizations.

Another mistake that people often make in leadership is not recognizing the importance of remote and flexible work arrangements. With advancements in communication technology, remote work options have become more feasible and popular. However, some leaders may still resist or overlook this trend, failing to understand the value of work-life balance and flexibility in attracting and retaining top talent. To avoid this mistake, leaders should acknowledge the benefits of remote work, such as tapping into a global talent pool, increasing employee engagement, and unlocking higher levels of productivity. By providing remote work opportunities, leaders can adapt to the changing workforce dynamics and create a positive work environment.

Furthermore, a common mistake in leadership is neglecting employee well-being and not prioritizing a human-centric approach. In the future, leaders will be expected to foster a sense of belonging and inclusion, create a positive work environment, and invest in their employees' growth and development. Some leaders may overlook the importance of these aspects and focus solely on productivity and results. To avoid this mistake, leaders should prioritize employee well-being, build strong relationships with their team members through regular feedback, coaching, and mentorship, and create a culture of continuous improvement. By valuing and investing in their employees, leaders can foster engagement, inspire their teams, and drive success.

Finally, a mistake that leaders often make is not being adaptive and open to learning. The pace of change is accelerating, and leaders need to continually upgrade their skills and embrace new perspectives. Some leaders may be resistant to change or complacent with their existing knowledge and skills. To avoid this mistake, leaders should stay informed about industry trends, attend conferences and workshops, and actively seek feedback. By demonstrating a commitment to growth and learning, leaders can inspire their team members to do the same and create a culture of continuous improvement.

By avoiding the mistakes of not embracing technological advancements, neglecting remote and flexible work arrangements, overlooking employee well-being, and being resistant to learning, leaders can thrive in the ever-evolving workplace of the future. It is crucial for leaders to embrace these emerging trends, deepen relationships with their teams, and cultivate the skills needed to succeed in this rapidly changing world.

MY #1 PIECE OF ADVICE

Now that we have discussed the common mistakes to avoid in leadership, it is important to share what I believe is the #1 piece of advice to overcome these challenges and excel in the future workplace. My #1 advice for improving leadership skills in envisioning the future of teamwork is to continuously embrace innovation and adaptability.

"The best way to predict the future is to create it."

- Peter Drucker

SUMMARY:

- Embrace the future of leadership by integrating AI and automation into the workplace, empowering your employees to focus on creative and critical thinking skills.

- Attract and retain top talent by offering remote work options, tapping into a global talent pool, and promoting work-life balance and flexibility.

- Prioritize your employees' well-being, foster a sense of belonging and inclusivity, and create a positive work environment to thrive in the evolving workplace of the future.

- Continuously upgrade your skills, stay informed about industry trends, and embrace new perspectives to inspire your team and create a culture of continuous improvement.

- Let's seize the opportunity to leverage these emerging trends, deepen relationships with our teams, and cultivate the skills needed to thrive in this rapidly changing world of leadership. Let's lead the way to a bright future of success and fulfillment in the workplace.

APPLICATION QUESTIONS

- What can you do to get more cross-generational collaboration and currently invisible voices to the table in your decision making and strategy process?

- Does your organization have a clear idea of the values you stand for and promote? As a leader, do you spend enough time reflecting and aligning your own values?

- How can you foster a culture of continuous learning within your organization, ensuring that your team is equipped with the skills and mindset needed to embrace emerging trends and drive innovation?

- What specific actions can you take to encourage collaboration and cross-functional cooperation, recognizing the importance of diverse perspectives in shaping the future of leadership in your organization?

- What steps can you take to empower your team members to become future-ready leaders by providing them with opportunities for growth, mentorship, and personal development?

QUIZ

1. What are some of the key trends that will shape the future of leadership?

   A. Integration of artificial intelligence (AI)
   B. Increase in remote and flexible work arrangements
   C. A shift towards a more human-centric approach
   D. All of the above

2. What is one of the potential impacts of delegating routine tasks to machines?

   A. Increased efficiency
   B. Increased job satisfaction
   C. Increased productivity
   D. All of the above

3. What is one of the benefits of offering remote work opportunities?

   A. Increased employee engagement
   B. Access to a global talent pool
   C. Improved work-life balance
   D. All of the above

4. What is one way leaders can stay informed about industry trends?

   A. Regularly attend conferences and workshops
   B. Read industry publications
   C. Seek feedback
   D. All of the above

5. What type of skills should leaders cultivate in order to thrive in a rapidly changing world?

   A. Adaptability

B. Openness to learning

C. Strategic decision-making

D. All of the above

Answer Key:

1. D - All of the above

2. D - All of the above

3. D - All of the above

4. D - All of the above

5. D - All of the above

As you contemplate the future and the potential impact of emerging trends and developments in leadership on creating efficiencies and engaging employees, it is equally important to consider the invaluable piece of final advice that can elevate leaders to achieve unprecedented success in this regard. Keep reading to discover the one essential piece of advice that will help you navigate the path towards creating efficiencies and fostering engagement like never before.

CHAPTER 25

THE JOURNEY BEGINS

ESSENTIAL ADVICE FOR LEADERS ON CREATING EFFECTIVE AND ENGAGED EMPLOYEES

"A leader is one who knows the way, goes the way, and shows the way."

- John C. Maxwell

AT A GLANCE

Five Essential Points for Creating Effective and Engaged Employees

- Discover the one piece of advice that can propel leaders to unprecedented success in creating efficiencies and engaging their employees.

- Find out why building strong relationships with your team members is crucial for achieving maximum efficiency and productivity.

- Learn how establishing genuine connections can spark creativity and innovation in your organization.

- Uncover the secret to fostering loyalty, dedication, and a sense of belonging among your employees.

- Get practical tips on how to implement this advice and transform your leadership approach, leading to a flourishing organization.

Five Questions Business Leaders Should Ask About Creating Effective and Engaged Employees

- What strategies or initiatives do you believe are essential for creating a sense of purpose and meaning for employees in your workplace?

- What approaches or practices have you found to be most successful in empowering employees to take ownership of their own development and growth?

- When it comes to fostering a diverse and inclusive workforce, what steps or strategies do you believe are essential for you to boost employee engagement and ensuring everyone feels valued and included?

- As a leader, how do you balance the importance of setting clear goals and expectations while still encouraging autonomy and flexibility in your employees, to foster a sense of empowerment and engagement?

- What are some effective ways you are prioritizing work-life balance and employee well-being to cultivate a more engaged and motivated workforce in the years to come?

As an executive coach and trainer who specializes in leadership and organizational effectiveness, I have seen countless leaders aspire to achieve unprecedented success in creating efficiencies and engaging their employees. From my experience, I have learned that one piece of final advice can make all the difference in propelling leaders toward their goals. So, if you are a leader seeking to excel in these areas, here is my unequivocal recommendation for you.

As you may have guessed by now, my final piece of advice to achieve unprecedented success in creating efficiencies and engaging your employees is to prioritize and invest in building strong relationships with your team members. I cannot stress enough the significance of establishing genuine connections and fostering a sense of trust within your organization.

Why is this so crucial, you may ask? Let me explain.

First and foremost, building relationships allows you to better understand the individual strengths, weaknesses, and aspirations of each team member. When you take the time to know your employees on a personal level, you gain valuable insights into their unique talents, enabling you to assign tasks more effectively and delegate responsibilities to the right people. This targeted approach ensures that your team is working at maximum efficiency, with each member playing to their strengths.

Moreover, strong relationships cultivate an environment of open communication and collaboration. When employees feel valued, heard, and respected, they are more likely to actively contribute their ideas and perspectives freely, sparking creativity and innovation within your organization. By inviting diverse opinions and genuinely listening to your team, you create an inclusive culture that celebrates different viewpoints, ultimately leading to higher employee engagement and increased productivity.

Beyond the impacts on efficiency and engagement, establishing meaningful relationships with your team members also fosters loyalty and dedication. People naturally enjoy working with leaders who care about them as individuals, not just as employees. When you invest in building relationships, you demonstrate your commitment to their growth and well-being, which in turn, inspires their loyalty and dedication to achieving collective success. Employees are more likely to go the extra mile when they feel a sense of belonging and a strong emotional connection to their leader and their organization.

Now, you may be wondering how to practically implement this advice in your leadership journey. As I have stated numerous times throughout the book, it begins with small but intentional actions. Start by taking the time to actively listen to your team members during one-on-one conversations, team meetings, or even informal gatherings. Show genuine curiosity about their experiences, challenges, and aspirations. Remember, effective communication goes beyond words – nonverbal cues such as eye contact, body language, and tone of voice convey your sincerity and interest.

Additionally, make it a habit to provide constructive feedback and celebrate accomplishments consistently. Recognize and acknowledge the hard work and contributions of each team member individually and collectively. Simple gestures like a handwritten note or a public acknowledgment in a team meeting can resonate deeply and strengthen the bond between you and your employees.

Lastly, invest in opportunities for team-building activities, both within and outside of the workplace. These activities create environments for colleagues to bond and build trust in a relaxed setting, allowing for personal connections to form. Whether it's a team lunch, a volunteering opportunity, or a fun outing, these events build camaraderie and reinforce the relationships you are cultivating.

Alright, let me share with you an exceptional company that perfectly fits the bill and is widely recognized for being ready to create effective and engaged employees: LinkedIn. This leading professional networking platform not only empowers individuals to find opportunities but also puts tremendous effort into fostering employee engagement and growth.

At LinkedIn, they understand that employees are the driving force behind their success. They have successfully built a culture that values continuous learning, collaboration, and personal development. One remarkable initiative they have implemented is the "Week of Learning," where employees are encouraged to dedicate a week to enhance their skills and acquire new knowledge. This promotes a culture of curiosity, growth, and engagement within the organization.

Another outstanding aspect of LinkedIn's approach is their dedication to employee well-being. They recognize that a happy and healthy workforce significantly contributes to employee engagement and productivity. They provide a range of wellness programs, flexible work arrangements, and initiatives to support work-life balance. By prioritizing employee well-being, LinkedIn ensures that their employees feel supported and energized to perform at their best.

LinkedIn's management also places a strong emphasis on open communication and transparency. They value feedback from their employees and actively seek their input through various channels. This helps create an inclusive and collaborative work environment, where employees' voices are heard, and their contributions are valued. This approach not only fosters engagement but also drives innovation and high-performance within the company.

When it comes to applying LinkedIn's success to your own organization, keep in mind the importance of prioritizing continuous learning and professional development. Encourage your employees to dedicate time to acquire new skills and knowledge that align with their interests and goals. Empower them with resources, learning platforms, and opportunities for growth.

Additionally, foster a culture of well-being by implementing wellness programs, offering flexibility, and supporting work-life balance. Show that you value your employees' holistic well-being, and create an environment where they feel supported and can thrive.

Lastly, emphasize open communication and transparency. Encourage feedback and create channels for employees to share their ideas and perspectives. Actively listen to their input and make them feel heard and valued.

By adopting LinkedIn's approach of prioritizing continuous learning, well-being, and open communication, you can create a future-ready workforce that is not only engaged but also empowered to excel. So, let's ignite that drive for growth and engagement within your organization and create a thriving workplace environment.

If you aspire to achieve unprecedented success in creating efficiencies and engaging your employees, remember to prioritize building strong relationships. By doing so, you will unlock the full potential of your team, foster a culture of innovation and collaboration, and inspire unwavering dedication to shared goals. Take the first step towards transforming your leadership approach and watch as your organization flourishes under your guidance.

Now that you have read the book, it's time to put these principles into action. To help you implement the advice given, I have created a checklist that outlines practical steps you can take to prioritize and invest in building strong relationships with your team members. By following this checklist, you can begin transforming your leadership approach and achieve unprecedented success in creating efficiencies and engaging your employees.

> *"If your actions inspire others to dream more, learn more, do more, and become more, you are a leader."*
>
> *- John Quincy Adams*

CHECKLIST

Checklist for Creating Effective and Engaged Employees:

- Prioritize relationship-building: Recognize the importance of building strong relationships with your team members and make it a priority in your leadership approach.

- Understand individual strengths, weaknesses, and aspirations: Take the time to get to know your team members on a personal level. Understand their unique talents and areas for growth to effectively assign tasks and delegate responsibilities.

- Foster open communication and collaboration: Create an environment of open communication where employees feel valued, heard, and respected. Encourage them to freely contribute their ideas and perspectives, sparking creativity and innovation.

- Celebrate and provide constructive feedback: Consistently recognize and acknowledge the hard work and contributions of each team member. Provide constructive feedback to help them grow and improve.

- Actively listen and show genuine interest: Actively listen to your team members during one-on-one conversations and meetings. Show genuine curiosity about their experiences, challenges, and aspirations. Use nonverbal cues to convey your sincerity and interest.

- Invest in team-building activities: Organize team-building activities within and outside of the workplace. These activities create opportunities for colleagues to bond and build trust in a relaxed setting, allowing for personal connections to form.

- Demonstrate commitment to growth and well-being: Show your commitment to the growth and well-being of your team members.

Invest in their professional development and support their personal goals.

- Be accessible and approachable: Create an environment where team members feel comfortable approaching you with questions, concerns, or ideas. Be accessible and approachable to foster open and trust-based relationships.

- Be authentic and genuine: Be yourself and let your authentic self shine through in your interactions with your team members. Genuine connections are built on authenticity and trust.

- Continuously work on relationship-building: Building strong relationships is an ongoing process. Continuously invest time and effort into strengthening your relationships with your team members.

By working on these areas, you can develop your effectiveness in building strong relationships, fostering employee engagement, and creating efficiencies within the organization.

Now that we have gone through this checklist, let's take a look at some examples that demonstrate how the leader has applied these principles in their interactions with their team members.

> *"Do what you can, with what you have, where you are."*
>
> *- Theodore Roosevelt*

EXAMPLES

Creating personal connection: A CEO of a tech company decides to prioritize building strong relationships with his employees. He starts by scheduling regular one-on-one meetings with each team member to get to know them on a personal level. Through these conversations, he learns that one of his engineers has a strong interest in AI technology. Recognizing this, the CEO assigns the engineer to a project that aligns with his passion and expertise, resulting in a highly efficient and successful outcome.

Impact on communication and collaboration: A manager in a marketing agency focuses on building relationships with her team. She creates an open and inclusive environment where everyone feels comfortable sharing their ideas and perspectives. As a result, team members freely contribute their thoughts during brainstorming sessions, leading to innovative solutions for client projects. The collaborative culture also encourages cross-departmental collaboration, as employees feel empowered to reach out for support or ideas outside of their immediate team.

Fostering loyalty and dedication: The leader of a non-profit organization takes the time to build relationships with his team members. He regularly checks in with them, showing genuine concern for their well-being. In turn, the employees develop a deep sense of loyalty and dedication to the organization's mission. They consistently go above and beyond their job responsibilities, volunteering their time and effort to ensure the organization's success. The strong emotional connection they feel to their leader and the organization drives their commitment to making a difference.

Implementing practical actions: A department manager in a retail company wants to prioritize building relationships with her team. She starts by actively listening to her employees during team meetings, making eye contact, and affirming their ideas. Additionally, she regularly provides constructive feedback, recognizing individual and team accomplishments. To further foster relationships, she organizes a team-building activity once a quarter, such as a department outing or a volunteer day. These actions create a positive and supportive atmosphere, where employees feel valued and motivated to perform their best.

Transformative impact on organizational culture: The CEO of a manufacturing company decides to focus on building relationships with his employees. He encourages open and honest communication, actively seeking feedback and suggestions from all levels of the organization. This shift in culture fosters a sense of trust and empowerment, leading to increased employee engagement and productivity. The company experiences a transformation, with employees feeling a strong emotional connection to their leader and a collective drive to achieve shared goals.

These examples illustrate the positive outcomes that can result from prioritizing relationships in the workplace. Now, let's take a look at some of the mistakes to avoid when embarking on a similar path. These mistakes can serve as a valuable guide for organizations seeking to achieve success through relationship-building initiatives.

> *"Coming together is a beginning; keeping together is progress; working together is success."*
>
> *- Henry Ford*

TYPICAL MISTAKES AND HOW TO AVOID THEM

One mistake that most people make in the area of leadership and organizational effectiveness is not prioritizing and investing in building strong relationships with their team members. This can be avoided by taking small but intentional actions such as actively listening to team members during conversations, showing genuine curiosity about their experiences, challenges, and aspirations, and using nonverbal cues to convey sincerity and interest.

Another mistake is not providing consistent constructive feedback and celebrating accomplishments. This can be avoided by recognizing and acknowledging the hard work and contributions of each team member individually and collectively, using simple gestures like handwritten notes or public acknowledgments.

Lastly, not investing in team-building activities both within and outside of the workplace is a mistake that can be avoided. These activities create environments for colleagues to bond and build trust, allowing for personal connections to form, and can include team lunches, volunteering opportunities, or fun outings.

By avoiding these mistakes and prioritizing building strong relationships, leaders can unlock the full potential of their teams, foster a culture of innovation and collaboration, and inspire dedication to shared goals.

MY #1 PIECE OF ADVICE

To effectively avoid these mistakes and foster a culture of strong relationships, there is one key piece of advice that stands out. Reflect on and identify your own leadership strengths and weaknesses in order to develop a personalized action plan for improvement.

> *"Action is the foundational key to all success."*
>
> *- Pablo Picasso*

SUMMARY:

- Prioritize and invest in building strong relationships with your team members - it's the key to achieving unprecedented success in creating efficiencies and engaging your employees.

- Building relationships allows you to understand your team members' strengths, weaknesses, and aspirations, leading to more effective task assignments and delegation.

- Strong relationships foster open communication and collaboration, creating an inclusive culture that sparks creativity and innovation within your organization.

- Meaningful relationships inspire loyalty and dedication from your team, as they feel valued and cared for as individuals, not just employees.

- Take small but intentional actions, such as actively listening, providing constructive feedback, and organizing team-building activities, to demonstrate your commitment to building strong relationships and watch as your organization flourishes under your guidance.

APPLICATION QUESTIONS

- How can you build strong relationships with your employees and create a sense of trust and loyalty, ultimately ensuring they stick around for the organization's future success?

- How can you authentically demonstrate your vision for the future in order to inspire your employees and keep them engaged?

- What steps can you take to further create a positive and inclusive work environment that celebrates diversity and encourages collaboration among your team members?

- How do you consistently demonstrate your appreciation and recognition for your employees' hard work and contributions to motivate and strengthen their commitment to the team?

- What steps can you take to continuously develop and enhance your own knowledge and skills?

QUIZ

1. What is the primary benefit of building strong relationships with team members?

    A. It creates an environment of open communication and collaboration

    B. It allows for better understanding of individual strengths and weaknesses

    C. It inspires loyalty, trust and dedication to the organization

    D. All of the above

2. What are some practical ways to build relationships with team members?

    A. Investing in opportunities for team-building activities

    B. Taking the time to actively listen to team members

    C. Spending time to learn about the personal and professional goals

    D. All of the above

3. What is the ultimate result of building strong relationships with team members?

    A. Improved efficiency and engagement

    B. Increased loyalty and dedication

    C. Increased creativity and innovation

    D. All of the above

4. What is the main benefit of taking the time to know your employees on a personal level?

    A. It allows for better understanding of individual strengths and weaknesses

    B. It creates an environment of open communication and collaboration

C. It fosters a sense of belonging and a strong emotional connection

D. It sparks creativity and innovation

5. What is NOT a recommendation for leaders seeking to achieve unprecedented success?

    A. Focusing solely on the goal of productivity above all else

    B. Only providing feedback during annual performance reviews

    C. Keeping work and personal lives completely separate

    D. All of the above

Answer Key:

1. D - All of the above

2. D - All of the above

3. D - All of the above

4. A - It allows for better understanding of individual strengths and weaknesses

5. D - All of the above

Now that you have a solid foundation on how to achieve unprecedented success in creating efficiencies and engaging your employees, it's time to Take Action.

UNLEASHING YOUR LEADERSHIP POTENTIAL:
TAKING YOUR SKILLS TO THE NEXT LEVEL

Congratulations. You have completed "The Effective Leader: How to Maximize Engagement and Cultivate a High-Performance Team." By now, you are armed with a treasure trove of practical knowledge, powerful advice, and inspiring examples to revolutionize your leadership style and inspire extraordinary results within your team.

As you close the final chapter of this transformative book, you may be feeling a surge of enthusiasm and eagerness to put your newfound wisdom into action. Well, my friend, let me assure you that this is just the beginning of an exhilarating journey towards becoming an exceptional leader.

Throughout your reading, you delved deep into the art of creating effectiveness and engaging your employees, recognizing that a high-performance team is the cornerstone of any successful organization. You explored strategies to overcome the challenges and obstacles that may arise on your path to greatness.

But remember, knowledge alone will not make you an exceptional leader; it is the consistent implementation of these principles that will truly propel you towards achieving unprecedented success.

Now is the time to transform your intention into action. Take that first courageous step, as this journey begins with you, embracing the responsibilities and possibilities of leadership.

To kickstart your transformation, I urge you to immediately identify your current leadership gaps. Go to **LornaWestonSmyth.com/Resources** to download your Leadership Development Plan Template to capture your gaps and action plan. Reflect on the areas where you feel less confident or where your team may be facing challenges. Perhaps it's communication, delegation, conflict resolution or building trust. Acknowledging these gaps is the first step towards growth.

Once you have identified these areas, shift your focus towards improvement. Seek targeted resources, be it mentorship, further reading, training programs, or workshops, to enhance your skills. Reach out to those who have already mastered the mentioned areas for guidance and mentorship.

But remember, every remarkable leader has a unique approach. The key lies in adapting these lessons and strategies to your own leadership style, aligning them with your values and goals. Authenticity is the secret ingredient to creating a team that resonates with your vision.

As you begin implementing what you have learned, be prepared to witness the ripple effect of your actions. The positive engagement and enhanced performance within your team will create a self-reinforcing cycle of success, inspiring others to reach their full potential.

Go to **LornaWestonSmyth.com/Resources** to download your Leadership Development Plan Template and the recommended reading list now to help you implement what you have learned from this book.

Remember that leadership is an ongoing journey, and continuous self-reflection is paramount. Regularly reassess your progress, celebrating successes and identifying areas for further growth. Embrace feedback as an opportunity for improvement and never stop striving to bring out the absolute best in yourself and your team.

Lastly, don't underestimate the power of genuine connection and open communication. Empathy, active listening, and a willingness to understand and support your team members will foster a culture of trust and collaboration.

Each day presents a new opportunity to challenge yourself, to inspire and be inspired. As you embark on this remarkable leadership journey, know that greatness is not achieved by chance, but through dedicated effort, a hunger for knowledge, and the unwavering commitment to cultivating a high-performance team.

So, seize this moment, my friend, and let the world witness the extraordinary results you are about to achieve. Unleash your leadership potential, and become the catalyst for change in the lives of those around you.

It's time to transform your leadership style and inspire greatness.

Now, go forth and lead with grace, conviction, and unwavering dedication.

Your team is waiting for you.

BECOME THE LEADER YOU WERE MEANT TO BE

Are you looking to take your leadership skills to the next level and achieve unprecedented success for yourself and your team, without feeling overwhelmed by the responsibilities of leadership?

The **LornaWestonSmyth.com/Resources** can help you do just that. With a variety of training and coaching services, including workshops, assessments, one-on-one coaching, and group coaching, you will develop stronger leadership skills, enhance your communication and interpersonal skills, and ultimately become the leader you were meant to be.

As an experienced executive coach, I will provide you with the tools and resources you need to become a successful leader and reach your goals. Whether you're a CEO, Manager, Entrepreneur, or Team Leader, I will help you hone your skills and become the leader your team needs you to be.

Ready to take the next step in your leadership journey?

Go to **LornaWestonSmyth.com/Resources** to download your Leadership Development Plan Template and the recommended reading list now and discover how the I can help you become the leader you were born to be.

Made in United States
Orlando, FL
29 February 2024

44244111R00200